Lincoln Christian College

W9-BUE-469

an INTRODUCTION TO CONTEMPORARY PREACHING

an INTRODUCTION TO CONTEMPORARY PREACHING

J. DANIEL BAUMANN

BAKER BOOK HOUSE   GRAND RAPIDS, MICHIGAN

TO FRIEND WIFE, NANCY

48107

A NOTE TO THE READER

This volume is introductory in nature. Consequently, not all of the stated concepts are exhaustively developed. Also, because this is an overview, I have intentionally utilized the writings of preachers, teachers of preaching, communication theorists and other pulpit allies. So much of value has already been written that it is neither wise nor fair to feign originality. I am debtor to a great host of friends. If any idea fascinates or intrigues, you are encouraged to trace the footnote, find the source, and do your own in-depth study.

As for the production of this volume, I am indebted to a number of people. Mrs. Eileen Voth, in the midst of all her pressures as Faculty Secretary, went "beyond the call of duty" and typed the manuscript. Mr. Bernard Johnson, a staff member of the Christian Laymen of Chicago, gave much appreciated advice regarding content and style. And, as always, my wife Nancy played an important part. She did the original typing and provided continual inspiration through the project. These three friends have served faithfully and well. They deserve much of the praise for any virtue this volume contains; the weaknesses are chargeable to no one but myself.

CONTENTS

INTRODUCTION

Jesus said, "Go into all the world and preach the gospel." Twenty centuries of church history record the story of God's people in response to the Master's command. At times the preaching has been life changing and nation shaking; but frequently the pulpit, partly as cause and partly as effect, has been so innocuous that the church merely survived, and that certainly not triumphantly.

Today many self-appointed prophets, both inside and outside the church, are declaring with devastating clarity that the church and its preaching are dead and henceforth destined for the cemetery of history. Both, these prophets insist, may still exist but they are lifeless forms.

The church is variously described as "incredible,"[1] "unrenewable,"[2] and "dead."[3] Preaching is anathematized as boring, dull, uninteresting, irrelevant, void of courage, and incomprehensible.[4] In addition, today's sermons supposedly contain too many ideas, are heavy on analysis and light on prescription. They are characterized as formal, impersonal, excessively propositional, and as giving no guidance for commitment and action.[5] Small wonder that preachers are tempted to scan the "help wanted" section of the Sunday newspaper as they lick their wounds following another ordeal in the pulpit. Who can blame them?

"And yet," you ask, "you have the audacity to attempt another volume on preaching?" Such a venture may appear presumptuous to some, the height of unmitigated gall to others, a response to that academic pressure evidenced in the pun "publish or parish," or another example of the ostrich mentality that habitually afflicts men of the cloth. My response takes the form of a testimony—I have a profound faith in preaching!

I believe the Bible is on my side. Preaching was the prophets' method (à la Isaiah, Jeremiah, Jonah, Amos, et al.). The disciples of Christ were sent out and instructed to preach (Matt. 10:7; Luke 9:2). To Timothy Paul said, "Preach the word" (II Tim. 4:2). Increasingly biblical scholars are finding it difficult to distinguish between teaching and preaching in the ministry of Christ, C. H. Dodd notwithstanding.[6] As one series of Yale Lectures is titled, *Jesus Came Preaching.* A teacher of preaching concludes that

> Jesus preached because people needed to discern the meaning of everyday occurrences and they also needed to interpret the signs of their time. He preached in order to spur men on to service. Always he preached to men's needs. . . . Why preach? Because Jesus did? Not necessarily. But for the same reasons that Jesus did. Our living, our time, needs to be put into perspective. We need the light that God is supposed to bring.[7]

The Bible, by example and admonition, commends the method.

I believe church history validates my faith in preaching. Although one may be hard pressed to deliver empirical evidence that will satisfy a test-tube oriented rhetorician, it is commonly acknowledged that the church has been most healthy when its pulpit was robust. It may just be an accident of history or a quaint instance of repeated coincidence, but this writer is prone to accept the view which states that

> whenever Christianity has made substantial progress, great preaching has led the way. In the history of Christianity there have been five great centuries of growth and development. These same five periods are the five centuries of great preaching: the first with the apostles, the fourth with Chrysostom and Augustine, the thirteenth with Francis of Assisi and Dominic, the sixteenth with Luther and Calvin, and the nineteenth with Spurgeon and Maclaren. Contrariwise, whenever preaching has declined, Christianity has become stagnant. In the Dark Ages, in the fourteenth and fifteenth centuries, and in the seventeenth and eighteenth centuries, in most countries preaching was weak and ineffective.[8]

The observation of astute analysts is that spiritual life and activity in the Christian church finds a comparable state in the pulpit. When one is strong, so is the other; and conversely, declension in one is accompanied by malady in the other.[9] To ascribe causality is an interesting game that may produce no unchallenged conclusions, but the phenomenon exists and haunts us whatever evaluation we attach to it.

After reading the literature that debunks contemporary preaching and listening to the representative fare that is heard from the typical American pulpit, it is relatively easy to accept the verdict that "people are not tired of preaching but of non-preaching, of the badly garbled, anachronistic, irrelevant drivel that has in so many places passed for preaching because there was no real preaching to measure it against."[10]

While it is conceivably true that "the men who derogate preaching are, for the most part, precisely those who cannot do it well,"[11] we must be sympathetic with the concern that underlies the multiple charges brought against preaching in our day. We must insist, however, that it is not necessary to dismiss the method to heal the church. We do not need a new form; we need a new reality! Preaching is a privilege with unrealized potential and flexibility.

> Though the time when it was easy to assemble a crowd is over, at least for the immediate present, it is still true that people will gather where they have reason to believe that something will be said, with clarity and conviction, about life's most important issues.[12]

It is my conviction that preaching has the potential for significant influence in our electronic era if the preacher will be sensitive to the changes dictated by the sovereign movement of the Holy Spirit. God cannot be domesticated, limited by our programming, nor restricted to the method of preaching; yet there is insufficient evidence to indicate that imaginatively conceived, faithfully executed preaching is not still the primary instrument chosen of God to proclaim the Good News of Christ.

Most books have a rationale for their format. This particular work is no exception. The volume unfolds as a commentary on my own definition of preaching: *Preaching is the communication of biblical truth by man to men with the explicit purpose of eliciting behavioral change.* You will note that this definition incorporates the shorter definition offered by Phillips Brooks,[13] a phrase popular with the empirical rhetoricians,[14] and some additional ingredients gleaned from personal observation and experience. Three elements of the definition are particularly noteworthy and hence serve as the major divisions of this work: (1) Communication, (2) Biblical truth, and (3) Behavioral change.

Unconscious plagiarism is always a danger for an author. So many personal experiences, conferences, and books have left their indelible impression upon me that I am not always certain who should receive credit for what. My indebtedness is great. I will, however, make every effort to identify sources when they are known. My hope is that theological students and pastors alike will find some truth that will illuminate the preaching path. My prayer is that people will "hear you gladly" and that listeners' lives will be influenced to the glory of God.

NOTES

1. Harvey Cox in lecture at UCLA, January 19, 1970.

2. N. Gordon Cosby, *Christian Advocate*, VII, No. 19 (September 12, 1963), 7-9.

3. Words on button at University of California, Berkeley.

4. Clyde Reid, *The Empty Pulpit* (New York: Harper & Row Publishers, 1967), pp. 25-33.

5. Reuel L. Howe, *Partners in Preaching: Clergy and Laity in Dialogue* (New York: The Seabury Press, 1967), p. 32.

6. Cf. Robert Mounce, *The Essential Nature of New Testament Preaching* (Grand Rapids: Wm. B. Eerdmans Publishing Company, 1960).

7. William L. Malcomson, *The Preaching Event* (Philadelphia: The Westminster Press, 1968), p. 25.

8. H. C. Brown, Jr., H. Gordon Clinard, and Jesse J. Northcutt, *Steps to the Sermon* (Nashville: Broadman Press, 1963), pp. 28, 29.

9. Edwin Charles Dargan, *A History of Preaching* (Grand Rapids: Baker Book House, 1954), I, 12-13.

10. John Killinger, *The Centrality of Preaching in the Total Task of the Ministry* (Waco, Tex.: Word Books, 1969), p. 21.

11. Elton Trueblood, *The Incendiary Fellowship* (New York: Harper & Row, Publishers, 1967), p. 48.

12. Trueblood, p. 48.

13. *Lectures on Preaching.* Reprint. (Grand Rapids: Baker Book House, 1969), p. 5.

14. Cf. Gary Cronkhite, *Persuasion: Speech and Behavioral Change* (Indianapolis: The Bobbs-Merrill Company, Inc., 1969), pp. 3-15.

communication

PART ONE

CHAPTER ONE • THE PROCESS

THE LEGACY OF CLASSICAL COMMUNICATION THEORY

INGREDIENTS OF THE COMMUNICATION PROCESS

1. Source
2. Message
3. Channel
4. Receiver

BARRIERS TO COMMUNICATION

CHAPTER ONE / COMMUNICATION—THE PROCESS

There is no such thing as perfect communication. No preacher, regardless of how carefully he prepares his sermon, can expect the message he "sends" to be "received" exactly as he intended it. Nevertheless, meaningful and adequate communication is possible and certainly serves as the objective in the preaching situation. The complicating factor is numbers. Communication is difficult enough between two persons. With the insertion of every additional person the process becomes more complicated. Raymond W. Mc Laughlin has suggested that "human relationships do not develop arithmetically, but geometrically—that is, the introduction of each new member to a group *multiplies* rather than *adds* to the relationships in that group.[1] Apply these mathematics to an average church congregation and you have a frightening communication problem. However, with a little effort at understanding the dynamics of communication processes, a preacher can legitimately hope to become a "communicator."

Definitions of communication are not difficult to come by. Every theorist and writer seems to have his own way of defining communication. Frank Dance has suggested an inclusivistic theory for communication as simply

> the eliciting of a response. This kind of definition of communication is as true for intra-human organisms as it is for man. Communication is something we share with the entire animate world. Dogs communicate by eliciting responses; porpoises communicate by eliciting responses. Even man-to-machine, machine-to-machine, and man-to-man communication all fall within this same general definition of communication as "the eliciting of a response."[2]

Robert S. Goyer suggests that any inclusive theory of communication should have five essential ingredients: generator, stimuli, projection, perceiver, and discriminative response. Communication, he insists, is inherently dyadic and intentional, with commonality of meaning being the goal. He illustrates this through an equation: $\frac{P.\,R.\,M.}{G.\,R.\,I.} = 1$. That is, "perceiver's response made" over "generator's response intended" equals 1. A "1" or unity quotient occurs whenever there is a perfect correlation between intention and perceiver's response. He is quick to add that communication is usually fractional. Certainly between humans communication is consistently fractional; between man and machines or between machines it is not necessarily so.[3]

A definition by Hovland, Janis, and Kelley is of help to the preacher because it speaks to the interpersonal nature of communication. These theorists suggest that communication is "the process by which an individual (the communicator) transmits stimuli (usually verbal) to modify the behavior of other individuals (the audience)."[4] Reuel Howe notes that communication occurs whenever there is a "meeting of meanings." Agreement may result but there is communication even when agreement is nonexistent.[5]

For years communication has been depicted graphically as linear; more recently it is described as circular. But now neither description seems adequate. Human communication is too complex, and thus a helical or "coiled" symbol for communication seems more in keeping with the present understanding of the process. As Frank Dance says, "Chardin talks about the progression of life as a spiral; likewise, in the model of the DNA molecule, which is a helix, we find a much more suitable model for human communication theory than the line of the circle, for a helix is three-dimensional."[6] It is important to remember that communication does involve the sending and receiving of messages and that this process is much more complex than earlier theorists believed. The helical view recognizes that communication never comes back full circle. There is always movement—hopefully, in a forward direction.

THE LEGACY OF CLASSICAL COMMUNICATION THEORY

Classical rhetoric isolated three modes of artistic proof. Aristotle labeled them ethos, pathos, and logos. Ethos referred to the speaker's credibility, pathos to his use of emotion, and logos to the use of reason or logic in public speeches.

Classical theory also defined five rhetorical canons: (1) *invention,* which included analyzing the proposition, gathering and selecting materials, and formulating approaches to be used; (2) *disposition,* which dealt with the order and arrangement of the materials within the speech; (3) *elocution,* or "style," which referred to all matters of language, the choice of words, and the arrangement of words into larger units; (4) *delivery,* which included voice, physical elements, gesture, posture, movement; and (5) *memory,* which has been dropped from modern approaches to speech.[7]

Wayne N. Thompson overstates the case, but nonetheless suggests the immense influence of classical theory when he says, "Aristotle produced a comprehensive system that in its Whatelian modification still is dominant, and the rhetorical history of the intervening twenty-three centuries can be written in terms of Aristotle's imitators, his modifiers, and his dissenters."[8]

It is not surprising that Aristotle and classical rhetoricians still have such an impact upon present theory when one considers that Aristotle built a system upon principles of behavior which are still essentially valid. Furthermore, the approach was philosophic, consisting of principles rather than rules. It was also very practical. It was moderate in statement with a significant place granted to reason. Due to its flexibility, it has stood the test of time.

Today, four communication trends are clearly distinguishable: (1) the rediscovery of the great classical writings on oral communication; (2) new developments in psychology related to public speaking (James Winans, Charles H. Woolbert); (3) quantitative research in human communication; and (4) related fields: semantics, linguistics, speech audiology and pathology, and group dynamics.[9]

While the classical approach to speech communication relies upon introspection, intuition, and rational authority to gain insights, the scientific approach, known as quantitative research or the behavioral approach, is dependent upon a scientific method. This places great stress upon controlled observation, manipulation, statistical analysis, and replication.

At present there is an unfortunate amount of infighting among classical, neoclassical, and behavioral communication theorists. This is regrettable since a blend of the three disciplines seems desirable. Whatever empirical study can add to the art of rhetoric would appear to be a plus. It is possible that through the influence of the behaviorists rhetoric can become more of a science and less of an art.

Gerald R. Miller contends that "the scientific scholar should concern himself primarily with the factual questions of speech communication . . . and that the humanist should direct his attention to the value questions of the area. . . . Certainly, if *what is* can be brought into closer harmony with *what ought to be,* the effort involved would be more worthwhile for all students of speech communication."[10]

This type of working agreement is to be commended. A study of preaching textbooks reveals that virtually without exception homiletics has been viewed from the classical perspective. Very little of the findings of psychologists and behavioral scientists has made its way into preaching textbooks. An attempt will be made in this volume to utilize some of the findings of the behavioral scientists as they are applicable to the preaching situation, the presupposition being that homiletics is a selective application of the knowledge and skill common to all public speaking. Preaching shares much with general speech. It is different at two significant points. First of all, it is concerned with biblical categories; and second, it finds a unique ally in the ministry of the Holy Spirit. Nevertheless, it is unwise for the preacher to shut his mind to the findings and insights of the communication theorist. The man who is called by God to preach the gospel ought to concern himself with gaining more proficiency in his task. Any useful insights ought to be incorporated into the service of Christ and His church.

INGREDIENTS OF THE COMMUNICATION PROCESS

Three behaviorists have combined their talents to provide a comprehensive theory of communication which indicates the various ingredients within the process.

It involves the reception of a signal; the processing of the information contained in this signal, i.e., the development of a message (meaning) in light of our past experiences through decoding (taking meaning out of the code in which the signal was received) and encoding (formulating a message which may be transmitted via the appropriate code); and then the transmission of the appropriate signals. While this process is going on, our central nervous system is constantly monitoring itself, to keep track of our physical and mental condition (called *internal feedback*) and also the condition of the communication situation we are in (called *external feedback*). The messages it receives from these two monitoring processes are an integral part of the total communication situation.[11]

Many elaborations on the communication systems have been provided by Berlo, Gerbner, Schramm, Westley and MacLean, and Shannon and Weaver.[12] Their descriptions are not identical and their point of view varies considerably. However, they—along with Borden, Gregg, and Grove—include the four basic elements of source, message, channel, and receiver in their description.

For purposes of analysis we will isolate these four ingredients, remembering this is impossible in the act of communication inasmuch as they are overlapping dimensions in a dynamic process.

1. Source

The source of communication is the preacher, who is equipped with communication skills, attitudes, a bank of knowledge, a social system in which he lives, and a culture in which he operates. As the sender of the message he is one who must encode his own thoughts, ideas, and cognitions into verbal, vocal, and physical messages.

2. Message

The task of the preacher is to take biblical truths and transmit them via verbal, physical, and vocal stimuli. His success as a communicator depends on the harmonious blending of the verbal, the physical, and the vocal. If he says one thing verbally and another physically, he has distorted his meaning. In addition, his effectiveness is dependent on an understanding of the language he uses. If his message has been encoded into language unknown to the listener or the receiver, an obvious breakdown in communication exists. His task is to declare the biblical message in understandable, harmonious fashion.

3. Channel

Most rhetoricians have focused upon either speaker, message, or receiver. Recently Marshall McLuhan urged that the medium or channel be the primary concern of the rhetorical critic. Thus all considerations about the speaker, the message, and audience would be subordinate to the requirements imposed by the medium itself.

McLuhan is an interesting person. Many academicians hate him. The ad men love him, and most other people feel that he is perversely and uncomfortably important.[13] His critics say he is not a scholar, that he only dabbles and as a result he does not have authority. Others say he is almost impossible to read and understand. One critic said, "The trouble with skimming Mc Luhan is that it's like trying to fill a teacup from a firehose; there is likely to be no second time."[14]

Some have noted that although he claims no particular point of view McLuhan's writing is opinionated and extremely dogmatic. Another has said, "One defect of *Understanding Media* is that the parts are greater than the whole. A single page is impressive, two are 'stimulating,' five raise serious doubts, ten confirm them, and long before the hardy reader has staggered to page 359 . . . rhetorical vagueness has numbed him."[15]

Michael J. Arlen muses, with more than facetious seriousness, regarding McLuhan's fascination with the electronic era and his rejection of the Gutenberg era that "it's hard to forget that the first thing that boring old Gutenberg printed was the Bible and the first thing television gave us was Uncle Miltie—and, on present evidence, there doesn't seem to be any pressing basis for tossing out the first because of the second."[16]

His friends, on the other hand, maintain that his style is frequently obscure because he is using a different kind of medium; that he is making probes and is not involved in the logical and the analytical. His whole approach is poetic and intuitive.[17] "His statements about communication, rather than being academic and theoretical, are prophetic. . . . He has opened up vistas that are closed to some of us, so that we can look in and see if they excite us."[18]

For the sake of academic integrity it must be acknowledged that Mc Luhan does play "fast and loose" with certain facts, that he does flit about historical data with an unfortunate abandon, that his language is esoteric, and that he is given to fits of dogmatism. We are, nevertheless, impoverished if we do not grant him a hearing. He is right in criticizing the smug assumptions of most of the media leaders. His work is full of insightful ideas that invite participation in the thought process. Amid obvious chaff there is important truth that for many of us opens up an awareness of dimensions previously hidden.

McLuhan is a prophet.

> He is not tempted in the slightest to dig in at some bygone historical moment. Accepting novelty as inevitable, he is not only a modernist but a futurist. . . . His position is to be inside change; he is given over to metamorphosis on principle. . . . It is this appreciation of innovating forms that distinguishes McLuhan from other writers on popular culture.[19]

McLuhan hypothesizes that all media are extensions of man. The wheel is an extension of the foot, clothes are an extension of the skin, computers are an extension of the central nervous system, and so on. He then discusses two types of media, hot and cool. "A hot medium is one that extends one single sense in 'high definition.' High definition is the state of being well filled with data." "Hot media are . . . low in participation, and cool media are high in participation or completion by the audience."[20] When he talks about hot media he includes radio, movies, and photographs. When he speaks of cool media he includes the telephone, TV, cartoons, and speeches. For example, he contrasts a photograph to a cartoon in the following fashion. A photograph is high in definition; it is completed. It allows or demands little on the part of the observer. A cartoon, however, is a cool medium because it is simply an outline of, and is not the total definition. It involves the reader or the observer. It therefore demands more of a participatory nature. Radio is a hot medium. It is high in definition. It does not demand much from the listener. TV, on the other hand, is a cool medium for it has a number of dots and the observer is called upon to fill in and take from this field of dots and make a picture. He reaches out; he becomes involved in; he participates in a way that he never participated in listening to the radio.

Unfortunately one must accept some of these categories on faith alone because McLuhan is quite arbitrary in his distinctions. However, to describe media and to categorize them according to the degree of participation required by the audience is a helpful approach. John H. Sloan maintains that "the degree of auditory *participation* or involvement may provide us with a new perspective on describing speaker-audience relationships."[21]

Another idea basic to McLuhan's thought is the concept of the medium being the message. In his volume *The Medium Is the Massage* he contends that "all media work us over completely. They are so pervasive in their personal, political, economic, aesthetic, psychological, moral, ethical and social consequences that they leave no part of us untouched, unaffected, unaltered. The medium is the massage. Any understanding of social and cultural change is impossible without a knowledge of the way media work as environments."[22] He further notes that "societies have always been shaped more by the nature of the media by which men communicate than by the content of the communication."[23]

The problem with these two statements is that they need to be taken with a great deal of skepticism in order for the real truths to emerge. They run false when they are treated in a literal sense. The medium is not the entire message just as it does not totally control the message. An insight has been escalated into an ironclad generalization and therefore becomes a falsification. The truth of his statement is simply that *a message and a channel are intimately bound together, each to some extent an inseparable part of the other.* The channels, however, are generally distinguishable and the content cannot be downgraded. Whereas others have given almost total attention to content, McLuhan inverts the emphasis and treats the media almost to the exclusion of the content. If McLuhan was accurate, it would be as one man suggests:

> If TV had never gotten beyond broadcasting test patterns, its effect upon American society would, according to McLuhan, have been precisely the same and just as total—*if* you could have gotten the whole society to watch test patterns, which you couldn't. For Mc Luhan "content" is "the juicy piece of meat carried by a burglar to distract the watchdog of the mind." Only that and nothing more. . . .[24]

The reader is urged to consider seriously the thesis of McLuhan's two books, *Understanding Media: The Extensions of Man* and *The Medium Is the Massage.* Both suggest areas of concern regarding the channel which most preachers have never considered. It is true, as McLuhan contends, that the medium does matter. It is also true, as McLuhan maintains, that some media call for participation on the part of the listener and others minimize participation.

4. Receiver

The receiver in the communication process is one who receives from a source an encoded message via a channel or medium and then decodes that message. Decoding is translating the observable, verbal, vocal, and physical stimuli into forms of internal response. These responses result in some overt behavior. Every receiver has his own frame of reference and his own particular experiences which help him to select from the source whatever is of meaning to him. For example, suppose that an automobile accident occurred at an intersection observed by four witnesses: a doctor, a lawyer, a clergyman, and a mechanic. Their reports would very likely represent their own frame of reference. The doctor would probably notice the injuries and the resultant seriousness of the medical condition. The lawyer, because of his training and perspective, would probably notice the position of the automobiles and concern himself with the assessment of liability. The clergyman would perhaps note the physical condition of the people in the accident and whether they were in need of any spiritual assistance. The mechanic by virtue of his peculiar training and experience would probably note the condition of the automobiles and make some mental estimate regarding the cost of repairs and the subsequent difficulties in getting the cars back in running condition. Each of the observers would have seen the same accident but each would have selected from the event the things or aspects he felt were significant.

"Several studies reveal that most individuals practice what we may call *selective exposure;* that is, when allowed to exercise a choice, they expose themselves to 'favorable' messages and refuse to heed 'unfavorable' ones." [25]

The following conversation was overheard on an elevator in the UCLA Research Library. Girl A (referring to a professor): "Well, he isn't very good at communication anyway." Girl B: "He is if you listen real hard." The question may be raised whether effective communication demands listening "real hard." Doesn't effective communication command rather than demand a hearing? Must it of necessity require "hard" listening? If the source is effective, the receiver will be drawn into listening. It will not be a difficult assignment.

William D. Thompson has written a helpful book titled *A Listener's Guide to Preaching.* In this easy-to-read little volume he talks about the ingredients of good listening as well as some of the barriers to concentration: distractions, overstimulation, and tangent following. He suggests that the listener needs to note main ideas, anticipate the speaker's next point, identify with the ideas in the sermon, review the things that have been heard, and put the principles to work in every listening situation.[26]

The receiver would be well advised to refrain from agreeing or disagreeing with the speaker until he is certain what the speaker's views are. To prejudge before the entire message has been heard is an unfortunate practice of all too many listeners. S. I. Hayakawa suggests that

> listening means trying to see the problem the way the speaker sees it—which means not sympathy, which is *feeling for* him, but empathy, which is *experiencing with* him. . . . All too often, we tend to listen to a speaker or his speech in terms of generalization: "Oh, he's just another of those progressive educators." . . . once we classify a speech in this way, we stop listening, because, as we say, "We've heard that stuff before."[27]

The receiver becomes involved in a process known as "feedback," which is any information that the source gains from his receivers about the probable reception of his message. These would include such things as a smile, a frown, attention, inattention, questions, and comments.[28]

The successful preacher is one who has learned to read this feedback and thereby alter or modify his message when necessary, so that a desired response will be elicited from the congregation. If there is no sensitivity to audience response, distorted and unsuccessful communication results. Feedback is of two types: positive, which includes smiles, applause, nodding, or apparent close attention; and negative—hissing, inattention, yawns, frowns, and so forth.

It is perhaps a fair assessment to say that of the many specific charges leveled at the preaching of our day none is more basic than the heresy of treating preaching as a one-way process. Preaching is a process that is dialogical in nature; the monological stance is an illusion. This means that the preacher and the congregation are caught up in a dynamic relationship in any preaching situation.

When we view communication as a process we are acknowledging that it does not have a clear-cut beginning and end. There is a continuous inter-action between source and receiver. At points the receiver becomes the sender and the sender becomes the receiver so that there is a dynamic interplay between them. Communication is multidimensional. There is no simple A sends X to B. It is a dynamic, moving process. Gerald R. Miller summarizes the meaning of the process as follows:

> First, the notion of process hinges on the two key concepts of interaction among variables and of changes in the values taken by these variables. Second, a process viewpoint stresses the extreme psychological complexity of speech communication; it asserts the near impossibility of capturing the full richness of this everyday activity in which each of us participates.[29]

BARRIERS TO COMMUNICATION

There are any number of ways in which communication can break down. It can be through language, through attitudes, through poor ventilation, or it may simply be the hour. Most breakdowns in communication are at one of two points: the preacher or the listener. James T. Cleland, in a fascinating discussion of the "homiletical battery," speaks of the preacher as being a pitcher. He throws either a good pitch or a wild pitch. A wild pitch produces a breakdown in communication. The listener, on the other hand, is likened to the catcher. The pitch is caught when the communication is good. There is a passed ball when a breakdown arises. The failure can be at either end.[30]

Let us note a few of the breakdowns.

(1) Often the church has emphasized man's relation to the world-to-come and failed to give him adequate direction for a this-worldly mode or meaning of existence.

(2) There has often been an easy ethic proclaimed which does not allow the listener to handle the gray areas of life. Sermons treat the "black and white," and the listener is ill equipped to cope with the ambiguous.

(3) Many of the concepts articulated in the pulpit are, according to the man's present condition, too advanced for his Christian experience. Ideal states and ideal conditions articulated through ideal illustrations serve to discourage the listener rather than assist him. The distance between the proclaimed ideal and the listener's situation is often so great that he surrenders through frustration and does nothing—"What's the use. . . . It's impossible." The sermon should, instead, suggest the next step in the direction of the ideal. Unless proximate steps are spelled out, there is a breakdown in the communication, for all communication needs to end in some form of behavioral change.

(4) Week after week we pour out more and more ideas with a resultant

communication overkill. There is frequently too much demand and too little application. Elton Trueblood put it this way: "People are sermon-hardened; they've heard too much."[31] The implication of this type of charge is that we ought to preach less and do a better job in the application and integration of truth into daily life.

(5) We have not found ample means of communication that will reach people through all of their senses and henceforth demand a greater degree of participation. Much preaching has allowed listeners to maintain neutrality without involving them in the communication process.

(6) A further breakdown is in integrity, where the preacher has not been nearly convincing enough because of the low correlation between his words and his deeds.

(7) The experience of many churchgoers has given them low expectations regarding the pulpit fare. Their extensive and frequently exhausting experience in the church has not been what it could have been and therefore they come with low expectations.

(8) The image of the church has suffered at the hands of the public press and the sociological writers. A bad name has developed for the church and its message. The preliminary tuning is therefore negative.

(9) Overcommunication has trained the listener to sit without hearing. There has been dullness, and he therefore puts in time. Communication suffers.

While we admit the many breakdowns in communication—some the responsibility of the preacher, some because of content, others because of media, still others due to listener failure—we must acknowledge the fact that the preacher has certain contemporary allies that will aid communication if he will be alert to them. One of the allies of the preacher is the anxiety of men. There is a loss of identity and purpose in our society. Men seek security, identity, and purpose in life. They want to know who they are; they are desirous of an authentic existence; they want "to be."

A second ally of the preacher in the communication process is the basic religious nature of man. Current interest in astrology, folk music, the drug culture, and communal living—all these attest to man's basic religious quest and his religious concern which we believe to be God-implanted. Another is the concern for persons and society on the part of many young people. The recent success of the Peace Corps, VISTA, along with the numerous demonstrations related to race, pollution, environment, ecology, population explosion, economic inequity, housing discrimination, war and peace—all these speak of an idealism and concern that may not characterize the so-called establishment.

A fourth ally is the rootless character to life. The excessive mobility that characterizes much of American life produces job insecurity, changing communities, and a concomitant desire on the part of people for some stability.

The gospel can communicate to such persons if the preaching task is purposefully and creatively undertaken.

Communication is not, and never has been, an option for the preacher. It is a moral imperative. "How shall they hear without a preacher?" And how will they be changed unless the preacher communicates?

NOTES

1. Raymond W. McLaughlin, *Communication for the Church* (Grand Rapids: Zondervan Publishing House, 1968), pp. 66-67.

2. Frank Dance, "Communication Theory and Contemporary Preaching," *Preaching*, III (September-October 1968), 23.

3. Robert S. Goyer, "An Inclusive Theory of Communicative Process," Western Speech Association 40th Annual Convention, San Diego, California, November 25, 1969.

4. Carl I. Hovland, Irving L. Janis, and Harold H. Kelley, *Communication and Persuasion* (New Haven: Yale University Press, 1964), p. 12.

5. Reuel Howe, "The Responsibility of the Preaching Task," *Preaching*, IV (November-December 1969), 8.

6. Dance, p. 27.

7. Thomas M. Scheidel, *Persuasive Speaking* (Glenview, Ill.: Scott, Foresman and Co., 1967), pp. 13-16.

8. Wayne N. Thompson, *Quantitative Research in Public Address and Communication* (New York: Random House, Inc., 1967), p. 3.

9. George A. Borden, Richard B. Gregg, Theodore G. Grove, *Speech Behavior and Human Interaction* (Englewood Cliffs, N.J.: Prentice-Hall, Inc., 1969), pp. 188-190.

10. Gerald R. Miller, *Speech Communication: A Behavioral Approach* (Indianapolis: The Bobbs-Merrill Company, Inc., 1966), pp. 27, 30.

11. Borden, Gregg, Grove, p. 9.

12. Erwin P. Bettinghaus, *Persuasive Communication* (New York: Holt, Rinehart and Winston, Inc., 1968), p. 12.

13. Tom Nairn, "McLuhanism: The Myth of Our Time," *McLuhan: Pro and Con*, ed. Raymond Rosenthal (Baltimore: Penguin Books, 1968), p. 140.

14. Howard Luck Gossage, "The New World of Marshall McLuhan," *McLuhan: Hot and Cool*, ed. Gerald Emanuel Stearn (New York: Signet Books, 1969), p. 20.

15. Dwight MacDonald, "Understanding M.," *McLuhan: Hot and Cool*, p. 205.

16. Michael J. Arlen, "Marshall McLuhan and the Technological Embrace," *McLuhan: Pro and Con*, p. 85.

17. John M. Culkin, S.J., "A Schoolman's Guide to Marshall McLuhan," *McLuhan: Pro and Con*, p. 245.

18. Dance, p. 21.

19. Harold Rosenberg, "Understanding M.," *McLuhan: Hot and Cool*, p. 197.

20. Marshall McLuhan, *Understanding Media* (New York: Signet Books, 1964), p. 36.

21. John H. Sloan, "Understanding McLuhan: Some Implications for the Speech Teacher and Critic," *The Speech Teacher*, XVII (March 1968), 142.

22. Marshall McLuhan and Quentin Fiore, *The Medium Is the Massage* (New York: Bantam Books, 1967), p. 26.

23. McLuhan and Fiore, p. 8.

24. Theodore Roszak, "The Summa Popologica of Marshall McLuhan," *McLuhan: Pro and Con*, p. 261.

25. Borden, Gregg, Grove, p. 202.

26. William D. Thompson, *A Listener's Guide to Preaching* (Nashville: Abingdon Press, 1966), pp. 87-91.

27. S. I. Hayakawa, *Symbol, Status, and Personality* (New York: Harcourt, Brace and World, Inc., 1963), p. 33.

28. Bettinghaus, p. 207.

29. Miller, p. 41.

30. James T. Cleland, *Preaching to Be Understood* (New York: Abingdon Press, 1965), pp. 101-126 (Chapter V).

31. Clyde Reid, *The Empty Pulpit* (New York: Harper and Row Publishers, 1967), p. 91.

CHAPTER TWO • THE PREACHER

CHAPTER TWO / COMMUNICATION—THE PREACHER

What are you doing, you man, with the word of God upon *your* lips? Upon what grounds do you assume the role of mediator between heaven and earth? Who has authorized you to take your place there and to generate religious feeling? And, to crown all, to do so with results, with success? Did one ever hear of such overweening presumption, such Titanism, or—to speak less classically but more clearly—such brazenness! . . . Who dares, who can, preach, knowing what preaching is?[1]

Karl Barth's challenge, originally spoken in July of 1922, cannot be easily dismissed. It reminds us of the audacity and unmitigated gall that allows a man to think he has a right to speak the Word of truth. To think that a man will stand and declare that he is a herald of God or a servant of Christ does seem highly presumptuous. Some may even be tempted to ask if anyone has the right to consider himself a preacher. Who is really equal to the task?

And yet it must, in the final analysis, be humbly acknowledged that God's sovereign purpose in the world is to be accomplished through men; men whom He has called—finite, sinful, frail men. This is admittedly difficult to comprehend. It requires an act of faith—in God, who ordained it, in the Word where this purpose is revealed, and in the Spirit through whom this surprising mode of operation is to be accomplished.

QUALIFICATIONS

The New Testament uses the words *bishop* and *elder* interchangeably to refer to the pastor. Qualifications for the office of bishop are carefully spelled out in two passages, I Timothy 3:1-7 and Titus 1:5-9. It is obvious that the office of bishop cannot be carelessly entered into nor can it be regarded simply as an option among the available vocations for men of any era. The standards are extraordinarily high, unusually demanding, and almost idealistic. While at first the qualifications seem somewhat unrealistic, they must be treated seriously for they represent goals for the man who will stand as a preacher in the church's pulpit. Consider, if you will, the following goals for God's man—the kind of person, it seems to me, God uses to proclaim the gospel of Christ.

1. A Called Man

God's servant is first of all *called to sonship*. No one has a claim to the pulpit of the Christian church who has not experienced the redemptive touch of Christ upon his life. What right does a man have to declare *the* story (the gospel) until it has first of all become *his* story? It may be possible for an advertising man to extol the virtues of the Volkswagen automobile while he continues to drive a Cadillac. The preacher, however, is denied the luxury of declaring a message that he has not personally appropriated. Preaching is essentially a form of testimony, though it is much more than that. It implies a dynamic relationship with the Lord of the church. Notice the definition of the gospel found in I Corinthians 15, which closes with the words, "Last of all he was seen of me also." Various sermons within the New Testament (The Sermon on the Mount, Acts 2 where it says "we are all witnesses," Acts 7, Acts 17, etc.) suggest that preaching was a sincere account of the speaker's own personal faith. Truth that is preached must first of all be experienced. The preacher is not a spectator; he is a participant.

Christ must not only be spoken of; He must be an observable part of the preacher's person. Historians tell us that much of the success of George Whitefield's preaching was that he *was* the sermon. The messenger is one in whom the message has already taken on flesh. This is in keeping with the incarnational character of the Christian faith.

While it does not matter significantly what you call this relationship—conversion, redemption, regeneration, being born again, being saved, having a vital encounter, being transformed—it does matter that you experience reconciliation to God whereby one is adopted into the family of God as a son. The fact of a radical commitment to Christ is so essential to service within the life of the church that deep heart searching is not simply recommended; it is imperative. Richard Baxter asked the question years ago, "Can it be reasonably expected that [God] should save any through offering salvation to others, while they refuse it themselves; or for telling others those truths, which they themselves neglect and abuse?"[2] A man does not earn his salvation through service; he serves because he is saved. "For by grace you have been saved through faith; and this is not your own doing, it is the gift of God—not because of works, lest any man should boast. For we are his workmanship, created in Christ Jesus for good works, which God prepared beforehand, that we should walk in them" (Eph. 2:8-10).

It is a valid assumption on the part of God's people that when you stand to declare the mighty acts of God in Christ you have first of all been mightily acted upon. Only a son can speak with deep conviction, born out of personal experience with the Father. Perhaps this is why Paul warns that a pastor "must not be a recent convert, or he may be puffed up with conceit and fall into the condemnation of the devil" (I Tim. 3:6). More than one church has experienced deadness because its pastor has not been alive in the things of the Spirit. Unconverted preachers are not conductors of resurrection vitality. A changed man is in a position to assist others in their need of change. Power in the pulpit is not simply a rhetorical art; it arises in part from the recesses of a transformed life. Jesus told Nicodemus that he "must be born anew" (John 3:7). The way to sonship is through repentance and acceptance of Christ as personal Saviour and Lord, through a faith commitment. That commitment ought ordinarily to precede ordination and the call to preach.

God's man is also *called to discipleship*. To be a disciple is to be a learner—to stand under the tutelage of the Spirit of God. Such a person is growing because of his encounter with Scripture and the Spirit of God in that continuing relationship with the Father through Christ the Son. The beginnings of the Christian faith were entrusted to twelve men who followed Christ for three years of His earthly ministry and learned firsthand the truth regarding the Kingdom of God. Those who stand in this tradition must likewise be taught and continue to learn what it means to be a servant of Jesus Christ.

Dwight E. Stevenson says, "No man can preach movingly on any text as long as he is using that text solely as a channel of revelation to other men. He cannot speak on behalf of God to another until he himself has listened to God."[3] While it is true that any follower of Christ is called to sonship and discipleship, the preacher has yet another claim upon his life, mainly that he is *called to apostleship*. John the Baptist responded to this type of call and it was said of him that he "was a man sent from God. . . . He came for testimony, to bear witness to the light, that all might believe through him. He was not the light, but came to bear witness to the light" (John 1:6-8).

Christ in an intercessory prayer addressed to the Father on behalf of the disciples said, "As thou didst send me into the world, so I have sent them into the world" (John 17:18). An apostle is one who feels himself peculiarly sent; not only recognizing his place within the body of Christ, not only concerned about maturity as a child of God, but sensing also that the Spirit of God has uniquely touched him to be a preacher of the gospel.

In the letter to the Ephesians the gifts of the Spirit are enumerated: ". . . some should be apostles, some prophets, some evangelists, some pastors and teachers, for the equipment of the saints, for the work of ministry, for building up the body of Christ" (Eph. 4:11-12).

While it no longer seems fashionable to speak about your call to the ministry, it is just such a call with its "oughtness" and imperative note that will deliver the man called to serve within the life of the church from being bound, confused, and frustrated. The call of God will grant a transcendent perspective and provide as well the certainty that the same God who called the church into being has called a man to serve within its corporate life.

There are numerous ways to account for this call of God in a man's life. For some it is the impact of Scripture, and for others it is prayer. For still others it may be a sense of need or perhaps some combination of all three of these. To some a place of service is discovered and a need is felt personally. Happiness is also a worthy ingredient in the understanding of God's call. When a man senses God's touch upon his life this is frequently endorsed by a sense of personal joy. For such individuals, happiness and the will of God become synonymous categories.

Peace, which is a difficult thing to define, but which is certainly experienced, can be a further recognition on the part of God's man that this is a call from God Himself. This call to apostleship is further recognized by a local church. Having first of all been called to preach the gospel, he is then assured of this call when a local congregation corporately recognizes this is indeed God's man and calls him to serve among them as pastor.

2. A Healthy Man

At the risk of flirting with the heresy of faculty psychology, allow me to distinguish between health of spirit, body, and mind, recognizing at the outset that man is one, that he is *gestalt,* that he is total, and that no part of him may be separated except for analysis. These (spirit, body, mind) are not distinguishable parts of man in terms of the ongoing function of persons.

A healthy man is one who provides food for his interior life, whose spirit is thereby kept alive. This occurs as time is spent away from people in private. Time is allotted to personal devotional experiences, the reading of Holy Scripture, meditation, and prayer—personal, private, and intercessory. James S. Stewart says, "Is it not . . . evident that the weight of his peculiar responsibility must drive him to his knees?" He adds:

> And when you look into their faces on the Sunday, as you lead their worship and proclaim to them afresh the all-sufficient grace of Christ, that background of your hidden intercessions, of your pleading for them name by name, will lift your words and wing them with love and ardour and reality. God will not refuse the kindling flame when secret prayer has laid its sacrifice upon the altar.[4]

That which is experienced in private is inevitably recognized in public without being acknowledged. It is true that people are sensitive to one who has been in the presence of God. Some time each day should be set aside for this devotional experience. For many the morning hours are best. On the other hand, there is nothing contrary in Scripture, church history, or theology that says a man cannot have this in the middle of the day or late at night. A time personally chosen when one can be alone to have a tryst with God is the important matter. The fact of a devotional experience takes precedence over concern for the time or place.

The interior life of the pastor is further enriched by reading hymns of the church, interacting with devotional literature, both classical and contemporary, and by reading and studying sermons. One of the paramount values of reading other sermons is that the busy pastor seldom has time to hear sermons preached, but his faith can be strengthened as he reads them. The immensity of man's need coupled with our own needs compels us to pray with Frances R. Havergal:

> Lord, speak to me, that I may speak
> In living echoes of Thy tone;

As Thou hast sought, so let me seek
Thy erring children lost and lone.

O teach me, Lord, that I may teach
The precious things Thou dost impart;
And wing my words, that they may reach
The hidden depths of many a heart.

O lead me, Lord, that I may lead
The wandering and the wavering feet;
O feed me, Lord, that I may feed
The hungering ones with manna sweet.

O strengthen me, that while I stand
Firm on the Rock, and strong in Thee,
I may stretch out a loving hand
To wrestlers with the troubled sea.

O fill me with Thy fullness, Lord,
Until my very heart o'erflow
In kindling thought and glowing word,
Thy love to tell, Thy praise to show.

O use me, Lord, use even me,
Just as Thou wilt, and when, and where;
Until Thy blessed face I see,
Thy rest, Thy joy, Thy glory share.

A healthy man also gives attention to his body. It is sad that so many pastors give themselves in an all-out effort to the cause of Christ and die young because they foolishly avoided some elementary wisdoms regarding a healthy body. Proper rest should be a cultivated habit. On occasion, to be sure, the pastor is called upon to give himself to some crisis, thereby minimizing sleep. But overall, Christian stewardship demands that he give proper time to rest. A recreational program is also highly recommended. Attempt some form of recreation, whether it be golf, tennis, volleyball, handball, basketball, or . . . (you fill in the blank). It is important that a recreational program be regularly maintained to keep the body toned and the blood coursing through the veins to assist vibrancy. No apology is necessary when a man devotes one day each week to recreation. Everyone needs a change of pace from the routine demands of study and parish.

Perhaps the most common area where pastors are guilty of undisciplined living is at the kitchen table. It is unfortunate that cartoons frequently depict pastors as paunchy types with that unseemly "bishop build." Good eating habits permit a man to control his weight and thus lengthen his usefulness. Overweight pastors stand the risk of an early death through excessive strain on the heart. Proper diet keeps the body clean and healthy while cutting down on cholesterol and other problems related to cavalier eating.

God's man should also seek to cultivate a healthy mind. It is an acknowledged fact that many church problems and even church splits arise not because of theological differences, but because of personality conflicts related to emotional immaturity. The preacher is one who ought first of all to know himself, to recognize his strengths as well as his limitations; to practice being honest with himself and learning the fine art of self-acceptance. This, of course, must never be an excuse for indolence; but the real limitations, the things which cannot be changed, ought to be accepted without resentment. I once heard a layman comment that his pastor was a nice guy, but when he stood in the pulpit he was an entirely different person. His tone and his attitudes changed. He became a scolding, judgmental, authoritarian person. Such a breakdown in integrity arises from an unfortunate bifurcation of the preacher's role as a man and as a servant of the Word. Such a division is unreal, to say nothing of being unhealthy.

Robert Raines, Bruce Larson, Keith Miller, and a score of kindred spirits have recently called the church to a new kind of honesty. Churches, we all know, are filled with confused, frustrated, frightened, and guilty people. People have often found it difficult to let their feelings be known lest they be castigated, rebuked, and even ostracized. The preacher stands where they stand. He too experiences temptation. He too knows anxiety. He too has walked their "vale of tears." To assume in the pulpit that such is not true is to create an illusion, to undercut authenticity, and to raise questions about ministerial integrity.

Abraham Maslow indicates that one of the problems in social science research is that scientists often forget "that much of human communication is skillfully executed subterfuge, practiced with a finesse acquired from a lifetime of learning—that we spend much time trying to avoid becoming known."[5] Discrepancies between the preacher's life and message render him unauthentic and often label his gospel as irrelevant. All men, and certainly preachers, are called to be themselves, their best selves; to accept themselves; to recognize who they are and not parade as someone else. Role playing is a touchy game with impossible rules.

William L. Malcomson reminds us of a very important fact.

> The best preachers are those who love themselves. If you love yourself, you accept yourself, you like yourself, you forgive yourself, you enjoy being yourself, you have decided that you are of worth. . . . You will find it very difficult to love other people if you do not love yourself. Instead, you will be wanting them to give you something that only you can give yourself. You will be wanting them to tell you, to prove to you, that you are of worth. That is too much to demand of another person. It isn't fair.[6]

This is in keeping with the twin commands to love God and your neighbor as yourself. The man who finds it difficult to love his neighbor may find that he does not love himself. He cannot accept another because he has not first of all learned to accept himself. Self-love, the kind that is appropriate and not a form of neurotic pride, is commended by the apostle Paul in Romans 12:3, "Do not think of yourselves more highly than you should. Instead, be modest in your thinking. . . ." In other words, think realistically of yourself, neither with pride nor self-abnegation.

3. A Disciplined Man

There are many areas in which the preacher can become careless. Perhaps the most commonly neglected discipline is that of the clock. Because the man of the cloth does not punch a time card, it is possible for him to get by, to use personality, "the gift of gab," and let the clock degenerate into an uncomfortable friend. A wise steward is one who has domesticated time, who finds that the clock can be a servant and not a master, who schedules things, who arises at an early hour, who spends time in his office, who spends time doing the things that must be done because he has a sense of personal accountability to God and the church.

The regularity of Sunday with its inevitable preaching demand and the frequency of crises that arise in the life of the church all commend a discipline of time. Time must be domesticated to be useful.

A wise man learns the delicate art of neglect. There are certain things that demand his time. He learns to establish priorities. It is necessary to major on major issues and minor on the minors. The pastor will necessarily court misunderstandings. To do justice to the demands of the preaching situation he will discover the wisdom of absenteeism at unnecessary meetings. The "hail-fellow-well-met" type will protest his pastor's absence at certain official affairs, but the concerned persons will applaud their pastor's discretion when they see how effectively he serves. The ladies of the parish may question his studied absence at their meetings, but his ministry of the Word ought to reveal his wise stewardship of time.

This disciplined approach to life will also make him more knowledgeable. As he functions not only in the church but also in the community he will find that an awareness of life, of people, and of issues will be the reward. A man's relation to his society may be described as follows: He is in society and he is of society, but he is not a prisoner of that society. "The fully functioning personality is not . . . fully adjusted."[7] An undisciplined man finds himself absorbed in society and therefore unable to speak a redemptive message to the society of which he is a part. He becomes an echo of culture rather than a prophet in its midst.

4. A Compassionate Person

God has loved us into fellowship and sonship. Because of His love we are therefore enabled to love. This love cannot be initiated; it can only be reflected. We can love because we have been loved. And this love is an unconditional love. One Catholic layman shared his concern,

Fall in love with us as *we are*—don't hold back your love until we are

> beatified. And if this good fortune should be yours, that you are in
> love with or that you fall in love with your people, for God's sake
> don't hide it, but take all the risks that go with love even to the point
> of saying things to us which your love urges you to say, even though
> they may be the kind of things likely to make you seem ridiculous in
> the eyes of Philistines and vulgar people.[8]

There are always risks if a man wants to love his people. But risk it we must.
Jesus had a reverence for individuals: Mary Magdalene, Zacchaeus, the
woman at the well, the disciples (as individuals), Mary, Martha, Lazarus.
Christ did not go around seeking crowds. He sought individuals and the
crowds sought Him. The servant of the Master is likewise called to focus
upon people, people in their need.

Charles Schulz, the cartoonist, who doubles as an astute theologian,
portrays Linus talking to Lucy saying, "I love mankind . . . it's PEOPLE I
can't stand."[9] Persons expect and have a right to be respected. Love for the
person makes respect a live possibility. A loving person is approachable. The
stance of aloofness symbolized in the old traditional New England pulpit
with its lofty elevation must be recognized for what it is—an occupational
hazard which will undercut usefulness to the church and guarantee sterility
in the pulpit. The dichotomy of pastor and preacher is an anachronism. It
represents two dimensions of a single call to serve the people of God. The
man who is not available renders the gospel irrelevant. The approachable
man has been equipped with ears—ears that really hear. One thoughtful
observer of preachers has noted, "The best way to have listeners is to be
one."[10]

Reuel Howe relates this listenability to the total process of communication when he says,

> God gave us two eyes, two ears, and only one mouth. A lot of people
> never learn a lesson from that—which is that you ought always to use
> your eyes and ears twice as much as you use your mouth. Another
> way of putting it in electronic terms . . . is that the purpose of the
> eyes and ears is to program the mouth. The problem with a lot of
> human relationships is that there is too much unprogrammed talk.[11]

People are saying, "If you love me, hear me." "If you love me, feel with
me." Christ has liberated the Christian and has enabled him to love. For the
preacher this means that his tongue is engaged only after his heart and ears
are in gear.

Consider the following conversation.

    B: Why do you want a bigger church?
    A: So I can help more people.
    B: Why don't you practice polygamy so that you can love more
        women?
    A: Brother, I haven't begun to love the one I have as deeply as I
        should.
    B: How about that?[12]

5. A Humble Person

One of the occupational hazards of the preacher is pride. It is not an attractive thing to see a man have a love affair with himself in public, but it is a rather common fact. To all those tempted with the Messianic complex, the words of Paul to the Corinthians are still worthy of consideration. "For consider your call, brethren; not many of you were wise according to worldly standards, not many were powerful, not many were of noble birth; but God chose what is foolish in the world to shame the wise, God chose what is weak in the world to shame the strong, God chose what is low and despised in the world, even things that are not, to bring to nothing things that are, so that no human being might boast in the presence of God" (I Cor. 1:26-29). An understanding of this biblical truth makes a man teachable. He has the spirit of a scientist who recognizes that he may not have the last word, but only the latest. He maintains an ability to listen, to rethink, to put to the test, to make certain that the things he says are indeed true. He does not confuse himself with Scripture. Scripture is inspired; he is not. He speaks the truth but does so humbly, recognizing that he may get in the way and that the Spirit of God may not be given a complete hearing.

> The preacher . . . is a catalyst, seeking to be the agent which causes the encounter of God with man to actually take place. When he regards himself as the expert, he manages God and man. As the catalyst he is at the service of both, and he gets out of the way.[13]

This kind of spirit enables a man to recognize his own biases so that he maintains a willingness to change and a flexibility when the truth dictates such a move. He stands *on* the Word of God and he stands *under* the Word of God, which means that he is judged by the Word of God, as the Spirit interprets it in a meaningful and personal fashion.

6. A Courageous Person

God's man stands in that magnificent tradition that includes Amos (5:24), Micah (6:8), and Jesus Himself (Matt. 22:37-40). When there is injustice or unrighteousness, sin of any sort, personal or social, the preacher must have the courage to speak the truth. "No true minister of Jesus Christ cuts his convictions to fit community feeling nor does he trim his message to the shape of his congregation."[14]

There has always been a place in the church for the peacemaker who applies the balm of Gilead. But when this is done at the risk of tailoring the truth or because of irresponsibility, the transgressor must be condemned as lacking in courage. That which is evil should be condemned. There needs to be a call for reform of what is bad in society, an encouragement to preserve what is good, and a willingness to pioneer in creating what ought to be characteristic of a culture.

IMPLICATIONS

The qualifications we have reviewed are very demanding. Such goals may not be realized in our lifetime, but they nonetheless serve as standards toward which all of us can aspire. They are goals which the Spirit of God can help implement so that we may be more effective in fulfilling the call of God.

These ingredients combine to make up what the rhetoricians have traditionally called *ethos*. Note the well-known comments of Aristotle regarding ethos.

> Persuasion is achieved by the speaker's personal character when the speech is so spoken as to make us think him credible. We believe good men more fully and more readily than others: this is true generally whatever the question is, and absolutely true where exact certainty is impossible and opinions are divided. This kind of persuasion, like the others, should be achieved by what the speaker says, not by what people think of his character before he begins to speak. It is not true, as some writers assume in their treatises on rhetoric, that the personal goodness revealed by the speaker contributes nothing to his power of persuasion; on the contrary, his character may almost be called the most effective means of persuasion he possesses.[15]

Twenty-five centuries of history have not seriously altered this conclusion. The possibility exists that Aristotle was wrong in assuming that ethos is the most powerful of the three means of persuasion, but modern experimentation does support the conclusion that ethos contributes to persuasiveness.[16]

There are many influences that combine to influence and persuade listeners, and ethos is one of the decidedly important variables. Gary Cronkhite observes:

> It seems safe to conclude that a speaker who is "agreeable" in Norman's terms, "trustworthy" in Berlo's sense, "safe" in Lemert's, or possessed of good "character" as McCroskey puts it, is likely to be more persuasive. Further, if he has "culture" and "conscientiousness" (Norman), "competence" (Berlo), "qualification" (Lemert) or "authoritativeness" (McCroskey), he will enhance that persuasiveness.[17]

For our purpose it is helpful to note that ethos is of two basic types: *antecedent ethos,* which is the role, title, position that a man brings into a situation; and *manifest ethos,* which is what the man actually projects in the speaking situation.

Even if a man has no antecedent ethos to speak of, he may earn status with his hearers during his message or address.[18] Ethos may also be altered in addition to being created. The dress, voice, manner, perceived sincerity, the introduction given to the speech—all these may have their effects upon changing the speaker's ethos.[19]

Contemporary studies of ethos have settled on the following elements in defining this concept operationally: "(1) Expertness, (2) Trustworthiness, (3) Personal dynamism."[20] It can be argued with empirical evidence as support that the personal life and character of the preacher does have its impact. And the things that have been said in homiletics textbooks for many years are basically true: there must be integrity, the man who says one thing and does another cannot be trusted, and the man who lives the good life does have a claim to listeners. Integrity breaks down when there is "separate existence of the house of life and the house of doctrine."[21]

A man's whole life makes up the antecedent ethos so that not only his behavior in the pulpit but also his behavior as a family man, as a man in community, as a man with human frailties, as a concerned man, as a Christian, contributes to the communication situation. Such a challenge is rather obvious. John Knox states it in this fashion: "How good we are as preachers depends—not altogether but (make no mistake!) primarily—on how good we are as men."[22]

A significant form of preparation for preaching is preparation of the preacher. Effectiveness in the pulpit is indeed tied to the life, the integrity, the Christian character of the man who declares the gospel. Good men are full of their message and will be heard.

NOTES

1. Karl Barth, *The Word of God and the Word of Man,* trans. Douglas Horton (New York: Harper & Brothers, 1957), p. 126.

2. Richard Baxter, "The Reformed Pastor," *Young Minister's Companion: A Collection of Valuable and Scarce Treatises on the Pastoral Office* (Boston: Samuel T. Armstrong, 1913), p. 428.

3. Dwight E. Stevenson, *In the Biblical Preacher's Workshop* (Nashville: Abingdon Press, 1967), p. 67.

4. James S. Stewart, *Preaching* (London: The English Universities Press, Ltd., 1955), pp. 175, 177.

5. George A. Borden, Richard B. Gregg, Theodore G. Grove, *Speech Behavior and Human Interaction* (Englewood Cliffs, N.J.: Prentice-Hall, Inc., 1969), p. 82.

6. William L. Malcomson, *The Preaching Event* (Philadelphia: The Westminster Press, 1968), p. 63.

7. S. I. Hayakawa, *Symbol, Status, and Personality* (New York: Harcourt, Brace & World, Inc., 1963), p. 55.

8. Desmond Fennell, "What I Miss in Sermons," *Preaching,* II, (November-December 1967), 1-10.

9. Robert L. Short, *The Gospel According to Peanuts* (Richmond: John Knox Press, 1964), p. 122.

10. Sister Thomas McNeela, D.C., "Eliciting Listener Response," *Preaching,* II (September-October 1967), 32-35.

11. Reuel Howe, "Responsibility of the Preaching Task," *Preaching,* IV (November-December 1969), 10.

12. Malcomson, p. 83.

13. Arndt L. Halvorson, "Preaching Is for People," *Lutheran Quarterly*, XX (November 1968), 360.

14. Daniel D. Walker, *The Human Problems of the Minister* (New York: Harper & Row, Publishers, 1960), p. 144.

15. Aristotle *The Rhetoric and the Poetics of Aristotle*, ed. Friedrich Solmsen (New York: The Modern Library, 1954), p. 25.

16. Kenneth Anderson and Theodore Clevenger, Jr., "A Summary of Experimental Research in Ethos," *Speech Monographs*, XXX (June 1963), 77.

17. Gary Cronkhite, *Persuasion: Speech and Behavioral Change* (Indianapolis: The Bobbs-Merrill Company, Inc., 1969), p. 175.

18. Jon Eisenson, J. Jeffrey Auer, and John V. Irwin, *The Psychology of Communication* (New York: Appleton-Century-Crofts, 1963), p. 289.

19. Wayne N. Thompson, *Quantitative Research in Public Address and Communication* (New York: Random House, Inc., 1967), p. 54.

20. Thomas M. Scheidel, *Persuasive Speaking* (Glenview, Ill.: Scott, Foresman and Company, 1967), p. 10.

21. Helmut Thielicke, *The Trouble with the Church: A Call for Renewal*, trans. John W. Doberstein (New York: Harper & Row, Publishers, 1965), p. 13.

22. John Knox, *The Integrity of Preaching* (New York: Abingdon Press, 1957), p. 59.

COMMUNICATION—THE AUDIENCE

AUDIENCE ANALYSIS (GENERAL)

1. Urbanization
2. Industrialization
3. Leisure Revolution
4. Concern for the Individual
5. Communication Revolution

AUDIENCE ANALYSIS (SPECIFIC)

1. Prior to the Sermon
2. During the Sermon
3. Following the Sermon

SOME IMPLICATIONS OF AUDIENCE ANALYSIS

1. Consideration for Location
2. Uniformitarianism
3. Preaching with Children in Mind

CHAPTER THREE • THE AUDIENCE

CHAPTER THREE / COMMUNICATION—THE AUDIENCE

Of all the possible approaches to oral communication, few treat the listener as a primary consideration. This can be understood when one recognizes that the listener is not the most overtly active nor the most easily studied feature of the communication process. Most rhetoricians, homiletics teachers, and preachers themselves have been concerned about the speaker. They are either concerned with his health, spiritual power, oratorical gifts and similar personal qualities, or their attention has focused on the sermon: its clarity, freshness, illustrations, structure, language, contemporaneity, theology, and similar message oriented items.

But what about the audience? If communication is a process that includes sender, message, channel, and receiver, are we warranted in giving almost exclusive consideration to the sender and the message? Obviously, we are not. One of the most significant contributions made by a behavioral approach to communications is its focus on the audience, a focus which notes effects on the audience in terms of changed attitudes, beliefs, and values. As such, modern communication theory has served as a corrective to the imbalance that classical theory created by limiting attention to speaker and message.

AUDIENCE ANALYSIS (GENERAL)

Any congregation is a slice out of the general populace. What then are the current trends and influences in American life of which the speaker ought to be aware? Five considerations are noteworthy.

1. Urbanization

Urbanization is more than a geographical issue. It is a frame of reference, an attitude, a mind-set. While it is true that the population has shifted primarily to the city, it is also true that individuals who presently live in the rural sector of our nation have been urbanized. Grandfather may have lived on the farm, but Junior lives in the city, probably in one of the emerging megalopolises. But for those who have maintained a rural residence, there does exist an urban mentality. This is traceable to the impact of mass media. A man may plow, disc, plant, and cultivate his soil during the day, but he can sit down at night before the television set and be immediately immersed in the life of Times Square or Hollywood. He can move from Manhattan to Los Angeles by a simple twist of the dial. His attitudes, his orientation, and frame of reference are thereby being influenced, though ever so subtly, by the impact of television, radio, and the printed page.

Most Americans live in the city. There are millions rubbing shoulders with each other in the neighborhood, passing each other on the freeways, stumbling over each other in the shopping centers. Americans are economically, socially, and spiritually interdependent. The so-called rugged individualist is passing into legend. Urbanization is partly responsible for the trend. It is an interesting reversal that whereas once man fled from the country to the city to find employment and housing, now he retreats from the city to the country to find a slower pace. A place is sought where he can find rest, leisure, and recreation removed from city pressures.

2. Industrialization

Some prophesy that within a generation "2% of the people in our country will be able to supply all the material needs of the other 98%."[1] This cybernetic age is extremely threatening to masses of people who fear they may be replaced by machines. Social scientists continue to describe the IBM age in terms of depersonalization. It is such an understanding that motivated an imaginative principal in a slum area to provide each student in the school with a photograph of himself. The classrooms were abundantly supplied with large mirrors. The result was an outstanding increase in the learning rate. The slum child has had very little visual orientation and very little sense of authentic existence. He needed to realize that "I am somebody."[2]

3. Leisure Revolution

With all of the pressures placed upon contemporary man, it was inevitable that there would be a retreat from city life and the demands of employment. One is not surprised to discover the pressure from unions for shorter work weeks and longer weekends. Camper trailers, boats, cabins, snowmobiles, and even foreign travel have become common in a society that is both prosperous and mobile.

On Friday afternoon and evening the freeways are choked with urbanites retreating from the city. Again on Sunday afternoon and evening the freeways are choked with the returning traffic. The leisure revolution has affected even the person of moderate means. Such a movement in society has been threatening the church, which has built its whole program around a stable Sunday congregation. When the members move either to the country, to the desert, or to the beach, it is difficult to maintain any type of homogeneity and congregation. This has prompted some churches to initiate drive-in services where people may come on Sundays in beach clothes, worship, and then drive to their place of recreation without ever entering a church building. A few have tried services within the sanctuary at an earlier hour and invited people to attend in their sports attire.

Some churches have provided a mid-week service which is a replication of the Sunday service. In that way members of the congregation who will be absent on Sunday are encouraged to have their worship experience during the work week when they are at home.

4. Concern for the Individual

America is witnessing a concern for persons perhaps unparalleled at any time in our short history. While industrialization has depersonalized, there has been a counterreaction on the part of many who sensed that loneliness and emptiness was being experienced by vast portions of America's "lonely crowd." The counterreaction has been expressed in various ways. The peace movement across the States has arisen in part out of a consideration of the tragedy that occurs to any nation involved in national and international conflict. Demonstrations by young and old alike suggest that people are concerned that life be altered in the direction of humanness. The racial revolution speaks persuasively of people's concern for other persons. The church and social institutions have increasingly combined their resources to grant integrity to the Black, the Chicano, and other minority groups.

Environmental consideration in our times is person centered. Ecology has become such a popular concern that even Johnny Carson has been plugging for the control of the three "P's" (population, pollution, and pesticides). The message is starting to get across to millions of Americans. Paul Ehrlich penned a best-selling volume called *The Population Bomb*. In addition, he has gone from campus to campus promoting his views before throngs of enthusiastic students. David Dempsey, concluding a review of the literature on environment, maintains, "If environmental control fails, it will not be for lack of information. We can literally read our way to a solution, although perhaps not to the will for solution. Ironically, . . . thousands of trees will have to be cut down to get the message across. You 'trade off' in this business. If the program is successful, the wood pulp will have been well sacrificed."[3]

5. Communication Revolution

S. I. Hayakawa contends that the generation gap is perhaps more serious than any of us realize. In one analogy he speaks of the hours young children spend with that powerful sorcerer, TV. This sorcerer is

> a storyteller and a spinner of dreams. He plays enchanting music; he is an unfailingly entertaining companion. He makes the children laugh; he teaches them jingles to sing; he is constantly suggesting good things to eat and wonderful toys for their parents to buy them. Day after day, year after year, children for a few hours a day live in the wonderful world created by the sorcerer—a world of laughter, and music and adventures and incredible goings-on, sometimes frightening, usually fun, and always entrancing. . . . Parents and teachers scold and

make unreasonable demands. But the sorcerer is always friendly and fascinating, so that the children sit there as if drugged, absorbing messages that their parents did not originate and often do not even know about. For one-fourth or more of their waking hours from infancy onward, they live in a semantic environment their parents did not create and often make no attempt to control. ... The present generation of young people is the first in history to have grown up in the television age. A significant proportion of these born after 1946, although brought up in parents' homes, had their dreams, their expectations and their imaginative lives created for them by others. Is it any wonder that some of these children, as they grew to adolescence, turned out to be strangers in their own homes?[4]

Nicholas Johnson of the Federal Communications Commission estimates that children get more verbal impact from radio and television than from parents, schools, neighbors, and church combined. "By the time he enters first grade, the average child has spent more hours in front of a television set than he will spend in a college classroom."[5]

Marshall McLuhan's analysis of mass media includes a division of history into three distinct eras: (1) In the primitive period men lived absorbingly with one another, eating, fighting, loving, and sharing in a face-to-face relationship where all the senses were in balance. (2) The Gutenberg era (approximately 1500 to 1900) created the portable book and man could separate himself from others and live in isolation. Typography gifted man with "detachment and noninvolvement."[6] (3) The electronic era was initiated with the invention of the telegraph in 1844. McLuhan concludes that electronics will ultimately retribalize man by restoring his sensory balance and returning him to a more primitive form of absorbing existence with fellow men. This technological advance created the TV child·and the *participation mystique.*[7]

Youth today are not interested in the detached patterns of the nineteenth century. Their music, their whole life style is one of shared participation, not of noninvolvement. It is a world of allatonceness.[8] The TV child is tuned to all of the adult news—rioting, war, inflation, taxes, crime, and bathing beauties. He is bewildered when he enters an environment characterized by a nineteenth century rear-view mirror approach to education.[9]

Youth are restless. They face and become involved in adult problems and yet are compelled to live as children. In an earlier era it was possible for the adolescent to be provided with a rain check and he was prepared to wait it out. But since TV the drive to participation has ended adolescence.[10] "The television generation is a grim bunch. It is much more serious than children of any other period—when they were frivolous, more whimsical. The television child is more earnest, more dedicated."[11]

Father was educated in sequential linear fashion, but his son is being educated by mass media which are all at once, total, a return to sensory balance. The pull of the media is toward participation. Noel Jordan concludes, "It cannot be denied that mass communications exert some influence on us all."[12] McLuhan feels that the use of hallucinogens is related to the electronic environment. Such activity shows a kind of empathy with this environment and also a way of repudiating the old mechanical world.[13]

There is ample evidence to believe that there is truth in the dictum that "we become what we behold."[14] Our basic cultural medium is no longer the written word. The medium now is the electronic image. Prentice Meador summarizes the influence of secular society upon modern American audiences by noting the following characteristics: "1. Conformity, 2. Sophistication, 3. Materialistic self-interest, 4. Respect for time-saving efficiency, 5. Search for personal adjustment, 6. Strain for superiority and status, 7. Respect for progress, 8. Respect for universally accepted ideals—equality, justice, the brotherhood of man. . . ."[15]

In addition to the aforementioned trends in American life, there are some general needs that are as broad as humanity itself. Abraham H. Maslow classifies human needs into five categories: physiological needs, safety needs (represented in established economic, social, political, religious, and educational institutions), belongingness and love needs, esteem needs, and the need for self-actualization.[16]

Jesse Jai McNeil refers to the three basic urges of man.[17] (1) *The urge to do—activity.* Everyone desires to be active, to be involved in meaningful and significant ways. All too much is busywork or meaningless activity. (2) *The urge to belong—community.* A cynic said, "Give an American a red badge and a certificate and he will join anything." It is inherent within human nature to desire socially rewarding relationships. Yet, he is often living on an island in the midst of people, experiencing some form of alienation. The church exists to provide a fellowship or community in which man is accepted as he is. (3) *The urge to be—authenticity.* It is easy to lose our individuality and become cogs in civilization's giant wheel. We can become numbers instead of persons. In the words of T. S. Eliot we become "hollow men." Authentic existence is a paramount contribution of the Christian faith.

AUDIENCE ANALYSIS (SPECIFIC)

It is never easy for a preacher to analyze his congregation. A sizeable congregation of two hundred or more is almost impossible to know in any depth. There is a tendency for parishioners to role play in the presence of a pastor and thereby deprive him of accurate analysis. It is unlikely that the preacher will use scientific instruments, either because of his lack of ability to handle them or his lack of information regarding which ones are available. Therefore, the pastor is usually limited to impressions or perceptions which are susceptible to distortion. Contrary to a popular image of the church there is a great deal of heterogeneity in a congregation. A further difficulty inherent in a mobile society is the phenomenon of "unknown" visitors, thus introducing an unpredictable cluster of variables on a regular basis.

Two sets of tools are available to the preacher in his task of audience analysis. The first type is the mechanical—interest inventories, membership records, questionnaires, any form of testing, sometimes a sophisticated attitude scale, and other means of accomplishing statistical information collection.[18] A sociologist could assist the preacher in his selection of tools for this task.

A second tool available to the preacher is that of his own sensitivity. While he will not mechanically look for knowledge of his people, he can keep his eyes open to observe how people talk, think, live, and feel. People will discuss their problems, laying bare their souls to the faithful preacher. He will ask questions, discerning questions, designed to cultivate understanding. He will also be alert to feedback from committee interaction, feedback that comes in formal worship as well as from counseling relationships during crises experiences. Regular visitation and social contacts will also enlarge his understanding if he trains himself to be sensitive. No worthy shepherd ever felt he could care for his sheep by reading about them in the library. He must live among them and thereby be sensitized to their weaknesses, pressures, and multiple concerns which inevitably arise in the process of living. This is to say that there ought to be no bifurcation between the pastoral and the preaching roles. The good preacher is a good pastor. One task feeds the other.

It was said of Phillips Brooks:

> There was someone in the study almost continuously, while others were waiting in the reception room or in the dining room. Yet the person in the study was made to feel that, at the moment, this was the one thing that Phillips Brooks had to do and that he was interested only in this person's problem. And, at that moment, this was true.[19]

This serves in part to explain the effective ministry of the great Boston preacher. He not only preached from his books but he preached from people. He worked among them. He analyzed them. He spoke to their needs.

The pastor may also secure information secondhand. This information is shared by teachers, officers, lay people in formal and informal settings, staff, and outsiders. All serve as useful sources in audience analysis.

What should the preacher look for? Inasmuch as "the success of the persuader will depend upon his having a complete and accurate catalog of his listeners' attitudes toward a large number of . . . concepts," it is imperative that he be selecting and collecting information as regularly as possible.[20] He ought to be looking for images, values, beliefs, and reigning affections. What are the basic issues that concern his people? Specifically, this means that he ought to be alert to their areas of indifference, where they maintain a form of neutrality or lack any consistent interest, the areas where they become defensive and touchy or subject to a lack of emotional control. What are their hurts and anxieties? When do they cry for help? In what situations? At what points are they preoccupied in thought and in word? What about their hidden agendas when they are in meetings or in group settings? To what groups do they make appeals? From what frame of reference do they speak? Is their membership in or sympathy with organizations the basis of their action or motivation? At what points are they ambivalent? What about their knowledge of the Bible, their Christian faith, life in general? At what points do they maintain prejudices or biases? Are their minds open or are they closed?

For example, people maintain images in their minds which form a complex of associations which can affect or be affected by a listening experience. The "auditor carries his images with him into the listening situation. Whatever effect the message has upon him will occur through stimulation of that set of images, and some of the most profound effects of communication may take place in the image system itself."[21]

We have an apparent dilemma at this point. We cannot treat a large group—for example, two hundred parishioners—as if they were alike. None-theless, for the sake of coherence we must treat them as a group, although behavior is always individually and not collectively determined. We cannot consider each auditor in a large audience and we cannot consider the audience as if it were a single auditor.

> What we require to extricate us from this dilemma is some way of thinking about the audience that will permit us to summarize briefly the similarities and differences among its separate auditors. Our summary can then be regarded as a shorthand description, which tells us how things are typically or on the average in the audience as a whole.[22]

Our analysis is as valid as it is typical. Or to put it another way, when we speak about our congregation on the average, then it is useful and accurate for the largest cluster of persons.

For most of us this process of audience analysis has been conducted very informally in the very process of living and associating with other people. It is necessary for the sake of effective communication that we make this task more formal, which implies that we do it more systematically. For all of the people that sit before us bring to that situation a complex skein of physical and psychological needs coupled with theological variants that must be understood if meaningful communication is to exist.

This background of experience, attitudes, beliefs, motives, and habits is referred to as the "antecedents to their interaction."[23]

There are three major dimensions to specific audience analysis: prior to the sermon, during the sermon, and following the sermon.

1. Prior to the Sermon

There is no single step in speech preparation that deserves more careful attention than the analysis of the particular audience to which the particular message is to be presented. Yet it is a step that is very frequently omitted. But even then the speaker does make some assumptions about them. He assumes at least that his auditors are in the same circumstances as he and that they will respond to his ideas in the same way that he responds to them.[24]

First of all, a demographic analysis should be conducted in order to ascertain general information: age, sex, marital status, place of residence, vocation, income, schooling, and political party preference of the congregation. Then, more specifically, on a weekly basis, he conducts a purpose oriented analysis. What level of understanding does my audience have regarding this subject? What past experiences have they had regarding this subject? He may then proceed to divide his listeners into three broad groups: partisans, neutrals, and opponents. This division forms a guideline in selecting the specific purpose for his speech on the chosen subject.

Each new sermon requires a fresh assessment of the congregation's relationship to a subject. What frame of reference is likely to color the audience's response? What experiences and exposure color the subject and will therefore demand further consideration and understanding from the preacher in his process of preparation? Does the congregation understand the topic? Are they neutral or antagonistic toward the topic? The answers to these questions may dictate the particular method that will be chosen in the type of illustration or authority that may be drawn upon in presenting and emphasizing that subject. It is well for the preacher to do·some form of pretesting with representative persons (such as opinion leaders, staff members, officers, wife) in order to minimize faulty perceptions.

Walter Russell Bowie gives the following earthy counsel:

> It is well that at some time he should go into the church and kneel there in one of the pews and remember those who will be sitting there. Here in one place will be a businessman, burdened and often bewildered by the difficulty of keeping his business from being a failure and at the same time keeping himself a Christian. Here will be a woman bringing in her heart some secret wound of domestic wretchedness. Here will be the young man undecided whether to resist or welcome some hot temptation. Here, seated side by side, will be two who have fallen in love and before whom life seems to be opening into the wonder of new romance. Here they are, these different personalities with their different joys and sorrows, their opportunities and their needs. What can the message he plans to preach on Sunday be made to mean to them?[25]

Even after the manuscript or notes have been completed, it would be well for the preacher to rethink the whole business to be certain he has not allowed any pride of discussion or lure of rhetoric to deflect him from the major purpose of sharing some profound biblical truth.

2. During the Sermon

Audience analysis continues while the sermon is being delivered. And as Monroe and Ehninger maintain,

> No prior analysis of an audience is proof against mistaken judgment. Moreover, the audience's attitude may change even while you are speaking. For these reasons, it is important to keep a close watch on the reactions of your listeners when your subject is announced and throughout your entire speech. The way your hearers sit in their seats, the expression on their faces, such audible reactions as laughter, applause, shifting about, or whispering—all these are vivid symptoms of their attitude toward you, your subject, or your purpose. If you are wise, you will develop a keen sensitivity to these signs and learn to adapt your remarks accordingly.[26]

Attitudes change under the influence of the speaker's word choice, his language usage, message organization, appearance, gestures, and voice characteristics. It is impossible to assume that prior attitudes will be maintained through the sermon. The preacher's effectiveness is predicated upon his ability to interpret audience cues accurately and to react in a way that will increase the persuasiveness of his message. Recent studies have concluded that it is possible to read rather accurately the cues given by an audience. [27] These studies also suggest that there is at least some improvement in the accuracy of audience analysis as the speaker becomes more experienced. [28]

The implications are interesting. It means at least that a man's ability can be improved through practice, and also it suggests that the sermon is not a group of written or memorized words but is a message for people. The preacher is not preaching to a group but to persons, and congregations are not interchangeable. Not only is the preacher influencing the responsiveness of his congregation, but the members of the congregation are influencing one another. And these influences depend upon any number of factors: audience size, group feeling, preliminary tuning, homogeneity, orderliness, common focus, and polarization.[29]

This continuous sequence of behavior known as communication is only partially under the apparent control of the speaker. Skilled speakers have found that their effectiveness is not dependent upon manipulation of an audience. It is rather in their ability to "feel" their audience and therefore fit their speeches to ongoing patterns of behavior and tendencies discovered in the audience during the dynamic moment of presentation.

3. Following the Sermon

Many preachers visit with their congregation once the service has ended. This practice has merit. The sensitive preacher is able to pick up signals, cries for help, the need for further clarification, trends, and feelings. Such a practice may serve to trigger a personal visit with persons who have given some indication of further concern regarding the sermon. The time at the door or at the front of the church should not be depreciated as a meaningless ritual. It can be a time of mutual significance for a pastor and his people.

Preaching represents challenge to the preacher and each member of the congregation is an individual challenge. There is, as Webb B. Garrison reminds us, "always the possibility that one who came to scoff or preen may remain to pray."[30] The sensitive preacher will discover in his postsermon analysis that even messages which he is inclined to dismiss as relatively insignificant have had some effect. This effect may differ with individuals.

SOME IMPLICATIONS OF AUDIENCE ANALYSIS

1. Consideration for Location

Geographical consideration is an important dimension in audience analysis. Wise preachers have recognized that using New England illustrations in the Midwest or Midwest illustrations on the West Coast is ineffective communication. A preference ought to be made for local identification. Billy Graham in his crusades has followed this lead. He usually begins each crusade with comments about that area, producing identification with him and therefore attracting his audience. This conveys a feeling of concern about them as persons. The author once experienced a serious communication breakdown in Canada because he failed to use local illustrations and chose, quite naively, illustrations drawn exclusively from his stateside experiences. The geographical concern is most important.

2. Uniformitarianism

There is a pulpit tendency to stereotype Christian experience. Careful audience analysis denies a preacher the privilege of assuming that a common standard of excellence can be applied to all. Christian grace can be understood only in terms of the individual, biological, psychological, or social situation.

3. Preaching with Children in Mind

The preacher should learn to be brief and to the point. Succinctness is a virtue for which every preacher ought to strive, particularly for the sake of children in the congregation. No small fry weaned on Saturday cartoons can endure sermons that drag on needlessly. Nothing is sanctified by the sheer weight of its duration.

A further concern of the preacher who would address children is to use understandable language. This applies as well to adults. Too many preachers have literally followed the wag who said, "If you can't convince them, confuse them." Only the insecure preacher needs to flaunt the esoteric language of the seminary. All that talk about anthropology, eschatology, existentialism, Calvinism, mythology, pneumatology, plus Greek and Hebrew terms is beside the point. Not even the learned professionals care about these things. What they want to hear is a simple word from God about forgiveness, love, hope, peace, assurance, and meaning in life.

Illustrations must be earthy, for that is where people live. You will recall that in the first century it was the disciples who tried to keep children from Jesus. Today it is sometimes the preacher. Preaching with children in mind is to preach to the point, in language children know, with illustrations they understand and appreciate. We will not always succeed in the endeavor, but any successful communication with the young is worth the effort.

NOTES

1. Elwood Kieser, C.S.P., *Preaching*, II, No. 5 (September-October 1967), p. 4.

2. Marshall McLuhan, *Understanding Media*, p. 120.

3. David Dempsey, "Environmental Bookshelf," *Saturday Review* (March 7, 1970), p. 61.

4. S. I. Hayakawa, "The Sorcery of Television," *Santa Monica Evening Outlook* (March 9, 1970).

5. Hayakawa, "The Sorcery of Television."

6. McLuhan, *Understanding Media*, p. 157.

7. McLuhan, *The Medium Is the Massage*, p. 114.

8. McLuhan, p. 63.

9. McLuhan, p. 18.

10. McLuhan, *Understanding Media*, p. 74.

11. McLuhan, *The Medium Is the Massage*, p. 126.

12. Noel Jordan, "Mass Communications: The Absurdities," *University of Denver Magazine*, Vol. 6, No. 5 (Spring 1969), p. 19.

13. McLuhan, *War and Peace*, p. 77.

14. McLuhan, *Understanding Media*, p. 18.

15. Prentice Meador, "Toward an Understanding of Today's Listener," *Preaching*, II, No. 5 (September-October 1967), 38-39.

16. Abraham H. Maslow, *Motivation and Personality* (New York: Harper & Brothers, 1954), p. 91.

17. Jesse Jai McNeil, *The Preacher-Prophet in Mass Society* (Grand Rapids: Wm. B. Eerdmans Publishing Co., 1961), pp. 56-66.

18. Winston Lamont Brembeck and William Smiley Howell, *Persuasion: A Means of Social Control* (Englewood Cliffs, N.J.: Prentice-Hall, Inc., 1952), pp. 321-327.

19. Charles F. Kemp, *Life-Situation Preaching* (St. Louis: The Bethany Press, 1956), p. 55.

20. Gary Cronkhite, *Persuasion: Speech and Behavioral Change* (Indianapolis: The Bobbs-Merrill Company, Inc., 1969), p. 76.

21. Theodore Clevenger, Jr., *Audience Analysis* (New York: The Bobbs-Merrill Company, Inc., 1966), p. 87.

22. Clevenger, p. 14.

23. Thomas M. Scheidel, *Persuasive Speaking* (Glenview, Ill.: Scott, Foresman and Company, 1967), p. 47.

24. Clevenger, p. 29.

25. Walter Russell Bowie, *Preaching* (New York: Abingdon Press, 1954), p. 28.

26. Alan H. Monroe and Douglas Ehninger, *Principles and Types of Speech*, 6th ed. (Palo Alto: Scott, Foresman and Co., 1967), p. 137.

27. Milton Dickens and David H. Krueger, "Speakers' Accuracy in Identifying Immediate Audience Responses During a Speech," *The Speech Teacher*, XVIII (November 1969), 303-307.

28. Dickens and Krueger, pp. 303-307.

29. Clevenger, p. 13.

30. Webb B. Garrison, *The Preacher and His Audience* (Westwood, N.J.: Fleming H. Revell Company, 1954), p. 43.

CHAPTER FOUR • THE SETTING

CHAPTER FOUR / COMMUNICATION—THE SETTING

Preaching, historically, has been in the context of worship. There are, of course, exceptions to the rule. Noteworthy attempts to "preach" the gospel have been made in such unlikely places as on the Sunset Strip in Hollywood and on Bourbon Street in the midst of the French Quarter in New Orleans. The "liturgy" that precedes and follows such preaching is not generally considered part of what we would call the worship experience. Such imaginative ventures by people like Arthur Blessitt and Bob Harrington deserve the support and encouragement of concerned Christians, even though discussion of their forms is not within the scope of this chapter.

Our concern in this chapter is with the more conventional phenomenon of a sermon in the context of worship in a church building. We limit ourselves to this setting not because there is anything wrong with other settings, but simply because most preaching does not occur outside the church building. Other forms and other attempts are to be applauded and need to be considered in other works on the subject.

Christians are commanded, "Thou shalt worship the Lord thy God" (Matt. 4:10). Worship may be defined simply as the response of the creature to the creator. Ronald A. Ward defines worship as "an adoring mental attitude toward God and an outward expression in corporate speech and act."[1] It includes a recognition of the holiness, goodness, and love of God. If God is utter perfection, then certainly He ought to be praised.

The psalmist gives us the purpose of worship when he says, "Give unto the Lord the glory due unto his name; worship the Lord in the beauty of holiness" (Ps. 29:2 KJV). Or, as it is in the modern rendering, "Ascribe to the Lord the glory of his name; worship the Lord in holy array" (Ps. 29:2 RSV).

S. Barton Babbage is correct when he notes that "the primary purpose of worship is not moral uplift nor ecstatic feeling nor aesthetic pleasure; on the contrary, worship means giving to God that of which he is worthy (the root word means 'worth-ship'), that which is his due."[2]

The criteria by which we judge the propriety of worship and the aids to worship are summed up in the question, Does it give glory to God? The spirit of worship is always more important than its form, order, or logistics. When the spirit is right, irregularities or even omissions may be readily excused.

In the Lord's parable regarding the publican you may recall that this man confined himself to supplication and confession. In the eyes of God his worship was acceptable, although it may be criticized as being both defective and disordered. He had, however, offered to God something acceptable and of genuine worth. People need to know how important their attitude is in the worship experience. Going to church is not similar to going to a football game, where you watch others perform but do not participate. "If they go to be entertained, they will be disappointed; if they go to criticize, they will find flaws; but if they go to worship they will find values regardless of the architecture of the room or the subject of the sermon."[3]

The attitude commended by the Master in His discourse on prayer is perhaps appropriate for the worshiper as he seeks a meaningful meeting with his Creator. "Ask, and it will be given you; seek, and you will find; knock, and it will be opened to you" (Luke 11:9 RSV).

It is hoped that the revival of interest in worship and liturgy will help signal the fulfillment of the words spoken in 1922 by Karl Barth: "On Sunday morning when the bells ring to call the congregation and minister to church, there is in the air an *expectancy* that something great, crucial, and even momentous is to *happen.*"[4] Such a setting would lend itself most naturally and purposefully to the preacher's task of declaring the good news that God was in Christ reconciling the world unto Himself.

GOALS FOR WORSHIP

1. A Reasoned Approach

It is to be hoped that all worship will be done purposefully and not haphazardly. God is a God of order. He deserves to be worshiped in a thoughtful manner. Time given to consideration of the act of worship is time well spent. For some this means the development of a worship rhythm. Isaiah 6 has frequently been used as a directive for a reasonable and purposeful scheme in worship. Isaiah the prophet describes a vision he had in the temple. It occurred in the year King Uzziah died from leprosy. God's holiness was revealed and the seraphim called to one another and said, "Holy, holy, holy is the Lord of hosts; the whole earth is full of his glory" (Isa. 6:3).

Following Isaiah's vision of the holiness of God, he could only cry out in repentance and confession, "Woe is me! For I am lost; for I am a man of unclean lips, and I dwell in the midst of a people of unclean lips; for my eyes have seen the King, the Lord of hosts!" (6:5).

Then one of the seraphim flew to Isaiah and taking a burning coal from the altar touched his mouth and said, "Behold, this has touched your lips; your guilt is taken away, and your sin forgiven" (6:7). Following the revelation of God's holiness and Isaiah's response in terms of repentance, confession, and cleansing, the voice of the Lord is heard saying, "Whom shall I send, and who will go for us?" The reaction of the prophet is explicit, "Here am I! Send me" (6:8).

God challenges the prophet and the prophet responds. Four distinct elements arise out of the consideration of the prophet's experience.

(1) **Adoration.** God is adored. His name is recognized as holy. There is pure, open recognition of who God is in the perfectness of His person. The only response is that of "holy, holy, holy." Worship is initiated in such an endearing stance.

(2) **Confession and cleansing.** All too frequently confession and cleansing or confession and absolution have been omitted in the liturgy of churches within the free church tradition. Such a deletion is unfortunate. There is much to say for introducing a time and a prayer of confession early in the liturgy. Contemplation of the holiness of God does awaken a sense of sin, and as soon as the congregation is ready there ought to be an opportunity for confession of sin and the assurance of forgiveness. The clergyman who leads worship can direct the members of the congregation in areas where they might make their own confession, if a printed confession is deemed inadvisable. The form is incidental. The inclusion of confession is, however, integral to the worship rhythm.

(3) **Instruction.** The choir anthem may be part of this, as is the reading of Scripture and the sermon. These ingredients ought to reveal a plan or motif. Each aspect of the worship service ought to "fit" and be integral to the overall direction of the experience. Whether acted upon or not, the thought and focus of a particular worship service ought to be identifiable.

(4) **Response to the challenge that has been offered.** Increasingly the offering is included at this time as a corporate response to the goodness and grace of God. Opportunity for personal response to the challenge offered in the sermon may take any number of forms. The traditional invitation or more innovative formats are worthy of consideration. Invitations to silent prayer, private confession, or singing a song that captures the spirit of dedication and desire represented by the congregation are all meaningful responses which find a reflection of the spirit of Isaiah who when challenged to go said, "Here am I! Send me" (6:8).

For some a reasoned approach to worship suggests psychological progression in which feeling tones are directed. John Knox prefers to speak of various moods or movements: "Adoration and thanksgiving, confrontation with God's will, confession of sin, the seeking of forgiveness and of other help we need, affirmation of faith, consecration of life."[5]

One senses that in the worship rhythm or psychological progression the one thing often overlooked and yet imperative to proper worship is the sense of exuberance which characterized Old Testament worship as well as the enthusiastic joy apparent in New Testament worship. Jesus said, "These things I have spoken to you, that my joy may be in you, and that your joy may be full" (John 15:11). The disciples were full of the Holy Spirit and joy (Acts 13:52). Paul reminded the church at Galatia that the fruit of the Holy

Spirit includes joy (Gal. 5:22). The Epistle of I John was written "that our joy may be complete" (I John 1:4).

The modern church does not seem to experience the exuberance and joy that the church in the Old and the New Testament experienced. This is not because worship has ruled it out, but because worship has been misunderstood as a sober, doleful experience rather than a relationship to the creator marked by celebration, festivity, and joy.

The New Testament was not written by a committee and then kept safe in the church for security purposes, but arose instead "in the context of a joyful, worshipping church."[6]

2. Thematic Coherence

There ought to be a clearly defined focus which affects sermon topic selection, Scripture, selection of congregational and special music, content of prayer, and other ingredients in the liturgy. At times thematic coherence is simply an accident unrelated to purposeful planning. When a guest speaker comes to fill the pulpit it just may be that his sermon subject does "fit" into the worship theme, but such a chance approach to worship is not to be commended on a weekly basis. The framework of the service is determined by the theology and tradition within which the church fashions its own ministry. But the materials that form the substance of that worship experience—the hymns, the prayers, the anthems, the sermon, the Scripture—are unified in a single theme.

Donald Macleod speaks of the sermon as the central idea which becomes the "integrative factor" in the choice of subjects.[7] A relation of harmony which avoids the problem of fragmentation draws together all the elements of the liturgy into a single meaningful experience. If thematic coherence is to exist, it necessitates early planning: a minimum of three weeks prior to the actual worship experience. There is need for coordination of efforts between organist, choir director, preacher, and other worship participants. Some choir directors plan the music at least one month in advance, printing this data after careful consultation with the preacher so that there is a minimum of fragmentation and a maximum use of topic concentration.

While every attempt should be made to seek a dominating theme for any given service which will focus on some particular truth, it is also to be noted that there may be those who "go away unhelped unless the other aspects of Christian worship have also found a place within the service, and have not been neglected in the eagerness of emphasizing a part."[8]

This means that there ought to be times within the liturgy for the worshiper to be free to pray, to confess, to reflect, and to be alone with God without being directed. The organ prelude, offertory, and postlude can become meaningful times within the flow of the service when there is a time for nondirective worship. This implies that the organist should choose nondirective music that will allow the worshiper to be alone with his God to pray, to think, and to meditate without being thematically caught up in a predetermined direction. For this reason, music with familiar words is to be avoided.

3. A Quest for Excellence

The concern for quality should encompass at least the following:

(1) **Leaders of worship.** Not just anyone will do. Those who assist in the worship experience should be trained and prepared, so that their contribution will not detract from but contribute to the experience of the worshiper. It is better to pay for outside help that contributes to worship than to settle for local talent that may distract.

(2) **Advertising and printed aids.** The outdoor bulletin board becomes an obvious advertisement of the church and its ministry. It ought, therefore, to be neat in appearance and have a crisp, succinct message. When the bulletin board becomes encumbered with the details of every meeting during the week, it becomes impossible to read and unattractive to the passerby. If it is to be used appropriately it will be kept current, with only the most important items listed there every week. For some this means just the sermon title and the hour of the morning service and also the hour of the evening service if there is one. The name of the church, the clergyman, his staff, and the phone number may also be included. All other details are available to the interested person when he calls the church. To feel that every detail must be included on the bulletin board adds disorder and discourages interest and attention.

The worship folder which is supplied to the worshiper on Sundays giving directives for worship ought to be carefully laid out with reproduction that is accurate and attractive. It is possible that printing professionally done will be almost as reasonable as a secretary's time used to run off worship folders on a mimeograph machine. The appearance of the printed folder is generally more attractive. The worship folder should not be a newspaper filled with parish news of endless detail. If necessary a periodic newsletter can be used to take up the slack of material that would detract from the central purpose of the worship folder. An insert suggesting devotional readings for the week which are correlated to the preacher's topics for the following Sunday has been profitably used by some. It is wise to append a question for the adults and perhaps another question for the children, for each of the daily listings, to guide them as they worship at home together.

The newspaper and other mass media can also provide helpful aids to worship. When these are used the quality of presentation should be commensurate with the character of worship itself.

(3) **Physical considerations.** No church building committee should accept its responsibility without due consideration to the immensity of its task. The architecture of a church proclaims a message that either augments the preached word or conflicts with it. The nonverbal impact is greater than most building committees recognize. "If the Gospel of Christ is worthy of accurate verbal proclamation week by week, it is also worthy of faithful architectural proclamation, where its message speaks year after year."[9]

What is required for the contemporary church building is not a fake or fictitious imitation of the past. For instance, gothic architecture was fine for the thirteenth century, but a church built in the 1970s should be an authentic and honest expression of the faith in the materials and forms of today. "We then indicate the timeless relevance of the Gospel for all men, at all times, in all places."[10]

The contemporary church has had a difficult time working its way through the "edifice complex." It is a travesty of stewardship when congregations invest millions and millions of dollars in buildings, rationalized away as monuments of aesthetic beauty dedicated to God while, if the truth could be known, one would not be surprised to discover that frequently they were monuments to the building committee or the massive egotism of a "successful pastor." In our day we need to recover a sense of being a pilgrim people where we do not build buildings that last forever, but where investments are made primarily in people, which inevitably includes programs and staffing. Buildings are means, not ends. Therefore, there ought to be simplicity. Ornateness is admired but simplicity encourages use. Quality workmanship is to be encouraged. It may be an instance of false economy when we attempt to do a cheap job. Flexibility is also a necessity. Permanent seating may be a thing of the past. The so-called sanctuary ought to have some use during the week. Symbolic representations also deserve consideration, for each becomes a form of proclamation. Certainly the building ought to be indigenous, representing its culture and its setting—growing out of the culture, not being distinct from it, so that it fits into its geographical locale.

The placement of chairs or pews is of no small importance. While it is true that there are no significant studies that tell us the most satisfactory arrangement of members in situations that involve large groups, the best advice to the communicator is that he ought to discover some arrangement in which the source has the ability to direct the flow of communication rather than one in which there is an opportunity for cliques to form, or for private discussions to start wherein leadership can shift to someone else in the room.[11]

Theater style seating is very common in those American churches where the church may contain as many as one hundred to one hundred and fifty rows. More recently some architects have helped a congregation to do something symbolic of the *koinonia* or fellowship that ought to characterize the Christian church. As a result we have the "wrap-around church" or church in a semicircle, in which the communion table and the pulpit are centered with the congregation around them. This lends itself to a more theologically defensible structure and also assists the listeners. The farther a man is from the speaker, the greater the distractions and the less the likelihood that effective communication will occur. It is possible to build a church that has no more than eight or nine rows that will seat 350 people if constructed in a semicircle around the pulpit.

It is also better to raise the seating slightly as it moves away from the pulpit than to raise the pulpit. The symbolism of a raised pulpit suggests that the preacher is above contradiction rather than being a part of the fellowship of the church, where preaching becomes part of the church's ministry and not simply the ministry of the preacher.

Physical discomfort and good listening are not synonymous. Proper temperature must be maintained; for if it is too warm or if there is poor ventilation, drowsiness and discomfort occur. Adequate lighting will also be beneficial in worship. Enough lights should be provided so that the hymnal and the Bible may be read by the congregation without strain. Dimly lit churches seem to depress the spirit of the congregation.

Concern for acoustics is also to be urged. Every congregation has some people with deficient hearing. Poor acoustics or an inadequate or nonexisting public address system will prevent good communication.

Attention to other minor details such as the pulpit Bible being opened beforehand, hymns properly indicated on the hymn board, the organist having been provided an order of service, earphones and amplifying system tested before each service, the clock regulated, and a punctual beginning must not be overlooked. Environmental barriers should be kept at a minimum so that ample consideration is given to the dynamics of the total communicative event.

In the final analysis there are two standards by which our quest for excellence may be judged. First, does it glorify God? Second, does it "build" the worshipers (I Cor. 10:23; 14:3 ff., 12, 17, 26)?

(4) **Lay participation.** Modern authors remind us that the Christian church has been guilty of too much passivism. In response to this charge it is not sufficient simply to have laymen make announcements, lead in prayer, or read Scripture. There needs to be a form of corporate participation. When this does not occur it is not always the pastor's fault. The church often places him in a situation in which lay people prefer to be led, prefer to have someone else be active, and

thus they choose to maintain their passivity. I recall an occasion when the chairman of the trustees was asked to share a matter of concern with the entire congregation. He spoke for some five minutes regarding the building of a Christian education unit. Following his short message he passed me on his way to his pew and said with a quivering voice, "You can have this job." He was saying something that others have said: Let the preacher do it. We want to sit back; we want to listen; we want to watch; we would prefer not to be involved.

But a kind of participation and corporate response in worship can occur, say, through informed hymn singing. An insert in the worship folder giving the background of a hymn, followed by three or four Sundays in which a new hymn is sung until it becomes known and loved, can be a great aid to involvement. The introduction of fresh litanies, more attention to confession, and the encouragement of testimonies are also helpful. On a visit to the East Harlem Protestant Parish I heard George Webber talk about his congregation in its experimentation with worship. One element they refused to delete from their service was a time of "sharing." This part of the service in which they could give a word of testimony became for them the one important ingredient that they did not want to dispense with at any cost.

Lay participation may also be encouraged through dialogical sermons and sermons designed for actual feedback sessions. These forms will be discussed in detail at a later time.

(5) **Flexibility**. If we admit (as we must) that the Holy Spirit is sovereign, it is necessary for us to be deprived of the luxury of frozen forms. "Service as usual" may quench rather than enhance the worship experience. It is very easy to fall into worship ruts. Some churches have tried to vary their format on a regular basis. One church, for example, introduces a new order of service every three months in its quest to discover ways by which the congregation may more effectively meet with God in a meaningful worship experience. This flexibility distinguishes means from ends. The worship, adoration, and recognition of God is primary. The means for the accomplishment of that goal and the building of God's people in the process determine all that the church attempts to do. Isn't it interesting that the church of the "immaculate perception" which we have in the contemporary scene would be embarrassed with the confusion that characterized the congregation on the day of Pentecost. There must be a place for the Holy Spirit to come and disrupt, change, and modify so that the purposes of God may be achieved.

RELATION OF WORSHIP TO THE SERMON

1. Integral, Not Distinct

The sermon needs the service of worship just as the service of worship needs the sermon. Each becomes significant in the light of the other.

> Unless we conceive of preaching as being itself an act of worship, we miss what is most essential in it and what distinguishes it most radically from other kinds of teaching, religious or secular. . . . Either preaching contributes to, provides a medium of, worship, or it is not preaching at all.[12]

Just like "love and marriage go together like a horse and carriage," so the sermon and worship go together in a wholistic, *gestalt* experience. It is heresy of the first order to set preaching and worship over against each other. Preaching is an act of worship. When this is not accepted, extremes can develop; undue importance is given to either preaching or to liturgy. Lycurgus M. Starkey, Jr., describes it as follows:

> The prima donna of the pulpit considers the worship service with its appropriate mood music and lighting devices as no more than a proper setting for his moment on the stage. The liturgical fanatic retreats into the aesthetic to escape the terrible discipline of preaching and becomes little more than the manipulator of exotic rituals.[13]

Such extremism is unfortunate but it does exist.

2. Equal in Importance, Not Subordinate

The "opening exercises" heresy in which all the ingredients of the service become subordinate to the sermon, which becomes the important element in the worship service, is to be discredited. Any part may be for some worshiper the most meaningful element on any given day. It may be the prayer, or music, a litany, Scripture reading, or the anthem that will meet the person as he attempts to have an audience with God. It is important to remember that one never knows in advance through whom or through what God may choose to speak.

Hymns, confessions, and prayers do not simply or merely prepare the way for the sermon, but become equal in importance to the preached Word. In all of these elements God is at work, meeting with His people. The sermon as an essential part of the worship program is no more or less important than the other constituent parts. "The preaching of the Word should complement and endorse all that has gone before."[14] This means that the so-called preaching service is an inaccurate term. It is a worship service that includes among the other elements the preaching of the Word. The concern that gave rise to preaching as something of primary importance is valid. It represents a departure from sacramentalism and a movement toward concern for God and His address to His people through His Word. But it must be readily acknowledged that God does speak His Word through the reading of Scripture, through prayer, through litany, through music, as well as through preaching.

3. Definite Preparation

The liturgy of the worship service is a preliminary tuning for the sermon itself. Preliminary tuning is "a state of readiness to respond to some particular person or thing in a uniform and predictable fashion."[15] This concept takes note of a certain amount of inertia in auditors' moods and thought patterns. Once the listener has been channeled into a particular train of thought or emotion, the subsequent message related to that thought or emotion will elicit from the listener a stronger or more uniform response than would otherwise be the case.[16]

This underlines the importance of thematic coherence, a focus on a single concern which finds its final emphasis in the sermon. The worship service functions as a psychological ally, establishing the feeling tones, changing the moods of the congregation, drawing the veil on other distractions from the outside world, and bringing attention to the primary concern of that worship hour.

Worship is part of the total preaching event, which includes congregation, message, preacher, and channel. The setting will either contribute or detract. Concern for the setting of worship will do much to contribute to the effectiveness of the preached Word.

NOTES

1. Ronald A. Ward, "Worship: The New Testament Basis," *Baker's Dictionary of Practical Theology*, ed. Ralph G. Turnbull (Grand Rapids: Baker Book House, 1967), p. 364.

2. S. Barton Babbage, "Worship: Aids to Worship," *Baker's Dictionary of Practical Theology*, p. 401.

3. Charles F. Kemp, *Life-Situation Preaching* (St. Louis: The Bethany Press, 1956), p. 209.

4. Karl Barth, *The Word of God and the Word of Man*, trans. Douglas Horton (New York: Harper and Brothers Publishers, 1957), p. 104.

5. John Knox, *The Integrity of Preaching* (New York: Abingdon Press, 1957), p. 78.

6. Ward, p. 365.

7. Donald Macleod, "The Sermon in Worship," *Baker's Dictionary of Practical Theology*, p. 68.

8. F. S. Fitzsimmonds, "Worship: General or Regular Services," *Baker's Dictionary of Practical Theology*, p. 398.

9. Babbage, p. 402.

10. Babbage, p. 402.

11. Erwin P. Bettinghaus, *Persuasive Communication* (New York: Holt, Rinehart and Winston, Inc., 1968), p. 205.

12. Knox, pp. 75, 76.

13. Lycurgus M. Starkey, Jr., *The Holy Spirit at Work in the Church* (New York: Abingdon Press, 1965), p. 80.

14. William Prior, "Worship: Constituents of Liturgy," *Baker's Dictionary of Practical Theology*, p. 408.

15. Theodore Clevenger, Jr., *Audience Analysis* (New York: The Bobbs-Merrill Company, Inc., 1966), p. 11.

16. Clevenger, pp. 11, 12.

COMMUNICATION—THE MEANS

ESTABLISHED STRUCTURES

1. Deductive
2. Inductive
3. Psychological
4. Dramatic (Narrative)

EXPERIMENTAL METHODS

1. Dialogical
2. Drama
3. Mixed Media
4. Visual

CHAPTER FIVE • THE MEANS

CHAPTER FIVE / COMMUNICATION—THE MEANS

Communication is a dynamic process with an almost unlimited set of variables—time, place, environment, sender, message, channel, receiver, to name just a few of the recognized categories within which there are even further dimensions of influence. It is our purpose in this chapter to isolate the structure (channel) variable. For some, such as Charles Koller, this variable is of utmost importance.

> The structural specifications for a good sermon are comparable to the specifications by which the primitive Indian fashioned his arrows. He realized that his very survival might depend upon the excellence of his arrow. The shaft must therefore be absolutely straight, lest it wobble in flight; the point must be sharp enough to penetrate; the feathers must be in just the right amount to steady the arrow in flight, yet not to retard its flight or dull its thrust. Similarly, the sermon must have a clear thought running straight through the length of it, a sharp point at the end, and just enough "feathers" to cope with the atmosphere through which it must pass on its way to the target.[1]

While the channel must be recognized as important, excessive attention to this variable can be detrimental to the total communication event. Forms are not to be served so much as to be used. McLuhan's hyperbolic thesis that the "medium is the massage" has helped to refocus the attention of communication theorists on the oft neglected channel, at the same time that it underscores the fact that a channel is its own form of message. Michael Bell, speaking from within the Roman Catholic tradition, makes comments that are equally appropriate to most Protestant situations.

> There are continuing attempts to renew the traditional parish mission but many of these miss the mark because their concern is with content—"updating" the mission sermon, making it more liturgical, more scriptural, etc. The real problem is not at all with content but with the medium. Because it remains a non-participational listening experience the mission cannot compete with the new communications environments created by mass media.[2]

To say, moreover, that the content of the message "has about as much importance as the stenciling on the casing of an atomic bomb"[3] is hyperbole gone awry. The other side of the case is presented by Wayne N. Thompson, who maintains in the light of existing quantitative research in communication and public speaking that "although good organization certainly does no harm, it is not the critical distinction between good and bad speaking. The speaker should not spend so much time and effort on organization that he sacrifices the attainment of other strong qualities."[4]

We insist, and Thompson would probably concur, that although organization is not the critical distinction, it is an important ingredient which deserves proper consideration and ample time. It is not to be treated with indifference, but rather as a necessity in sermonic preparation.

Technique, content, and delivery all play a vital role in the crisis moment when the Word is preached. Each can add to or subtract from the total effect. Sound structure will not make up for deficiency of content, but other things being equal it will generally enhance the possibility of effectiveness. A thoughtful attempt at structure will aid the speaker as well as the listener whose inbuilt sense of timing, progress, and proportion must be respected. John E. Baird says, "A good speaker never arranges his speech by accident."[5] Order may not be "heaven's first law," but it does serve the purpose of those who still honor logic and abhor chaos.

Simplistic approaches to structure are all too common. Henry Grady Davis lumps such phenomena into the rubric of homiletical carpentry.

> Speeches can of course be knocked together with a saw and hammer. There is always much lumber of moral and religious platitudes lying around—prose, verse, stock anecdotes, glittering generalities, all over the place—kites in the wind of fashionable thought. A man can cut, splice, and nail it together exactly as he would build a doghouse.[6]

Let us now consider the structural options that open to the preacher of the Word. First we will examine the more established structures which have already proved useful to speakers. Second, we will look at the more recent experimental formats. We will attempt to define and illustrate each of these types.

ESTABLISHED STRUCTURES

1. Deductive

The deductive structure is logical in form. It states a proposition, central idea or theme, and then develops it through the use of particulars such as exegesis, exposition, or illustration. There is little question about the direction of the preacher's thought. This is established at the outset and unfolded through the course of the sermon.

In *Expository Preaching Without Notes* Charles W. Koller commends a deductive structure which he calls "the basic pattern." The first step after a sermonic passage has been determined and the exegetical and expositional work has been completed is for the preacher to formulate a *proposition* or thesis which becomes the heart of the sermon. This proposition indicates the course of the discussion which is to follow. It must be formulated with scrupulous accuracy. If it is too broad, the development will fall short of its promise. If it is too narrowly determined, the expectations of the audience will be too low for appreciative listening. It should be in effect a generalization establishing some universal truth stated modestly and clearly without embellishment or exaggeration. Normally it takes the form of a simple sentence. Structurally, this is the most important sentence in the entire sermon. It must, therefore, be free from even the slightest touch of ambiguity. If it is to stimulate some expectation, it should not disclose too much, but should simply indicate the direction that the sermon will take. Of course, it must be sufficiently important to warrant the elaboration that follows in the body of the sermon.[7]

The second step after the proposition has been established is to ask an **interrogative** of that central idea. This is a critical point since the interrogative is the connective link between the thesis and main points of the sermon. The procedure is to ask one of the seven well-known interrogatives (who? which? what? why? when? where? and how?) of the proposition. Only one of the seven is used in any single sermon of "the basic pattern" type. The points that follow answer the question which is asked of the proposition. While the interrogative is generally not expressed in the sermon, it is always there inasmuch as every affirmation (i.e., main point) is in effect an answer to this single interrogative.[8]

A third homiletical device in basic pattern sermons is the establishment of a "key word." This is a noun or noun form of a verb or adjective. The key word must be specific. For instance, *things* is too general. The range of possible key words is practically unlimited. For example, such words as *barriers, dangers, elements, examples, details, manifestations, opinions, resources,* and *values* can be utilized. If there is structural unity in a sermon there is a key word, recognized in the development of that sermon, which characterizes each of the main points and holds the structure together, Koller says:

> The value of a clear cut thesis and a "Key Word" that exactly fits each of the main divisions can scarcely be overstated. The "Key Word" opens a corridor down the length of the sermon structure, with direct access from the front entrance to every room, instead of leaving the preacher and his hearers wandering uncertainly from room to room.[9]

Generally in basic pattern sermons a **transitional sentence** helps to link the introduction of the sermon to the main body. This transitional sentence usually includes an interrogative substitute, the key word, and the proposition, followed by the fourth homiletical device, namely, the main points. The main points, designated by Roman numerals, are stated as sentences or clauses, concise but complete. They are to be mutually exclusive. They should be coordinated in terms of proportion, unity, and sequence, inasmuch as there ought to be progression discernible to the audience, which leads cumulatively to a strong finish. They should be parallel in form, so far as possible. Parallelism should be maintained although alliteration is not necessary. Each of the points is to be coextensive with the proposition and should be undergirded by scriptural backing. This scriptural undergirding should be visible, logical, and not open to debate. It establishes the authority of the sermon.

Koller offers the following as an example of a basic pattern sermon.

Title: "How to Deal with Temptation"
Scripture: Matthew 4:1-11

> Introduction:
> 1. Temptation to sin is our common lot.
> 2. Temptation, successfully withstood, can be a means to spiritual blessing.

Thesis: 3. Temptation can be successfully resisted.
>   (Interrogative: "How?")

Transition: Like Christ, we must meet certain conditions:
>   (Key Word: "Conditions")
> 1. We must know the Word of God. ("It is written.")
> 2. We must believe the Word of God. ("It is written.")
> 3. We must obey the Word of God. ("It is written.")

> Conclusion:
> If we, like Christ in the wilderness, know . . . believe . . . obey
> . . . we too shall rise in triumph. . . .

Further developments of this sermonic pattern are to be found in the writings of Faris Daniel Whitesell and Lloyd M. Perry. Numerous types of the deductive method abound in homiletical literature. Most of them, to be sure, are less elaborate than the basic pattern. For example, there is the **jewel** or **diamond** approach in which the thesis is stated and then the various facets are developed. For instance, a sermon on the doctrine of justification could take its textual support from three passages in the Book of Romans: (1) the ground of justification (5:9); (2) the proof of justification (4:25); (3) the means of justification (5:1). The central truth is justification, and the three points are facets of that single truth. Alexander Maclaren, the nineteenth century prince of expository preachers, in a sermon titled "Love and Forgiveness" took Luke 7:36-50 and developed his idea in the jewel pattern. Each of his points was based on one of the three persons in the story: (1) Christ "standing as a manifestation of the divine love coming forth amongst sinners"; (2) The Woman, representative of a class of character, "the penitent lovingly recognizing the Divine love"; (3) The Pharisee, "the unloving and self-righteous man, ignorant of the love of Christ."[12]

A further variation on the deductive structure is the **telescopic** or **ladder** approach. This is the expansion of an idea. Each point depends on the previous point. For example, John 17:19 could be developed as follows: (1) "I sanctify myself"; (2) "for their sakes I sanctify myself"; (3) "for their sakes I sanctify myself, that they also might be sanctified through the truth."

Another form of the deductive structure is the **single-point sermon.** Instead of developing a theme in logical, sequential fashion, point by point, a single proposition is chosen and treated rather exhaustively. The approach is deductive. The proposition is stated, defined, discussed, developed, illustrated, and applied. This approach avoids the potential difficulty of having two, three, four, or more sermonettes within a sermon. Coherence is maintained as a single point is established. The method, in the hands of the thoughtful preacher, is very effective; in the hands of the careless it can be oppressively redundant. Thomas Chalmers' well-known sermon, "The Expulsive Power of a New Affection," is a single-point sermon on I John 2:15. His proposition is that a man may attempt to displace from the human heart its love of the world by setting forth another object which is worthy of its attachment, so that the heart will be moved to resign an old affection and exchange it for a new one. The thesis is established and a few practical observations are deduced.[13]

In each of these approaches the points, with the exception of the single-point sermon, should be an outgrowth of the passage of Scripture on which they are based. Generally, the points should be clearly stated. There is no particular virtue in being subtle about structure. Donald G. Miller is one who seriously questions the value of "silent-transmission homiletics. While riding in a car it may not be imperative that the rider know in what gear the mechanism is moving. But listening to a sermon ought not to be such a passive experience. Listening to a sermon involves conscious thought."[14]

Expository sermons lend themselves naturally to the deductive pattern. A passage is unfolded logically or sequentially. A sermon on "the prodigal son" could be developed: (1) Sick of home; (2) Homesick; (3) Home.[15]

2. Inductive

In deductive preaching the tone and direction are established at the outset of the sermon. In the inductive method an element of surprise remains. That is, the proposition, central idea, or thesis is not elaborated until the particulars have been worked through with the congregation and only at the conclusion of the journey is the thesis clearly enunciated. The deductive method is most appropriate when the congregation is in sympathy with, or agrees to the thesis of, the speaker. When this is not true and the congregation must be persuaded of a proposition's validity, it is wise to consider the inductive method in order to avoid early resistance from the listeners. When the congregation can wrestle with the speaker en route to a conclusion that he hopes they will share, he spares them the early closure that is always present in deductive preaching.

One of the most popular structures in the inductive category is the **problem solution** pattern. This structure utilizes two points: (1) statement, development, and analysis of the problem with its complexity, its particular interest and relation to the audience; (2) a statement of solution and its application drawing from the resources of the gospel in the meeting of that particular need. Some prefer to call it the "need and satisfaction" pattern because it deals with a recognized need and a recommended solution. The first sermon preached by Arthur John Gossip following his wife's dramatic, sudden death was titled, "But When Life Tumbles In, What Then?"[16] This autobiographical sermon tells of his utter sense of disaster and despair, his loneliness, his questioning of Emerson's "chirpy optimism" and his identification with Shakespeare who said that it is not difficult to bear other people's toothaches, but when one's own jaw is throbbing that is another matter. He asks the inevitable question, "Why, why, why?" The evidence, he contends, looks fairly damning that God really does love when this sort of thing occurs. From a clear, moving presentation of the problem he proceeds to a solution. "You people in the sunshine *may* believe the faith, but we in the shadow *must* believe it. We have nothing else. Some things become very clear: (1) that the faith works, fulfills itself, is real, and that its most audacious promises are true, and (2) one becomes certain about immortality." The sermon concludes, "I, too, like Hopeful, can call back to you who one day in your turn will have to cross it, 'Be of good cheer, my brother, for I feel the bottom, and it is sound.' " (A reference to the Jordan River.)

The **Hegelian** pattern (named for the philosopher George William Friedrich Hegel, 1770-1831) employs thesis, antithesis, and synthesis, or exposition, complication, and resolution. To state it still another way, the structure employs the ideal, the actual, and the reconciliation. A Hegelian sermon might take the following form: (1) thesis—God is holy; (2) antithesis—Man is sinful; (3) synthesis—God has acted through Jesus Christ to reconcile sinful man to Himself.

The **syllogistic** approach cites a major premise, a minor premise, and a resolving conclusion. Such a sermon might, for instance, cite a major premise such as the fact that Christ died for sinners. The minor premise could be "You are a sinner." The conclusion emerges as "Christ died for you."

A further variation within the inductive category is **questioning to the point of satisfaction.** John A. T. Robinson in a sermon on the ascension pointed out that this is not a fact in history nor is it a reference to time and space. It concludes with a satisfactory answer, at least to his mind, that the ascension is a cosmic event regarding the Lordship of Christ.[17]

The **analogical** structure is another potentially useful inductive approach. Jesus spoke analogically of Himself as the door, the shepherd, or the vine. John Bunyan's *Pilgrim's Progress* is the best-known analogy with proven sermonic possibilities. It is a method which is easily abused when the analogies are pressed too far. Sangster notes:

> It is not always simple to know where to draw the line. Paul likens the Church to a body, and mentions the eye and the hand and the foot. Did the preacher overdo it who, handling the same analogy, told some members of his congregation, not that they were an eye or a hand or a foot, but that they were the tonsils ("We are not worse off when you

are gone"), and the appendix ("We did not know we had you till you caused us trouble"), and the artificial teeth ("Sometimes you are in and sometimes you are out")?[18]

The pros and cons of the deductive and inductive approaches have been repeatedly argued. The relative merits of organizational matters are still debatable but this much we know: A *climax order* arranges materials so that the most important materials are placed last; an *anticlimax order* is an arrangement in which the most important materials are presented first; and a *pyramidal order* has the most important materials placed in the middle.

> The researcher says . . . placing an argument or an important piece of material in the middle of a message does not seem to be as effective as placing it in either the first or last position. In choosing between the first and last, however, the evidence seems to show some slight preference for a placement in the final position.[19]

3. Psychological

Alan H. Monroe's "motivated sequence" is the best-known psychological approach to speech making. He discards the names of the conventional divisions (introduction, body, conclusion) in favor of a five-step motivated sequence, each of which is named to correspond with the function of that step in securing a particular reaction from his audience. The steps are labeled attention, need, satisfaction, visualization, and action. "In a speech to persuade, for example, the student would probably organize his speech using all five steps, trying (1) to gain attention, then (2) create a feeling of need for action of some sort, (3) satisfy that need by suggesting a proposal and proving its soundness, (4) make his audience visualize the satisfaction, and finally (5) impel his listeners to act."[20] All five of these steps are not needed in every speech, however. The structure may be used either in its entirety or in abbreviated form.

Viewing this approach from the audience's perspective, the five points would be: (1) I want to listen; (2) something needs to be done, decided, or felt; (3) this is the thing to do, to believe, or feel, to satisfy the need; (4) I can see myself enjoying the satisfaction of doing, believing, or feeling this; (5) I will do or believe or feel.[21]

Harry Emerson Fosdick's well-known sermon, "Forgiveness of Sins," is in the Monroe tradition. Fosdick begins by securing the attention of his audience by saying that he is going to talk only to those who are sinners. He shows them their need by discussing what sin is all about, including everyone in his definition. Then he provides a biblical satisfaction and in the process shows them what it would mean to be forgiven. Finally, he concludes by saying, "Take out that unforgiven sin. For your soul's sake, get rid of it! But there is only one way. Whatever theology you hold, it is the way of the cross—penitence, confession, restitution, pardon."[22]

4. Dramatic (Narrative)

This pattern can be either historical or biographical. If it is historical the preacher relates a chain of circumstances (facts, instances, experiences, cases, developments leading to the central truth he is trying to make). In the biographical approach he builds the sermon around a person, not around a particular truth. A seminary student delivered a poignant sermon on the prophet Jeremiah, using the entire book for his source material. The first-person sermon showed the wrestling of Jeremiah with the prophetic call, his temptation to resign, his conversation with God where he told of being tricked into service, and included a few items he wanted to get off his chest before he surrendered the prophet's robe. The sermon concluded, "I can't stand it. I will be your prophet. It is burning within me. There is fire in my mouth." Scripture abounds with potential material for biographical preaching. To be sure, the preacher must use his sanctified imagination as he fills in the details. The Bible was not written as an anthology of biographies. It requires some very careful study, study not only of the text but also of historical and geographical data available to the preacher, plus the preacher's imagination. Dwight E. Stevenson should be consulted for helpful guidelines in the development of this form of biographical preaching. He illustrates the method with a sermon on Jacob.[23]

The narrative sermon is a very interesting and dramatic form of preaching. But it is often misused and the impact ruined when the preacher feels obligated to append a conclusion. The meaning should be indirectly applied through the characters, their interaction, their conversation. To have an explicit "preachy" conclusion destroys the inherent force of the narrative. The teller must trust that his own sermon will convey the meaning without loading it with explanations. This is done through hints and suggestive touches here and there.

I presented a series of three sermons during the Lenten season in which the choir assisted by singing "Were you there when they crucified my Lord, were you there?" The sermon series took the form of an extended answer to that question—one sermon on Barabbas, another on the Centurion, and a third on Thomas. In the first two the response was, "Yes, I was there"; and the sermon unfolded in the first person. In the third sermon the response was, "No, I was not there; I should have been, but I wasn't"; and a first-person sermon followed.

The methods we have noted are the most popular to emerge from the preaching literature, though by no means do they exhaust the possibilities open to the creative preacher. Other methods can be found in sermon anthologies and preaching journals. Try them; they may be useful.

EXPERIMENTAL METHODS

Two preliminary observations are in order:

(1) **The gospel is changeless.** Man's problem has always been, and will

continue to be, sin with its resultant alienation from God and the inevitable loneliness, guilt, and meaninglessness which attend this condition. God's answer is still found in Jesus Christ. It is trite but true that the emptiness in man's life is God shaped and only Christ can fill that basic vacuum. The charismatic message of the death and resurrection of Jesus the Christ with its call to repentance and faith, described in Acts 2, is still the primary message of the preacher. It is folly to serve up half a Christ to modern man. Paul was willing to be all things to all men, but there were certain things that Paul would not be to anyone. He would not dilute the gospel in order to be heard. It is better to give no hope than false hope. The gospel states in no uncertain terms that man has a problem and God has the solution.

(2) **Methods necessarily change.** The best preaching of any age is preaching that is addressed to that particular age. Much preaching has unfortunately degenerated into disquisition on ancient history or a rehearsal of the problems of antiquity. People are not concerned with the Jebusites, the Philistines, or the Hittites. They are concerned about meaning and life. Methods must therefore be enlisted which grant a hearing to the timeless message. There is nothing sacred about structure. There is nothing sacred about classical or traditional patterns. The only thing that is sacred is the gospel itself.

There is always a need for freshness and vitality, a Christ-honoring worldliness, if you please. Experimental preaching is an attempt to impress the truth. We have to fight sameness. While advocating the need for experimentation, we must also listen to Helmut Thielicke who cautions:

> We need to test the spirits and determine to what spirit these advocates of the new belong—whether they are men who have been struck by the message and are now bearing witness to that message with new means, or whether they are merely clever fellows who are suffering from their brain waves or liturgical playboys who want to try a new twist.[24]

Consider the following experimental methods:

1. Dialogical

Preaching is a two-way street. It is not an active speaker and a passive listener. This monological illusion is being seriously questioned in our day and rightly so! The parishioner is not content to be preached at. He wants a slice of the action. He wants to be considered a participant in the preaching of the church. The day has come when we ought to consider cutting back on the frequency of our preaching. Our much preaching has not been very effective. We have presented newer ideas, concepts, duties, and responsibilities without any opportunity for people to talk back, to wrestle with those ideas, to absorb and integrate the content before we parcel out some more. The challenge is to preach less, to do a better job when we do, and in the process help people to become involved in the implementation of the truth being shared.

Participational preaching is such an important consideration for the contemporary preacher that we will devote the entire sixteenth chapter of this volume to the subject.

2. Drama

Increasingly we are discovering the value of drama in the church's ministry. Youth groups, adult groups, trained professionals, and even preachers themselves are becoming involved in this form of gospel presentation. Some churches have gone so far as to build movable stages, to provide sophisticated lighting, curtains, and any added apparatus necessary for an effective quality performance. For most churches there still exists a difficulty of stage space as well as equipment in the church building. "Just as the preacher has to compete with trained speakers on radio and television, so the actor in religious drama has to face comparison with the polished professionals who are seen nightly on television. A good cause will no longer excuse a miserable performance."[25]

In spite of these difficulties, drama does serve to state effectively a problem in graphic fashion and perhaps does so more effectively than the preacher in the traditional, verbal, monological role. Drama can also effectively make application of a solution. To be sure, it cannot provide exegesis and it may not be as effective as the verbal approach in the explanation of some theological idea, but drama does supply concreteness and vividness in a way that preaching alone cannot do.

One San Francisco area church has conducted an "on stage" performance for many years on Sunday nights. Various approaches are used. Some of the sermons are acted out, some are pantomimed, some are done by silhouette. The attendance generally exceeds that of the Sunday morning congregation. People living in a graphic, pictorial era are interested in seeing the gospel presented in this kind of dramatic fashion.

3. Mixed Media

This form of presentation is a "happening"—not a haphazard massage to the senses, but a very carefully structured program designed to leave the viewer free to draw his own conclusions out of the experiences.

> It is also meant to be an experience of sensory overload, a hyperstimulation of all the senses in one area of human life. The goal is a kind of catharsis, new insights into the human condition, new relationships rising out of the familiar, liberating a person to take a total, simultaneous approach to a question . . . something which most traditional teaching methods neglect.[26]

Materials for a typical mixed-media program may include slides, films, sounds, and songs by the likes of Simon and Garfunkel, Bob Dylan, and the late Beatles. These and others who speak prophetically about our kind of world can be most useful. Mixed-media programs usually revolve around a given topic like war, race, violence, or sex. They suggest the urgency of the hour and the crisis that the church faces. The purpose is to create an environment in which the gospel may be creatively applied through the Holy Spirit.

Helpful directives on this form of presentation are offered by Anthony Schillaci in an article called "A Multi-Media Program—On Preaching Today."[27] While it is true that people do not willingly expose themselves to information that threatens their frame of reference and they do practice selective exposure and even selective retention of the materials they have available,[28] mixed media do provide a fresh, mind-expanding experience for the congregation. It should further be noted that when the receiver fails to understand materials presented through a visual mode alone, the auditory explanation may be of some help. For materials that are relatively simple to grasp, single-channel presentation is likely to prove quite satisfactory.[29]

4. Visual

Dale's "Cone of Learning" suggests that seeing is more effective than simply listening to a message. The wise preacher takes advantage of the chalkboard, pictures, graphs, overhead projectors, and opaque projectors. One preacher in a Thanksgiving sermon titled "Lord, Make Us More Thinkful" used five objects: bell, hammer, lightbulb, Bible, and cross to depict areas in which Americans ought to be grateful.[30] My pastor once used twisted coat hangers to illustrate a sermonic idea. In an imaginative fashion he showed how lives get twisted and tangled. Then, using a pliers and shears showed how life could be corrected as he reworked the hangers into more meaningful forms.

No method ought to be discarded until it is seriously considered as a possible mode of presenting the gospel message. Any method that will serve to underline, underscore, and make fresh the age-old message is worthy of consideration and possible implementation.

CONCLUSION

What is the best method of preaching? Who knows? This much seems certain—more than one method must be in the preacher's repertoire. Predictability from the pulpit is deadening for the listener. Variety, surprise, and even novelty are imperatives if the congregation is to be aroused, challenged, and refreshed. All too many parishioners have ears and hear not, eyes and see not, due to routinized preaching. What method is best? Certainly not the one that is used all the time, although some notable preachers have been slavishly attached to one structure. Alexander Maclaren's sermons were always of the three-decker type: introduction, three points, and conclusion. It will be noted, however, that the preaching of this pulpit giant did not turn chiefly on his unvarying structure. His structure tended rather to monotony. His sermons were gloriously redeemed by other gifts he possessed. Grady Davis reminds us:

> There is no ideal or standard form which every sermon should take. . . . There is no preexistent mold into which the substance of thought must be poured in order to make a sermon. . . . That unusual sermon we occasionally hear of, that good sermon which is supposed to break all homiletical rules—generally its preacher is the one who proudly admits that it does—is a fiction. If it is a good sermon, it does not break good rules; it breaks only the unnecessary and artificial rules.[31]

In summary we note: (1) No structure is sacred, only the gospel is. (2) Any structure may be helpful—it is naturalness, usefulness, and effectiveness that matter in the determination or selection. (3) Variety should be developed. You and your people need it—predictability is deadening. Any method that gets in the way of effective communication ought to be immediately discarded. Any method, moreover, that enhances communication serves as a viable option.

NOTES

1. Charles W. Koller, *Expository Preaching Without Notes* (Grand Rapids: Baker Book House, 1962), p. 41.

2. Michael Bell, C.P., "Preaching in Our Mass Media Environment," *Preaching,* IV, No. 1 (January-February 1969), 23.

3. "Playboy Interview: Marshall McLuhan," *Playboy,* Vol. 16, No. 3 (March 1969), 56.

4. Wayne N. Thompson, *Quantitative Research in P.A. & C.* (New York: Random House, Inc., 1967), p. 68.

5. John E. Baird, *Preparing for Platform and Pulpit* (Nashville: Abingdon Press, 1968), p. 154.

6. Henry Grady Davis, *Design for Preaching* (Philadelphia: Fortress Press, 1958), p. 82.

7. Koller, pp. 72-73.

8. Koller, pp. 51-52.

9. Koller, pp. 52-53.

10. Koller, pp. 79-81.

11. Koller, pp. 74-75.

12. Andrew W. Blackwood, *The Protestant Pulpit* (New York: Abingdon Press, 1947), pp. 107-113.

13. Blackwood, pp. 50-62.

14. Donald G. Miller, *The Way to Biblical Preaching* (New York: Abingdon Press, 1957), p. 95.

15. W. E. Sangster, *The Craft of Sermon Construction* (Philadelphia: The Westminster Press, 1951).

16. Blackwood, pp. 198-204.

17. "Ascendancy," *The Pulpit,* XXXVI, No. 5 (May 1965), 4-6.

18. Sangster, p. 98.

19. Erwin P. Bettinghaus, *Persuasive Communication* (New York: Holt, Rinehart and Winston, Inc., 1968), pp. 152-153.

20. Alan H. Monroe, *Principles and Types of Speech,* 4th ed. (Chicago: Scott, Foresman and Company, 1955), Preface ix.

21. Monroe, p. 315.

22. Blackwood, pp. 191-197.

23. Dwight E. Stevenson, *In the Biblical Preacher's Workshop* (Nashville: Abingdon Press, 1967), pp. 91-106.

24. Helmut Thielicke, *The Trouble with the Church: A Call for Renewal,* trans. John W. Doberstein (New York: Harper & Row Publishers, 1965), p. 49.

25. W. A. Poovey, "Preaching and Drama," *Lutheran Quarterly,* XX (November 1968), 375.

26. Anthony Schillaci, O.P., "A Multi-Media Program—On Preaching Today," *Preaching,* III, No. 5 (November-December 1968), 32.

27. Schillaci, pp. 32-36.

28. Bettinghaus, p. 180.

29. Bettinghaus, p. 171.

30. Wayne Dehoney, "Lord, Make Us More Thinkful," *Pulpit Digest,* XLVI, No. 326 (November 1965), 33, 34, 36-38.

31. Davis, pp. 8-9.

BIBLICAL TRUTH

PART TWO

BIBLICAL TRUTH—PREACHING THE BIBLE

DEFINITION OF BIBLICAL PREACHING

PROCESS OF DEVELOPING BIBLICAL SERMONS

1. Exegesis
2. Exposition
3. Application

TYPES OF BIBLICAL SERMONS

1. Topical Sermons
2. Textual Sermons
3. Expository Sermons

THE USE OF THE TEXT IN PREACHING

1. Topic Source
2. Launching Pad
3. Garage
4. Railroad tracks
5. Trolley Wire

CHAPTER SIX • PREACHING THE BIBLE

CHAPTER SIX / BIBLICAL TRUTH—PREACHING THE BIBLE

"With preaching Christianity stands or falls."[1] Maybe so. The case appears to be well founded. It is far safer to say, however, that preaching stands or falls with its faithfulness to the Bible. It is a contradiction in terms to speak of preaching that is unbiblical. To preach is to preach the Bible. Any purported sermons that are unbiblical must be thought of as religious essays, addresses, or speeches, outside the aegis of the sermonic. To preach is to speak with authority, hence biblically. The preacher is appropriately called a "herald of God"[2] or a "servant of the Word."[3]

It is the preaching of God's Word that makes the church a unique institution in society. What other right does a man have to speak so brazenly unless he has a word from God? "The preacher is not in the pulpit to express himself, to impose himself upon the congregation, but to expose and express the divine truth in Scripture, with as little human interposition as possible."[4]

Half a century ago Karl Barth lamented:

Am I not at least partly right when I say that people, educated and uneducated alike, are simply *disappointed* in us, unspeakably disappointed? Have they been too often—perhaps for centuries—*put off?* Has the church, in spite of its very best of intentions to meet their needs, too often indulged in secondary utterances?[5]

All week long our people hear the words of man. They have been immersed in the news of war, racial crisis, political intrigue, economic unrest, and other national and international traumas. Is it unwarranted to expect that when they come to church on Sunday they will hear a unique word, a word from God? Does not the preacher dabble in foolishness and secondary utterances when he simply describes what they hear all week long? Preaching's unique claim to a hearing is that it is a word from God, a word revealed in the Word of God. Indeed, it is a word of hope.

Man seeks authority, and that authority for faith and action resides supremely and finally in the Bible. Some would challenge this statement and say that the church is the authority in questions of faith and practice. Unfortunately the church has often erred regarding such matters. "And when in error, she must be corrected by a norm outside and above herself— lest she correct herself by herself."[6] Still others appeal to conscience or reason for authority. Such authority as this, however, is extremely open to question and doubt, regardless of what may seem like impeccable judgment. Where authority is seen as conscience or reason, "each individual is his own authority, and the Christian faith becomes what *each* individual thinks it is."[7]

The authority of biblical preaching is founded on the internal persuasion of the Holy Spirit. Resting in Scripture as authority is an act of faith.[8] The Bible is authoritative on several bases, not the least of which is its own internal testimony to inspiration (II Tim. 3:16; I Peter 1:21). This act is complete. The official canon is closed. The Holy Spirit has completed the task of inspiring men to provide the church and world alike with an authoritative, self-authenticating guide to God's intentions for His creature, man.

Illumination, in contrast to inspiration, is an ongoing act of the Holy Spirit extending the truth found in inspired Scripture. Jesus said the Holy Spirit would "teach you all things, and bring to your remembrance all that I have said to you" (John 14:26). "When the Spirit of truth comes, he will guide you into all the truth; for he will not speak on his own authority, but whatever he hears he will speak, and he will declare to you the things that are to come. He will glorify me, for he will take what is mine and declare it to you" (John 16:13, 14).

Another basic concept in this context is that of interpretation. Assuming the text is inspired and the Holy Spirit illuminates that text, then it remains for the preacher to interpret the Word for his people. Here the task becomes dangerous in its subjectivity. The preacher is constantly making judgments which are susceptible to distortion, presuppositional bias, and theological nearsightedness. It is an ominous thing when the preacher confuses his interpretation with inspiration or illumination. The goal of the preacher is to work toward the greatest possible correlation of the three: inspiration, illumination, and interpretation. But mark it well, no interpreter is infallible and the Bible's authority is in no sense impaired by this concession.

DEFINITION OF BIBLICAL PREACHING

There is much that passes for biblical preaching which upon closer examination is nothing of the kind. Instead it is a form of topical address which erroneously enlists proof texts. Congregations are frequently numbed into an uncritical acceptance of this sort of thing as long as the so-called sermon is accompanied by Scripture verses and references. If it refers to the Bible it must be biblical—so some assume. It is possible, as John Knox notes, "to preach a quite unbiblical sermon on a biblical text; it is also possible to preach a quite biblical sermon on no text at all."[9] A magical view is sometimes fostered unintentionally by certain preacher types who believe that a sermon, if it is to be a sermon, must be heavily weighted with the exact words of Scripture. Although the concern which gives rise to this attitude is legitimate—namely, that there can be no unbiblical preaching—the absolute application of the principle is misinformed. A sermon can be biblical without any text at all, and a sermon with many texts can be most unbiblical. This is not to encourage a form of preaching which regularly uses the Bible in a covert fashion. Most biblical preaching should declare forthrightly and manifestly its dependence on passages from Scripture. We do, however, need to guard against a naiveté which maintains that a Scripture passage be either noted or references be quoted if a sermon is to be in fact biblical. This approach is simplistic and serves as an injustice to the church, the preacher, and the cause of Christ.

Preaching that cannot honestly be related to the Bible cannot establish its claim to be Christian preaching at all. A useful definition of biblical preaching comes from John Bright: "The exposition of a biblical text or of some segment of the Bible's teaching, and the proclamation of that as normative for Christian faith and practice."[10] John Knox adds that biblical preaching (1) remains close to the characteristic and essential biblical ideas; (2) [is] centrally concerned with the central biblical event, the event of Christ; (3) answers to and nourishes the essential life of the church; (4) [is] preaching in which the event in a real sense is recurring.[11]

A Christian sermon should have certain hallmarks:

(1) **It will be theistic**; that is, it will be a witness to God. He will not be somewhere in the background, but will be distinctly in the center of the sermon. It will be evidence of the creator's call to His creature.

(2) **It will be Christocentric.** "The Christian message is not a set of collected ideals, nor even of revealed truths: the Christian message is Christ, the Person. . . . We are ordained to follow and serve Him, and this takes precedence over any secondary ecclesiastical loyalty."[12] A legitimate question for the parishioner to ask of the preacher is, "Where is Christ in the sermon?"

(3) **It is dependent on both the Old and the New Testament.** It is a false choice to choose between the two. The minister of the gospel ought to know and preach from both Testaments. The Old Testament was normative Scripture to Jesus and it is normative as well for the church when properly understood.[13] The reader is encouraged to consider seriously the thinking of John Bright in *The Authority of the Old Testament* (Nashville: Abingdon Press, 1967), where a proper understanding of the Old Testament as normative Scripture is discussed.

(4) **The minister's sermon will be only a part of the whole gospel.** It is grossly unfair to demand that every sermon include the whole gospel; however, eventually the whole gospel must be declared. Every partial presentation points beyond itself to the direction of the whole gospel.[14] The evangelistic preacher must not limit his attention to the truth of John 3:16, and the social action preacher needs the balance of John 3:16 lest his message be lopsided. A total exposure to the full counsel of God should be forthcoming from the pulpit.

(5) **The sermon should be interesting.** Dullness is the worst sin of the pulpit. When the preacher fails to grip his people, he has no right to complain that they are reluctant to believe or attend his preaching.

People cannot be expected to come to church simply as a matter of course to be bored by dry sermons. The gospel is interesting; only teachers and preachers are dull. The inherent interest of the Bible needs to be captured by the proclaimer.

(6) **The sermon ought to be defensible.** No one has a right to stand in the pulpit and declare that which will have to be unlearned outside the stained glass building. The preacher will have to ask himself if this material is of such a nature that it will not be proved false by honest study. At times, to be sure, he will err; but the task of preaching is of such a nature as to call for this kind of preparation.[15]

(7) **The sermon should mediate the presence of God.** A faithful sermon will usher people into the presence of a holy God. The experience of Isaiah in the temple should not be so unique as to be looked at as a historical curiosity. James S. Stewart asks the preacher, "Did they, or did they not, meet God today?"[16] For an affirmative answer the preacher must fade into the background and allow the person of Christ to dominate the sermon, so as to mediate the divine presence.

PROCESS OF DEVELOPING BIBLICAL SERMONS

One of two routes is usually taken in developing biblical sermons. The first begins with a passage of Scripture, then develops the subject contained in it. The second starts with the subject (a concern, need, burden of the pastor, etc.), then works back toward Scripture to find legitimate biblical support. "The text may find the preacher or the searching preacher may find the text."[17] Now the task begins. How should a man go about developing a biblical sermon? James T. Cleland suggests three stages through which personal reflection must pass. Stage one is investigation or exegesis of the Word of God, which deals with the *then.* Stage two is interpretation or exposition of the good news at the heart of the message, which deals with the *always.* Stage three is the application of the eternal good news to the contemporary situation, which deals with the *now.*[18]

John Bright's approach is similar. He also begins with exegesis. The second step is *theological exegesis:* "an exegesis that is not content merely to bring out the precise verbal meaning of the text but that goes on to lay bare the theology that informs the text. . . . All biblical texts are expressive of theology in that all are animated, if at times indirectly, by some theological concern."[19] Step three is translation of the exegesis into the idiom of today. "Each sermon thus becomes at once a theological and psychological exercise (what someone has called an exegesis both of the text and the congregation)."[20]

1. Exegesis

The biblical interpreter begins by attempting to discover what the biblical text meant to the author who penned it. Scholars are generally agreed that the best way to discover what the Bible intends is through the grammatical-historical method. The text is taken as meaning what its words most plainly mean in the light of the historical life situation to which it was originally addressed. The grammar is then interpreted against the background of this history. What did the text mean to its writer and what did the writer intend it to mean to his first readers?

Using his linguistic and critical tools the interpreter, to the best of his ability, seeks to discover what Isaiah, Jeremiah, the psalmist, Mark, Peter, John, or Paul actually intended to say. A certain amount of factual data will aid the preacher in this exegetical task. Who spoke the words of the text? What kind of person was he? What was his background? Who was addressed? What kinds of persons were addressed? What was the situation socially, economically, and politically? When was it written? What was the significance in the time? Is any significance to be attached to the place? What were the circumstances that prompted the message? What was the occasion? What aim did the speaker or writer have in mind?

Though these are general questions they provide a meaningful background against which the specific questions of the given text may be answered. An authoritative sermon rests on a passage which can firmly support it. Eisegesis occurs when we read our own ideas into the text or find meanings which its author did not intend. Biblical scholarship exists in order to serve the ends of preaching,

> to provide the exegetical raw material out of which sermons may be fashioned; or, in perhaps a better metaphor, to supply (and I do not mean ready-made) the exegetical skeletons (and I do not mean sermon outlines) which the preacher will clothe with flesh and sinews, and God—if he see fit—will fill with his Spirit.[21]

James Cleland discusses three types of homiletical sinners guilty of eisegesis:[22] (1) *Ignorant* preachers who are unintelligent, unaware, and uninformed. For example, a preacher might take Colossians 2:21 and develop a temperance sermon, although the text does not validate this idea at all. (2) *Slovenly* preachers who are slipshod and careless. They know better, but the busyness of life or the foolishness of schedule has robbed them of valuable study time. I once preached a sermon on Hebrews 12:1. I identified the "witnesses" as the unbelieving world that surrounds Christians, when the author of the Book of Hebrews obviously intended "witnesses" to be the heroes of faith outlined in the preceding chapter. (3) *Dishonest* preachers. They prefer a lie to the truth because it preaches better. There was a student at Duke, according to Cleland, who preached on Job 13:15—"Though he slay me, yet will I trust him" (KJV). Though he had read Moffatt, the Revised Standard Version, examined the Interpreter's Bible, and discussed it in Old Testament class, he chose the King James Version because it made a better sermon.

Barrett tells of a discussion between his father and a well-known Methodist preacher of a bygone day. " 'When I have found a text,' said my father, 'I always begin by studying the context in order to make sure of its original setting and meaning.' 'When I find a text,' replied his companion, 'I never look up the context for fear it spoils the sermon.' That is dishonest; that is handling the Word of God deceitfully."[23]

The goal in exegesis is to be as completely objective as possible. To be sure, no scholar has completely succeeded at all times and with every text; but objectivity in exegesis, like holiness in life, is an ideal toward which the preacher is to strive. He allows his personal presuppositions to be corrected by the text. He does not use Scripture for his own homiletical devices.

2. Exposition

Exposition is the task of discovering what in the text stands for all time. What is always true of God and His work among men? John Bright articulates a compelling theory of biblical preaching which promises to lift the interpreter away from the occasional dilemma that is created by biblical injunctions or patterns of practice that seem to be culturally bound. The Old Testament in particular seems to have numerous events, practices, and injunctions that have a time-bound character. Bright, rather than becoming involved in this time-bound and timeless discussion, moves on to discover what theological concerns inform the text and give it abiding authority for today. He properly maintains that all of the Bible is valid for us, inasmuch as each of the texts in some way reflects or expresses some aspect of the structure of theology and therefore shares in the normative authority of Scripture.

> There are no non-theological texts in the Bible. We will continue to use some parts more than others; but it is not a question of selecting certain passages as valid and discarding others, but of laying hold in each passage of that theological concern that informs it.[24]

For example, Bright takes the historical narrative of David and Bathsheba (II Sam. 11 and 12), with its sordid tale of lust and adultery, treachery and murder; then, rather than simply salvaging a few stray morals from the story, gives its theological importance. It portrays the theology of the Mosaic covenant which establishes the overlordship of the divine King in those who are subject to His law. It shows that a crime against a brother is a breach against the covenant. This David is God's chosen and designated king to whom His promises have been given and through whose line His gracious purposes for His people will be set forward. The message that speaks to every generation is that through Christ there is an eternal promise for those who live in covenant with Him. Through Nathan it condemns us and drives us to confess our sin against our brother as a sin against Christ. It reminds us that nothing that I can do erases the wrong that I have done, and impels me to penitence, to seek no righteousness, justification, or merit of my own.[25]

Viewed in this way theological exegesis is a bridge between the past scriptural event and a present application to contemporary man. Heinrich Ott talks of this as a hermeneutical arch which helps to explain the inter-relation between theology and preaching. As he says, "If it won't preach, it's not much of a theology."[26] He defines theology as "the reflective function of preaching itself."[27] This theological concern when brought to the Old Testament requires a further step. Because the preacher is a Christian and has received the Old Testament from the hands of Christ who is its fulfillment, he is impelled to bring his text to the New Testament, as it were, for a verdict. Recognizing the reality of progressive revelation helps the preacher discern fulfillment in the New Testament. The Christian sermon is to be more than bare theism; it must be Christocentric. At the same time assiduous exegetical effort should insure each text, whether Old or New Testament, of its grammatical and historical accuracy.

Bright's insight delivers us from becoming involved in the normative nature of Israel's history or in historically conditioned forms, laws, customs, institutions, and ancient patterns of thinking. It helps us discover the normative nature of the Old Testament, which is precisely in its theology. True preaching, to speak theologically, is the story of God's redemptive activity in Jesus Christ, of God's personal approach and holy action regard-ing salvation, demanding surrender and faith.

Theological exposition, serving as a bridge between the past event and the present life, underscores Donald Miller's concern that "the central concern of preaching . . . is so to rehearse the story of God's redeeming action in Christ that this becomes a living reality in the act of preaching." [28]

Bright's emphasis is most helpful. It does contain, however, an overstate-ment regarding the homiletical use of the Old Testament. He warns against moralistic preaching; yet some of his own examples are guilty of the very thing he indicts. And who is to say that the Old Testament does not provide positive and negative illustrations of God's work among men and what God expects between men? It is legitimate to use the Old Testament to illustrate man's need, man's dilemma, and God's provision through the lives of men and women whose basic experiences were similar to ours. We need to be cautioned continually, however, against using the Bible solely as a book of illustrations which throw light on human situations. Such practice easily degenerates into shallow, moralistic preaching.

3. Application

The appeals for a return to biblical preaching have in some places strengthened the pulpit. In some places, however, the appeals have gone unheeded or, perhaps worse, "have resulted in dull exegesis from the pulpit or in irrelevant homilies about things that occurred long ago and far away."[29] People are tired of preachers who spend too much time illuminat-ing the text and shed no light on life today. Biblical preaching can never be, if properly understood, a lesson on ancient history or an elaboration on what was helpful to the Gerasenes, the Hittites, or the Jebusites. Authentic biblical preaching is relevant, vitally relevant, and is "always in the present tense."[30] It is not only "thus *said* the Lord," but "thus *saith* the Lord."

James Cleland speaks of a sermon as an ellipse.

> It does not have a single focus but two focuses. It is not a case of being Bible centered or man centered. It is the conscious, careful recognition of both the historic faith and the folk in front of the pulpit. There are always two centers of interest in a sound sermon—the historic faith and the present day. Which is more important? The answer is: which focus is more important in drawing an ellipse? Both are indispensable. Together they form the Word of God.[31]

What is the link that joins the past and present? Paul Tillich maintains that

> we must communicate the Gospel as a message of man understanding his own predicament. What we must do, and can do successfully, is to show the structures of anxiety, of conflicts, of guilt. These structures, which are effective because they mirror what we are, are in us and if we are right they are in other people also.[32]

All persons in every age, biblical and otherwise, know the dilemmas of life delineated by Tillich. As such we have a living link not only with the Bible but with each other. We are very much like the people of the ancient world. It is only in some superficial thoughts, rational beliefs, and mental moods that we are different. In all of the basic heart realities we are the same. We stand before God exactly as people in every age have stood before Him. We have all experienced David's guilt, the doubting of Thomas, Peter's denial, the falling away of Demas, perhaps even the kiss of the betrayer Judas. We are linked across the centuries by the realities and ambiguities of the human soul. The eternal message of the Bible addresses modern man. Until the sermon links past with present, not identifying them but linking them, the sermon is incomplete. It is a Bible lesson, not a sermon.

The preacher is caught up in the dynamic tension between past events and the ever new life in the Spirit. Such is both challenge and risk. For he who would venture to bring the Word of God into our time will tend to skirt the edge of heresy. When you speak to today and attempt to translate the message into the modern idiom, there is always the risk of distortion and heresy; but risk it we must, for preaching is present tense.

James Cleland summarizes the process of developing biblical sermons.

> If we think of the Good News as a diamond, then we have a threefold task before us. First, we chisel the diamond out of the rock in which it was found; that is investigation. Second, we polish the diamond and cut it to reveal all its glory; that is interpretation. Third, we place it in a contemporary setting, as in a ring, for all to see in this day and generation; that is application.[33]

TYPES OF BIBLICAL SERMONS 48107

Classification of sermons is an arbitrary business. An examination of sermon anthologies shows the difficulty of airtight categorization. Nonetheless, sermons may be helpfully classified with regard to form. Generally they are *topical, textual,* and *expository.* Although there is general agreement as to the terms, there is no uniformity in definition of the terms. Donald Miller, D. W. Cleverly Ford, and John Knox equate expository preaching with *any* preaching that is biblical; that is, if you are a biblical preacher then you are an expository preacher. "All true preaching is expository preaching, and that preaching which is not expository is not preaching."[34] For our purposes, however, all preaching must be biblical but not all preaching ought to be considered expository. Let us define a topical sermon as the elaboration of a topic, a textual sermon as the elaboration of a short text, and an expository sermon as the elaboration of a longer passage of Scripture. In addition, there are hybrids—topical-textual being the favorite.

In spite of the criticism that has been leveled against topical sermons, it is not necessarily true that a textual or expository sermon is more biblical than a topical sermon.

1. Topical Sermons

The topical sermon is built around a subject, an idea that bears no analytical relation to any one particular passage of Scripture. It is frequently the easiest type of preaching because it requires the least amount of background and biblical research. It grants greater freedom to the preacher without the restriction of a text, and lends itself to unity better than any other form. It is a very popular form due to its contemporary flavor and its concomitant pertinence for the listener. It is popular with the preacher because of its relative ease in preparation.

Problems reside in this form of preaching; namely, the tendency on the part of the preacher to play topical favorites and the tendency toward unbiblical preaching. The latter occurs because it lacks the safeguard of a text. James Stewart talks about a form of unbiblical topical preaching:

> It is deplorable that God's hungry sheep, hoping for the pasture of the living Word, should be fed on disquisitions on the themes of the latest headlines. It is calamitous that men and women, coming up to the church on Sunday—with God only knows what cares and sorrows, what hopes and shadowed memories, what heroic aspirations and moods of shame burdening their hearts—should be offered nothing better for their sustenance than one more dreary diagnosis of the crisis of the hour.[35]

Again, it is not proper to regard all topical sermons as unbiblical. The topical format does lend itself to very useful biblical preaching. Harry Emerson Fosdick's sermon titled "On Learning How to Pray" is developed

Lincoln Christian College

topically: (1) Pray receptively; (2) Pray affirmatively; (3) Pray dangerously; (4) Pray undiscourageably.[36] One cannot fault the points. They are both Christian and biblical. The unifying note of the sermon is no particular passage, but a meaningful topic.

2. Textual Sermons

The textual sermon is based on a verse or two from the Bible. The main theme and major sermon divisions come from the text. The thought of the sermon must always be consonant with the text. There must be no unwarranted inferences and the theme must unify the development of thought. One of the values of this type of preaching is that it is biblical and therefore restrains the preacher from perpetrating an exclusive diet of personal ideas upon his congregation. It also affords the opportunity for study in depth; that is, an intensive scrutiny of a single biblical concept found in a verse or two of Scripture.

The basic problem with textual preaching is that there is unlimited opportunity for selectivity. Texts that interest the preacher will become the diet of the congregation. And texts that do not interest the preacher will be neglected to both his and their loss.

Eisegesis is another potential problem in this form of preaching. This occurs when the total flavor or purpose of the longer passage is disregarded. Such a myopia bends and misuses the text rather than allowing it to be understood contextually and interpreted accordingly. When the Bible is appealed to in a proof-texting fashion it can be used as authority for most anything. Hence, it ceases to be a genuine authority.

A representative textual sermon is built on Romans 1:16 and titled "Unashamed of the Gospel of Christ." Four points are drawn from the text: (1) Power; (2) Power of God; (3) Power of God unto salvation; (4) Power of God unto salvation to everyone that believes. Another example is a sermon by Lyman Abbott titled "The Secret of Character" taken from John 1:13. (1) Character is not of blood—inheritance; (2) Character is not of the flesh—government; (3) Character is not of the will of man—education; (4) Character is of God—who has come in Christ.[37]

3. Expository Sermons

Expository sermons are based on a biblical passage longer than two verses. The theme and major divisions come from the text being considered. The thought is developed from the passage without importing ideas from other Scripture. It is unified by a single aim and subject, and attempts to present an ellipse of the past and present. It is not to be confused with a running commentary, pure exegesis, or a collection of miscellaneous thoughts on a subject. It has a single theme, developed from an extended passage, with that single theme acting as the basis of selection of material from the passage.

It is the best method for teaching the Bible as well as for the preacher learning the Bible. Charles W. Koller has said:

> Textual preaching has much to commend it; likewise, topical preaching. No one method should be employed exclusively. But as a prevailing method, for year-round ministering, expository preaching has the greater potential for the blessing and enrichment of both pastor and people.[38]

It covers a variety of subjects and needs without suggesting that the preacher is singling out individuals. It breaks as well the bonds of preacher preference. It has a built-in variety, particularly when consecutive expository preaching is done from a book or number of chapters. P. T. Forsyth maintains that "you have no idea how eager people are to have the Bible expounded, and how much they prefer you to unriddle what the Bible says, with its large utterance, than to confuse them with what you can make it say by some ingenuity."[39] One wag commented, "Now there abideth topical, textual and expository, and the greatest of these is expository." A facetious statement, to be sure, but sufficiently true to bear consideration.

Although with deep personal conviction I commend the expository method, it is not necessary to follow all the suggestions made by its proponents. For example, some think the expository sermon makes it necessary "for the homilist to derive all the subdivisions, as well as the main divisions, from the same unit of Scripture."[40] This is an unnecessary limitation upon the method. Expository preaching can be developed with subpoints taken from other Scripture as well as nonbiblical sources. The major thrust, theme, and the major points should, nonetheless, be drawn directly from the passage of Scripture under consideration. An expository sermon should be developed with clear-cut divisions that suggest the movement within the passage of Scripture.

This method has frequently been abused. Perhaps no one has done any worse than the one who preached on the Prodigal Son:

    I. His Madness
      (a) He wanted his tin
      (b) He surrendered to sin
      (c) He gave up his kin
    II. His Badness
      (a) He went to the dogs
      (b) He ate with the hogs
      (c) He hocked all his togs
   III. His Gladness
      (a) He was given the seal
      (b) He ate up the veal
      (c) He danced a reel

A noteworthy attempt at expository preaching using the same passage (Luke 15:11-32) includes three major points: (1) I want my way; (2) I want; (3) I am wanted. A sermon by Paul S. Rees titled "The Presence of God," using Psalm 139 as its text, is also exemplary: (1) The searching of God's presence, vv. 1-6; (2) The scope of God's presence, vv. 7-12; (3) The satisfaction of God's presence, vv. 13-18; (4) The severity of God's presence, vv. 19-22; (5) The supplication for God's presence, vv. 23 and 24.

THE USE OF THE TEXT IN PREACHING

The Bible has been wisely used, sometimes misused, and all too frequently abused by preachers. Let us review some of the ways in which the text has been used both legitimately and illegitimately.

1. Topic Source

A passage of Scripture has sometimes been used simply to isolate a topic without any further relation to the content of the sermon. For example, a denominational official delivered a sermon on the topic "Giants in the Earth" (Gen. 6:4). He spoke of the heritage of the denomination, referring to the founders as "giants in the earth." This is legitimate only when the purpose is acknowledged and no attempt is made to suggest that this is what the passage intended to teach.

2. Launching Pad

In this instance, the text is used as a point of departure. This occurs primarily in topical preaching. The foundation is biblical, sort of an ornamental frontispiece, and the building itself is extrabiblical. To change the metaphor, it is like an airplane that taxis down the runway on the terra firma of the text and then lifts off, with the pilot of the sermon taking it where he will. There seemingly is very little relation between the biblical base and what follows. In such cases the text is used as a pretext or motto and it does not really guide the thought of the sermon at all. Dwight E. Stevenson says, "If engaged in by young ministers it allows them to perpetuate a shallow knowledge of Scripture without compelling them to deepen it. . . . Moreover, they are using the text as its masters rather than serving the text as its ministers."[41]

3. Garage

This textual use occurs when the sermon unfolds in inductive fashion and concludes with the text. A college message delivered by a laywoman described the process that a family goes through when it prepares for a wedding. Using very graphic language she described all the pomp, preparation, detail, and color involved in this type of occasion. The listeners were intrigued as she caught them up in her portrayal of the event. It was not, however, until the last moments of the chapel hour that her biblical purpose was revealed. She simply concluded by reading Revelation 19:7-9: " 'Let us rejoice and exult and give him the glory, for the marriage of the Lamb has come, and his Bride has made herself ready; it was granted her to be clothed with fine linen, bright and pure'—for the fine linen is the righteous deeds of the saints. And the angel said to me, 'Write this: Blessed are those who are invited to the marriage supper of the Lamb.' " This is a proper and effective type of surprise conclusion. If properly done it involves the audience in the movement, thought, and idea of the preacher while not allowing it an early closure.

4. Railroad Tracks

Some preaching is little more than biblical teaching as it moves within the rigid bounds of exegesis. Great pains are taken with Greek words, Hebrew words, cultural setting, extended quotes from critical commentaries, but very little is done with present-day application. It is content centered and concurrently weak in exposition and practicality.

5. Trolley Wire

Years ago, when we lived in Chicago, there was a bus on Addison Street that was powered by an overhead electric line. The connection between the bus and the line was accomplished by means of a power pole. This pole allowed the bus to move in and out among traffic while still maintaining contact with the source of power. If the driver made too drastic a move, turned too far, or turned abruptly, the pole would disengage itself from the wire. The bus would grind to a halt. It was necessary to place the pole back in contact with the wire so that the bus could move once again. This is a parable on preaching. The best biblical preaching is that which transpires when there is an obvious relatedness to the source of power—namely, the text—while at the same time allowing for movement and flexibility in terms of the changing human situation. This is the paradox of freedom. There is great freedom as long as you stay within the boundaries already established.

Perhaps you recall the story of Toodle the engine, which is often recounted in books for small children. The engine, we are told, stayed in the train yard. He was denied the privilege of cross-country travel. One day he determined in his little engine heart to leave the limitation of his existence and move out into the fields to romp among the flowers and trees. So he left, but soon he got bogged down. It was necessary for a wrecking crew to go and rescue the little engine. When he was brought back to his proper sphere of life he said within his little engine heart, "True freedom is found by staying within the boundaries for which I was made." Just so, the sermon. The ideal is living within the boundaries while at the same time there is freedom to move within this context. We need to affirm both exegetical power and the dynamic nature of application.

Preaching worthy of the name is biblical. In a real sense there is no preaching that is not biblical. All too often preachers commissioned by the church and called of God have settled for secondary utterances, when all the while people are crying out, not simply for another exhaustive diagnosis of the human situation, but seeking a word from God. A word is desired about life, abundant life, about grace, about hope, about the provision of God in Jesus Christ.

The words of James Stewart are right on target:

> Give the strength of your ministry to expository (viz., biblical) preaching, and not only will you always have a hearing, not only will you keep your message fresh and varied, but, in the truest sense, you will be doing the work of an evangelist; and from many of those quiet words of grateful acknowledgment which are amongst the most precious and sacred rewards of any man's ministry, you will know that through the Scriptures God has spoken again, as He spoke to the fathers by the prophets.[42]

NOTES

1. Clyde Reid, *The Empty Pulpit* (New York: Harper & Row Publishers, 1967), p. 34.

2. James Stewart, *Heralds of God.* Reprint. (Grand Rapids: Baker Book House, 1972).

3. H. H. Farmer, *The Servant of the Word* (New York: Charles Scribner's Sons, 1942).

4. C. K. Barrett, *Biblical Problems and Biblical Preaching* (Philadelphia: Fortress Press, 1964), p. 30.

5. Karl Barth, *The Word of God and the Word of Man,* trans. Douglas Horton (New York: Harper and Brothers Publishers, 1957), p. 111.

6. John Bright, *The Authority of the Old Testament* (Nashville: Abingdon Press, 1967), p. 35.

7. Bright, p. 40.

8. John Calvin, *Institutes of the Christian Religion,* I, viii, 13; cf. also I, vii, 5.

9. John Knox, *The Integrity of Preaching* (New York: Abingdon Press, 1957), p. 19.

10. Bright, p. 163.

11. Knox, pp. 19-23.

12. Samuel M. Shoemaker, *Beginning Your Ministry* (New York: Harper and Row Publishers, 1963), p. 27.

13. Bright, p. 78.

14. Seward Hiltner, *Ferment in the Ministry* (New York: Abingdon Press, 1969), p. 65.

15. Francis A. Schaeffer, *The God Who Is There* (Chicago: Inter-Varsity Press, 1968), p. 166.

16. James S. Stewart, *Preaching* (London: The English Universities Press, Ltd., 1955), p. 28.

17. H. C. Brown, Jr., H. Gordon Clinard, Jesse J. Northcutt, *Steps to the Sermon* (Nashville: Broadman Press, 1963), p. 34.

18. James T. Cleland, *Preaching to Be Understood* (New York: Abingdon Press, 1965), p. 77.

19. Bright, p. 170.

20. Bright, p. 176.

21. Barrett, pp. 32-33.

22. Cleland, pp. 64-70.

23. Barrett, p. 37.

24. Bright, p. 152.

25. Bright, pp. 153-154.

26. Lycurgus M. Starkey, Jr., "Heinrich Ott—Theologian of Preaching," *Pulpit Digest*, I, No. 374 (April 1970), 9.

27. Heinrich Ott, *Theology and Preaching* (Philadelphia: The Westminster Press, 1965), p. 19.

28. Donald G. Miller, *The Way to Biblical Preaching* (New York: Abingdon Press, 1957), pp. 13-14.

29. Michel Philibert, *Christ's Preaching—and Ours*, trans. David Lewis (Richmond, Va.: John Knox Press, 1964).

30. Henry Grady Davis, *Design for Preaching* (Philadelphia: Fortress Press, 1958), p. 203.

31. Cleland, pp. 42-43.

32. Paul Tillich, "Communicating the Christian Message: A Question to Christian Ministers and Teachers," *Theology of Culture*, ed. Robert C. Kimball (New York: Oxford University Press, 1959), pp. 202-203.

33. Cleland, p. 79.

34. Miller, p. 22.

35. Stewart, p. 11.

36. Harry Emerson Fosdick, *Riverside Sermons* (New York: Harper & Brothers, 1958), pp. 112-121.

37. Lyman Abbott, "The Secret of Character," *Modern Sermons by World Scholars*, ed. Robert Scott and William C. Stiles (New York: Funk & Wagnalls Co., 1909), pp. 3-17.

38. Charles W. Koller, *Expository Preaching Without Notes* (Grand Rapids: Baker Book House, 1962), p. 28.

39. P. T. Forsyth, *Positive Preaching and the Modern Mind* (Naperville, Ill.: Allenson, 1957), pp. 112-113.

40. James Braga, *How to Prepare Bible Messages* (Portland, Ore.: Multnomah Press, 1969), p. 38.

41. Dwight E. Stevenson, *In the Biblical Preacher's Workshop* (Nashville: Abingdon Press, 1967), pp. 155-156.

42. Stewart, p. 97.

BIBLICAL TRUTH—PREPARATION FOR THE EVENT

GENERAL PREPARATION

1. Build a Quality Library
2. Read Widely
3. Listen Carefully
4. Record Insights

ADVANCE PREPARATION

WEEK BY WEEK PREPARATION

CHAPTER SEVEN • PREPARATION FOR THE EVENT

Henry Ward Beecher was once approached by a young divinity student who appeared troubled. "Doctor," the student said, "I am planning to enter the ministry. One thing that is worrying me is how long I should spend in preparing my sermons. I enjoyed your sermon so much this morning that I thought if you could tell me how long it took you to prepare I would have some idea of how much time I should use in preparing a sermon." Dr. Beecher looked at the young divinity student, smiled, and said, "Young man, I have been preparing the sermon I gave this morning ever since the day I was born." For the effective preacher all of life is preparation. There is nothing in life that is not part of a man's overall development. Every book he reads, every meeting he attends, every person with whom he visits is in some way contributing to his overall view of the world, his understanding of life, and his knowledge of communication.

GENERAL PREPARATION

The young preacher in particular should be encouraged to read books on the subject of speaking and writing. Such books as Rudolf Flesch, *The Art of Plain Talk;* Charlotte Lee, *Oral Interpretation;* Nedra Newkirk Lamar, *How to Speak the Written Word* should be known and read. Published sermons by other men ought also to be included in a man's reading repertoire. *The Protestant Pulpit,* edited by Andrew W. Blackwood, and *Master Sermons Through the Ages,* edited by William Alan Sadler, are two important anthologies. Attention ought to be given to the sermons of men like Alexander Maclaren, the gifted nineteenth century expositor; Joseph Parker, the imaginative nineteenth century British preacher; James Stewart, the contemporary Scottish preacher whose pulpit charm has left its mark on both sides of the Atlantic; Helmut Thielicke, the German preacher-theologian whose insights were hammered out on the anvil of crisis; Peter Marshall, the late chaplain of the United States Senate who had that enviable ability to paint pictures with words; and Harry Emerson Fosdick, the perceptive life-situation preacher of New York's Riverside Church. Many of the finest preachers are not only published but may also be heard on tapes, records, and cassettes. The depth of insight in great preachers is a mandatory resource for the young preacher.

As general preparation, one ought to do the following:

1. Build a Quality Library

A certain amount of money ought to be set aside for book purchases. Money from weddings and funerals or a regular "book allowance" can be resources for this. A listing of top priority books should be kept handy to avoid the danger of impulse buying. When one buys he should purchase the best. The majority of books at Christian bookstores do not qualify. Secure the recommendations of those who know books. Most seminaries are happy to provide such a list for interested preachers. Strive for variety in your books. An imbalance will be reflected in your preaching. No preacher's library is complete without ample works in church history, Old and New Testament theology, pastoral counseling, social and personal ethics, and administration. Book clubs can assist a person in keeping abreast of contemporary literature and thought. Knowledge in such fresh, current ideas is a definite asset. An unabridged dictionary, a pronouncing dictionary, and a volume of synonyms are absolutely essential as basic tools. In addition, a good lexicon of both the Old and New Testaments, an unabridged concordance, and a Bible dictionary should be purchased. Commentaries (preferably individual volumes of a critical, exegetical nature), books on Bible characters, a book of quotations, a quality hymnal, selections of poetry, classical essays, current best sellers (fiction and nonfiction) should all be included in the preacher's expanding library. A set like *Great Books of the Western World* is also commended for its classical offerings and breadth of coverage. As always, trusted resource persons such as experienced pastors and seminary professors are important guides to the particular books needed to fill out the above categories.

Every man must discover what volumes are of particular usefulness to him. What appeals to one will not appeal to another. What serves another will be of little use to a friend. Skim through volumes before they are purchased. Discover if they have usefulness and potential for you. If they do, buy them when funds are available. Do not spend money foolishly buying cheap books such as "snappy sermon starters," or illustration books, or books of sermons by unknown preachers unless you have very good reason for doing so.

Be discerning. A quality library may be the best set of tools that you will ever have. A denominational executive, after much travel across the nation, noted that almost without exception, when people complained about the quality of their pastor's preaching, it was discovered that their preacher had a deficient library.

2. Read Widely

Thoughtful preachers sustain their ministries through a disciplined reading of a diverse selection of books. In addition to what a man already possesses, he should keep abreast of best sellers—fiction and nonfiction—in order to understand current thought patterns. The novelists, biographers, writers of essays, and contemporary playwrights are frequently prophetic voices of the age. Magazines for the pastor's study should be selected carefully. Avoid an exclusive diet of easy-to-read popular magazines. Thought-provoking journals and material that challenges your point of view should be read regularly. Otherwise a man can quite unconsciously develop sloppy reading habits which stultify thought rather than stimulate it. R. E. O. White says,

> Not to be sure enough of your convictions to give a fair hearing to the opposite point of view is weakness indeed; and to evade that point of view because it disturbs, upsets, or frightens is just cowardice. And it reveals a lack of faith in truth's wonderful capacity to defend itself.[1]

Keep a good book going. When you finish one, start another. If you are preaching on the temptations of Christ, you ought to be reading Dostoevski's *The Grand Inquisitor,* or if you are speaking on sin, *The Fall* by Albert Camus. To be sure, modern writers are not always as theologically correct as we could hope, but they do supply profound insights unavailable in the commentaries.

Of course, the Bible ought to be read on a daily basis. Keep some part of the Bible under systematic study. Use a notebook and jot down ideas. It is unnecessary to distinguish systematically between devotional reading and a reading of Scripture for sermon preparation. That which is discovered devotionally may be used sermonically and the fruit of homiletical study may be personally enriching. This is as it should be. There are inexhaustible treasures in Scripture. No pastorate is too long to exhaust this wealth, but it requires that one be a student of Scripture if this is to be true.

Read with a pen in hand. Books are tools, not ornaments. Feel free to write in the margins, to underline, and to index your books. Whatever serves to make the books most useful and helpful ought to be done. Even scribbling is acceptable if it serves a purpose.

3. Listen Carefully

The one who professes to have something to say is one who has learned to listen. The false dichotomy that was once so honored—pastor and preacher—is a professional impossibility. It was once common to distinguish these two roles; they must now be hyphenated. To be a preacher without being a pastor or vice versa is disastrous. One role complements the other. James T. Cleland remarks that those who are locked in their study surrounded by commentaries, isolated from people, are "invisible six days in the week and incomprehensible on the seventh."[2]

Helmut Thielicke confesses:

> Every conversation I engage in becomes at bottom a meditation, a preparation, a gathering of material for my preaching. I can no longer listen disinterestedly even to a play in a theater without relating it to my pulpit. . . . Thus life in all its daily involvements becomes for me a thesaurus in which I keep rummaging because it is full of relevant material for my message.[3]

This does not mean, of course, that a man should look at everything through homiletical eyes so that every event becomes a potential illustration, but rather that every book he reads and every experience he has is related to his role as "servant of the Word." That is to say, one develops a frame of reference, an attitude which does not allow him to go through life with half-closed eyes, or with ears shut to the voices that surround him. All that he does, all that he says, all that he hears is preparing him to better communicate God's Word. It means that God's man maintains an open-door policy; he is available, "not in a hurry, not in the grip of his next appointment. He must have an eye for people and time for them."[4]

Phillips Brooks spent Monday mornings with his Clericus Club. These men discussed great ideas in his study. It is likely that they were not aware they were often considering a sermon idea for Brooks; nonetheless, they contributed much to the richness of his preaching.[5]

Listening to people will also prime a dry pump. In the midst of parish demands some preachers discover that they have no particular sermon to preach. It is then that they must go back to their people and hear again the agony of the community, to feel honestly and deeply, to become sensitive to individuals, returning then to the study and with Bible in hand bring together the eternal resources of God and the recently discovered needs of people.

4. Record Insights

Impression without expression is nil. New insights, meaningful disclosures of biblical truth, of psychology, or of contemporary problems once recorded are available to a man for the rest of his life. A notebook in which ideas are jotted and sermonic germs are stored is highly recommended. As a man reads, as he visits, as he counsels, impressions should be recorded which can blossom into future sermonic usefulness.

Every preacher needs a workable filing system. A number of complex systems are available, but unfortunately some have been purchased by pastors who have never utilized them to the full. A simple filing system may be preferable. Most important of all is that the system chosen be broad enough never to be embarrassed by new materials, flexible enough to allow anything to fit into it, and simple enough so that its resources are readily accessible to the busy preacher. "The unhappy experience of many ministers has been to establish a system, to become bogged down in its use, then to abandon it and have no system at all."[6]

ADVANCE PREPARATION

Planned preaching, preferably for an entire year, is heartily commended. It enables the preacher to know well in advance what he is to preach, thereby reducing the emotional pressure of week by week selection. It conserves time and energy and also allows greater opportunity for thoughts to mature prior to actual sermon delivery. When should this be done? Many have found summer vacation to be a helpful time when one is away from the details and confusion of pastoral demands. It seems best to get away from the pressures and expectations of the parish, to a setting where one can make an objective evaluation of materials and ideas for the upcoming year.

A man should begin by outlining the year. On separate sheets he should list each of the twelve months, noting holidays and events within the Christian year, including special meetings and recommendations of the boards, committees, and organizations of the church. Often a church's annual planning meeting will assist the preacher as he begins his outline of the year's preaching schedule. It is imperative that the past year's work be reviewed. What needs were unmet? What subjects were left untouched? What parts of the Bible were neglected? He can then review the needs of the congregation, keeping a church directory handy, to refresh himself on the specific areas of need. Finally, in the light of the congregation's needs and his own past failures to meet particular needs, a pastor can develop a year's preaching schedule, maintaining a balance between variety and in-depth treatment. He should keep in mind the fact that sameness produces dullness and loss of interest. The narrowly confined pulpit cannot hope to cover the myriad of problems, needs, and concerns represented in an average congregation. Pulpit offerings, spread over the year, should correlate with the multiplicity of needs manifest in the congregation.

Variety in a preaching plan is achieved in various ways: (1) *the Bible survey principle*—an occasional study of biblical books, biblical doctrines, the life of Christ, biographical studies, and themes from the Christian calendar; (2) *the pastoral principle*—ideas drawn from pastoral calls, congregational suggestions, and general observation; (3) *a trend of the times principle*—current developments in theology, religion, politics, morals, economics, world affairs; (4) *a denominational principle*—following the guidelines of denominational programming; (5) *the experimental principle*—using visual aids, printed materials, narrative sermons, dialogue sermons, or changes in style among various sermonic types.

Variety, while useful for interest's sake, may be a liability for the listener. Sermonic smorgasbord—a little bit of this and a little bit of that—produces Christians with superficial knowledge of much, but a mature understanding of little. The proposed solution is thematic preaching. For example, one could select a subject and then devote an entire month to it. He would live with that idea for this whole period, reading everything of worth on the subject, soaking it in, providing books for the congregation on the subject, relating it to interest groups within the church, and generally involving the entire church family in a single concern for a month. Selection of the theme is crucial. A theme must be important enough to sustain interest.

Once the entire year has been outlined, subjects and texts are selected for every Sunday service. Folders or envelopes are provided, then labeled, to store appropriate materials as they arise in a man's study and ministry. It was the practice of D. L. Moody to use large envelopes, one envelope per theme, in which he would place developing thoughts, relevant newspaper clippings, and other useful insights. When the week arrives for a particular sermon, the preacher will probably have anywhere from one to ten items already in the envelope. He is well on his way toward a sermon with the subject he chose in advance. The benefits are obvious: time is saved and the fruits of a man's study are conserved.

Planned preaching should be kept flexible. If an emergency arises, a man should feel free to dispense with his plans and speak on the subject that is pertinent. Any emergency, crisis, or felt need is reason enough for a preacher to alter his previous plans.

WEEK BY WEEK PREPARATION

It takes time to prepare. Discipline is absolutely essential. A secretary can assist the pastor in maintaining privacy for his morning hours, so that only crises break into his sacred preparation time. Ralph Sockman spent eighteen hours of study on a Sunday morning sermon. Harry Emerson Fosdick usually spent twenty-five hours, approximately one hour per minute of actual delivery.

Consider the sober words of W. E. Sangster:

> To the man who scamps his work by sheer laziness or inefficiency, or because he is a hireling and not a shepherd, or because he puts golf before the gospel, or has no faith in his message or love of the people, I have no word to say. The bitterness of his remorse in eternity, when he faces at last all the consequences of his sloth, will be in itself (I imagine) almost more than he can bear.[7]

There is an axiom that says "The Lord will provide." But the condition is that the preacher be faithful, unremitting in his sermon preparation.

Preparation begins immediately. It is best to finalize the subject and text for the following Sunday on the previous Sunday night so that a pastor can begin soaking in his subject immediately at the outset of a new week. John Killinger comments, "When you take the pulpit to deliver the Word you were ordained to preach, let it be a real Word, and not something compounded in fever Saturday night to be delivered in spasms on Sunday morning."[8] Instant sermons prepared just before Sunday have no time to mature and in the long run result in superficial preaching.

What method should a man follow? There is no perfect method. The best method will be determined by the man in the light of his own temperament and practice. Proposed methods are intended as suggestions. They offer a starting point, a point of departure. To become prisoner of a particular method runs the risk of excluding that divine spark which transmutes the dull metal of a labored sermon into the shining gold of a sacrament.

Possible procedures are outlined by Clarence Roddy in *We Prepare and Preach* and Donald Macleod, *This Is My Method.* Both volumes are anthologies of methods used by well-known preachers. In the volume *Steps to the Sermon,* an eight-step method is suggested:

1. A prepared preacher
2. An idea to preach
3. A text interpreted
4. Related materials collected
5. Maturity secured
6. Construction completed
7. The sermon polished
8. The message preached[9]

Koller suggests a little different format:

1. Gather the preliminary data.
2. Make a brief analysis of the Scripture passage.
3. Outline the sermon, noting lessons, truths, then characterize with a "key word," finding parallel points.
4. Find a common principle which becomes the proposition.
5. Identify subject and formulate a title or topic to suit the message.
6. Prepare an introduction and a conclusion.
7. Develop the outline.[10]

Regardless of what method is chosen, it ought to be indigenous to the preacher and should not call attention to itself. Preparation is a means. It should not advertise its presence.

Most methods include all or a majority of the following steps:

(1) **Preparing the preacher.** Prayer begins all preparation. This primary step is a recognition of divine help and need for illumination. Billy Graham, as a daily practice, reads five psalms and a chapter in Proverbs. He then concludes his devotions with prayer. Every preacher should have some devotional exercise that he finds personally meaningful as a preparation for life in general and his preaching ministry in particular.

(2) **Choosing the subject and text.** There is no rule for establishing which comes first. It may be the idea or the text. On occasion they will emerge simultaneously. If nothing emerges it may be necessary for the preacher to ask, What is the spiritual need here? What guidance or comfort, what awakening or sharpening of conscience or enrichment in God ought the congregation to receive? Those who follow the planned preaching method begin with the text and subject already chosen. Some seize upon a recent inspiration and begin to develop it in the light of biblical teaching. Others will have to search

until they uncover some text or subject that "strikes fire" in their life. Here, as in other steps of the sermon development, one needs to keep open to the ministry of the Holy Spirit.

(3) **Studying the text.** If possible, use the original languages. A preacher needs to have some facility in Greek and hopefully in Hebrew. An interlinear text can serve as a last resort. Next, the various renderings of modern translations provide fresh wording and expression. The preacher should note the contextual data, the speaker, addressee, time, place, occasion, and aim. He should discover as best he can the unity which characterizes that particular book of the Bible. Donald G. Miller says, "It is the initial task of the interpreter . . . to search for the purpose and plan of the whole book before coming to grips with its parts. Failure to do this is often fatal to true interpretation."[11]

Next, survey the passage, outline the text, and jot down ideas. This begins a creative process known to all artists, musicians, and creative writers, a process that taps the mind for available resources. Jot down every idea via free association and exhaust *your own* thinking. Let other resources remain on the shelf. Do not turn too quickly to outside sources lest you quench the personal touch, that unique element that is yours as a preacher. Take from others only after you've gleaned all you can from the reservoirs of your own mind.

Finally, consult the commentaries. Discover what the best recent critical scholarship has to say about the text under consideration. Through this process a given text can take on real life for the preacher.

(4) **Shaping the material.** This is the task of bridging the gap between available material and the needs of the congregation. William L. Malcomson achieves this on the topic of discipleship by asking, "Why do I care about discipleship? Why should the congregation care about discipleship? What do we do about it if we want to be disciples?"[12]

As material is shaped it is not the task of the preacher to create or to impose a form, but to "feel" its true, native, and inherent shape, then letting the material take its own form. In the process, one will find it helpful to spell out the proposition and aim. A preacher will finalize the outline, making it clear and memorable. Experienced preachers counsel the inexperienced to avoid an outline for the sermon too early in the preparation lest it stifle the imagination. It will be necessary in most cases for an outline to be determined as one moves toward the final steps of preparation, however. The structure (skeleton) will then be filled in by supporting material (flesh) such as exegesis, explanation, exposition, or examples. Illustrations chosen for inclusion must be appropriate. Next, a conclusion is developed and finally an introduction. ("Finally," because it is difficult to write an appropriate introduction until one knows what is to be introduced.)

(5) **Writing the sermon.** Ideally, the preacher will write the sermon in full to develop skill of expression, logic, and balance. Sue Nichols reminds us:

> When amateur communicators say the first thing that comes to mind, their material pours out in long, wordy sentences with featherweight verbs and trite, obvious sentiments. . . .A skilled communicator dams up the initial flow. He curtails it until he can sort out his precise message, until he can phrase it with strength and release it in an altered but more powerful form.[13]

Thus it is that a sermon needs at least one week to become as developed, polished, and on target as possible. Late preparation on Friday or Saturday shortens the incubation period. Ideas need to mature before they can be expressed in refined, clear style.

James Stewart suggests that regardless of the method of delivery a preacher ought to begin by writing out his sermons in full. "During the first ten years of your ministry—and perhaps over a much longer period than that—there is no substitute for this essential discipline."[14]

Discouragement comes easily, for most preachers "feel" more than they can ever "express." "This is just what Shelley had in mind when he lamented that we never feel 'the original purity and force' of a poem because 'when composition begins, inspiration is already on the decline.' "[15] Nevertheless, the concerned preacher, undaunted in determination, will continue writing to improve his mode of expression.

(6) **Preparing the preacher.** He will soak in the sermon. If it is finished by Friday or Saturday, as it should be, he can read it over and reflect on it. He can read it until it becomes a part of him, so that it begins to run through the juices of his own personality, so that it is not a foreign object. Thus, when he stands in the pulpit on Sunday the sermon is something he knows and knows well. Preaching a sermon aloud three or four times until it flows and feels natural is a great aid. Care should be taken not to overpractice during the week lest a sermon find its fire spent on Sunday morning. Careful preparation leaves a bit of the excitement for Sunday. Finally, rest well Saturday night. On occasion a man must study late into the night on Saturday. There may be a sick call or an emergency that draws him away from his home late into the night Saturday and early into Sunday morning. But generally he will make it a practice, when at all possible, to be well rested. Major strength is reserved for the task of preaching.

(7) **Preaching the Word.** Enter the sacred desk with expectation and with dependence on the Holy Spirit. One never knows who in that congregation needs just the word that God has placed on his heart. It

is an affront to the gospel to feel that such a high and lofty task can be entered into without careful, time-consuming preparation. God's man is called to preach, and hence to prepare.

NOTES

1. R. E. O. White, "Pastor's Predicament: When to Study?" *Christianity Today* (December 6, 1968), XIII, No. 5, 4.

2. James T. Cleland, *Preaching to Be Understood* (New York: Abingdon Press, 1965), p. 40.

3. Helmut Thielicke, *The Trouble with the Church: A Call for Renewal,* trans. John W. Doberstein (New York: Harper & Row Publishers, 1965), p. 22.

4. Samuel M. Shoemaker, *Beginning Your Ministry* (New York: Harper & Row Publishers, 1963), p. 64.

5. H. C. Brown, Jr., H. Gordon Clinard, Jesse J. Northcutt, *Steps to the Sermon* (Nashville: Broadman Press, 1963), pp. 93-94.

6. Charles W. Koller, *Expository Preaching Without Notes* (Grand Rapids: Baker Book House, 1962), p. 116.

7. W. E. Sangster, *The Craft of Sermon Construction* (Philadelphia: The Westminster Press, 1951), p. 192.

8. John Killinger, *The Centrality of Preaching in the Total Task of the Ministry* (Waco, Tex.: Word Books, 1969), p. 29.

9. Brown, Clinard, Northcutt, Preface viii.

10. Koller, pp. 57-60.

11. Donald G. Miller, *The Way to Biblical Preaching* (New York: Abingdon Press, 1957), p. 42.

12. William L. Malcomson, *The Preaching Event* (Philadelphia: The Westminster Press, 1968), pp. 101-102.

13. Sue Nichols, *Words on Target* (Richmond: John Knox Press, 1963), p. 26.

14. James S. Stewart, *Preaching* (London: The English Universities Press, Ltd., 1955), p. 154.

15. Frank Kermode, "The Galaxy Reconsidered," *McLuhan: Hot and Cool,* ed. Gerald Emanuel Stearn (New York: Signet Books, 1969), p. 177.

CHAPTER EIGHT • SUBJECTS
PROPOSITIONS, AND TITLES

CHAPTER EIGHT / BIBLICAL TRUTH—SUBJECTS, PROPOSITIONS, AND TITLES

Early in the development of any sermon satisfactory answers must be found for three questions: What will I talk about? What will I say about it? How will I advertise it? Response to the first is the "subject"; to the second is the "proposition"; to the third is the "title." We will deal with these sermonic ingredients in order.

SUBJECT

Webster says that a subject is "that concerning which anything is said or done...."[1] It is a synonym of "matter," "theme," and "topic." For our purposes, the subject states what the sermon is about. It is one word or phrase which defines the limits of sermonic consideration. General subjects, usually one word, are divisible into smaller, specific subjects. John E. Baird notes, "Subjects are like Chinese puzzle boxes: big ones contain a number of small ones, and these in turn contain others smaller yet...."[2] Salvation, faith, prayer, ethics, love, missions, hope, and evil are typical examples of "general subjects." Each, of course, is too broad to be the subject of any clearly defined sermon. Large topics of this nature need to be narrowed into smaller homiletical packages (i.e., specific subjects) which can be adequately considered in a single preaching event.

Consider the following breakdown of "specific subjects" which can be adequately covered in a single sermon.

Prayer
(General Subject)

Hindrances to answered prayer
The essence of prayer
Prayer as adoration
The purpose of prayer
The spirit of prayer

Salvation
(General Subject)

Salvation is a gift of God
The purpose of salvation
Christ's role in redemption
The way of salvation

Ethics
(General Subject)

Motivation for ethics
Ethics in business
Ethics in the home
The ethics of war
The ethics of race

Not only must a general subject be narrowed to a specific subject in order to adequately focus attention and consideration, but the specific subject which is chosen must have "a force that is expanding."[3]

A specific subject, then, must have potential for expansion. Like bread dough impregnated with yeast, it must be ready to rise. Unleavened sermons are inadequate conveyers of spiritual nourishment. Inasmuch as every sermon should have a subject, and assuming that the preacher has the liberty of choosing his subject, how does one go about the task of making that selection? A few rules cast in the form of questions have proved helpful.

(1) **Does it grip you?** Does it strike fire in your soul? If it doesn't, drop it. You may be driven back to your sermon starter file in order to discover some subject that will excite you, enthuse you, or otherwise invigorate you as the spokesman. Nothing can be shared enthusiastically unless it strikes an enthusiastic chord in the soul of the preacher. If it doesn't interest you it is rather unlikely that it will interest anyone else. Contagion is an important factor in communication. That which inspires, excites, thrills, grips, or in other ways moves the preacher is likely to cause a similar reaction in the congregation. If it grips the pastor, it will likely grip some of the congregation. If it does not grip the pastor, neither will it grip the congregation.

(2) **Is it narrow enough?** Has the subject been defined in such a way that it is capable of being covered in a single sermon? "Your first problem is to narrow your subject to the smallest specific area which will be appropriate to your audience, your time limit, and your purpose in speaking."[4]

How much can adequately be said in twenty or twenty-five minutes? If the subject under consideration takes an hour to be adequately treated, it is too broad. If the subject can be exhausted in ten minutes, it is too narrow. It must be narrow enough, but not too narrow. It is better to have one biblical passage covered thoroughly than two passages barely treated in superficial fashion. Some years ago I was preaching a sermon on "The Inescapable Christ," taking my texts from both Old and New Testaments. An insightful listener, himself a pastor, told me the idea was fine, but that it erred because of information overload. There was enough material for two sermons. The point was well taken. I should have limited my consideration to either Old or New Testament. Too much material in one sermon is just as unwise as insufficient material.

(3) **Is it needful?** Is it loaded with what Davis calls the realities of the human heart?[5] Frequently the pulpit has been oppressively irrelevant. For example, many theologically conservative churches have a Sunday evening service built around an evangelistic motif. The music and the sermon are geared to reaching unbelievers. Yet, if unbelievers attend church, they are more likely to be in the Sunday morning worship service. The already evangelized need something other than another challenge to trust Christ as personal Saviour. We need to ask, Is the subject under consideration a response to a *real* need?

I was asked to preach in a rural church in northern Minnesota on the subject of "church-related vocations." I went prepared to do so, but discovered with horror that the congregation was composed almost entirely of people in their late forties to sixties and above. The sermon was irrelevant. My experience is duplicated hundreds of times over every Sunday by pastors who should know better. There is no excuse for such gross error in audience analysis.

(4) **Is it clear?** Fuzziness in the study creates confusion in the pew. If the subject is not clear, it is probably ambiguous or vague, from now on destined to leave people with uncertainty. For example, "The Spirit of Christmas" is an indefinite subject which needs to be recast for pulpit consideration.

(5) **Is it appropriate?** What is the occasion? Do you follow the church year? Is it a legal holiday? Is it a special service geared to missions? Is the audience made up of youth or the elderly? Is it a heterogeneous audience? What in the light of your understanding of the time, place, and occasion is appropriate? A few years ago a well-known theological seminary sponsored a banquet for its board of trustees, faculty, students, and friends. The guest speaker for the evening chose to give an evangelistic sermon. Everyone was troubled by his selection of subject. The evening should have included some thoughtful word of encouragement or challenge, not what they heard. The speaker was oblivious to the occasion.

It is appropriate for the pulpit to address historical situations that are fresh in the minds of potential auditors. The death of a president, senator, or leading spokesman, or such issues as racial unrest and similar social problems deserve the response of the perceptive Christian pulpit.

Subject and text of Scripture should be correlated. The subject of the sermon should be the subject of the portion of Scripture on which it is based. W. E. Sangster recalls the story of a German preacher in the arid early years of the nineteenth century when the gospel had almost been lost in the land of Luther. He announced his text one Sunday morning, "Now on the first day of the week cometh Mary Magdalene early while it was yet dark" from John 20:1. His subject was "The Benefits of Early Rising." He had nothing to say about the resurrection. He talked entirely to the tune "It is nice to get up in the morning!"[6] Subjects and texts should be carefully chosen and carefully correlated.

PROPOSITION

Well defined structure and effective delivery depend on a clear proposition. Without a proposition the sermon lacks direction and design. It becomes a hodgepodge, full of "deformities of thought" and "anatomical monstrosities, like a three-headed calf."[7]

A proposition is the sermon in a nutshell, "the heart of the sermon,"[8] expressed in simple, unmistakable language. It is a succinct statement of the subject in sentence form. This distillation of the sermon (i.e., proposition, thesis, or central idea) guides the preacher in his selection of materials and provides the listener with a summary of the sermon. It will keep meandering to a minimum and save the listener from "miscellaneous" responses. A gifted craftsman of the pulpit, John Henry Jowett, says:

> No sermon is ready for preaching nor ready for writing out, until we can express its theme in a short, pregnant sentence as clear as a crystal. I find the getting of that sentence the hardest, the most exacting and the most fruitful labor in my study. To compel oneself to fashion that sentence, to dismiss every word that is vague, ragged, ambiguous, to think oneself through to a form of words which defines the theme with scrupulous exactness—this is surely one of the most vital and essential factors in the making of a sermon; and I do not think that any sermon ought to be preached or even written, until that sentence has emerged clear and lucid as a cloudless morn.[9]

1. Marks of a Good Proposition

(1) **A simple sentence.** Compound, complex sentences tend to create sermons with compound and complex ideas. A simple sentence guards against the possibilities of multiple major ideas and of sermonettes within the sermon. A simple sentence proposition guarantees unity. Unity, which is a law of the listener's mind and a guard against fragmentation, partition, and disorder, can be guaranteed with a simple proposition. "When the sermon is the embodiment of one vigorous idea, when the whole of it becomes simply the elaboration and extension of that idea, then it produces in the listener that concentration of effect which is called unity."[10]

Singleness of thought expressed through a simple sentence proposition guards against fragmentation. Otherwise, the listener is forced to combine thought fragments into his own sermonic unit, which may be quite different from the preacher's intention. It is better to say one thing well than many things poorly. A simple sentence is an attempt to clarify and maintain this unity.

(2) **Clarity.** A crisp, unambiguous proposition is the goal. Because it is prose and not poetry, one should avoid any metaphorical use of language in stating the essential idea. Baird adds, "Any twist of meaning such as that involved in the use of sarcasm would be out of place."[11]

(3) **State it as a universal truth.** Propositions should not contain historical references such as personalities, places, or events. A good thesis is timeless and universal. It should be in touch with contemporary life and obviously timely. It should be stated in a form of a truth which is good for all time.

(4) **An abridgment of the sermon.** The proposition as an abridged discourse should comprehend the whole thought of the sermon. If it does not contain all the essential thought, the sermon is faulty as is the proposition. The whole sermon should be comprehended in miniature in the simple sentence proposition.

Nobody can say everything at one time without exposing himself to the danger of saying nothing. Therefore the sermon, which should be an intellectual organism, must have a central point; each individual sermon must have an organizing center that grows out of the text.[12]

(5) **Sermonic in nature.** A proposition expresses or implies a response on the part of the audience, a response toward which the preacher is moving. In a sense, a good proposition is invitational.

2. Kinds of Propositions

Glen E. Mills lists six distinct kinds of propositions:

1. Legal fact—"X slandered Y."
2. Past fact—"Slavery was not a direct cause of the Civil War."
3. Present fact—"The party in power is to blame for the crime rate."
4. Prediction—"Curtailment of foreign travel will strengthen the dollar."
5. Value—"American foreign aid is wrong in principle."
6. Policy—"Professional boxing should be outlawed."[13]

The proposition of legal fact is appropriate for the courtroom scene, but not for the sanctuary. The proposition of past fact is also inappropriate because, although preaching looks to the past for authority, it states its truth in the present tense. The other four types (present fact, prediction, value, and policy) are very helpful. For example, one could take the general subject of love and create four propositions using these four kinds. Present fact—"God loves every man, regardless of race, color, or creed." Prediction—"Love will transform your enemy into a friend." Value—"Only a new love for God can expel the love of the world and the things in it." Policy—"Every Christian should love his neighbor."[14] The proposition of present fact is a claim. The proposition of prediction is a forecast. The proposition of value is an evaluative judgment. The proposition of policy is an urge to act.

Is the proposition stated? Generally yes. It need not be, however. A carefully worded proposition is necessary for guidance in the preparation and delivery of a sermon, but the preacher may choose not to divulge it in so many words. If it is clearly in his mind and in the minds of his listeners, that is all that matters. When is it stated? Any place that is appropriate. A deductive sermon, such as the "basic pattern" (see pp. 76-79), should make it clear at the outset, somewhere in the introduction. An inductive sermon may conclude with the proposition. A narrative type may weave it subtly through the fabric of the sermon. The question to ask is, Does the listener come away with a clear idea of what the sermon said? The proposition, latent or manifest, at the outset, middle, or conclusion of the sermon, is the best guarantee that a single truth will emerge in clarity.

TITLE

The title is an imaginative, suggestive word or phrase used in the advertising of the sermon. It is not to be confused with the subject, which defines the area to be considered, or the proposition, which is the sermon in a nutshell. The title is used solely for public purposes. It is not a guide for the preacher in his preparation nor his selection of materials per se. The subject and the proposition do that.[15] In other words, I take issue with Brown, Clinard, and Northcutt who say:

> An effective title furnishes the preacher a divisible whole from which he can develop the framework of the sermon body. Even a general idea of the title helps the preacher in collecting, selecting, and condensing materials. A precise title is an invaluable tool in limiting and unifying each and every item in the structural development of the sermon.

Titles should be placed conspicuously on the church bulletin board with clean, easy-to-read letters (preferably lighted to attract the "night people"), in the local newspaper, and in the worship folder. If it commands a hearing, stimulates interest, or suggests that something worth hearing is going to be said, it has served admirably.

Recently while fulfilling a four-month preaching assignment, it was necessary to pass the First United Methodist Church in Burbank, California. A strategically placed bulletin board listing the pastor's sermon titles fascinated me. Unfortunately, it was impossible to hear the advertised sermons, although I sensed repeatedly that something vital was going to be said. The pastor of the church, Dr. Harry W. Adams, graciously provided over 150 titles for my perusal. I have chosen to list twenty-five of these because of their manifest interest and appeal. Although tastes differ significantly, the universal element of intrigue resides rather conspicuously in the following list:

> "The Wages of Sin Is Aaaughh!"
> " 'Tis Best to Have Loved and Won"
> "Siamese Twins: Pulpit and Pew"
> "God Is Where the Action Is"
> "Lord of the Ordinary"
> "Those Four-Letter Words"
> "The Foolishness of Preaching"
> "Freeway Faith"
> "Believing Something When You Can't Believe Everything"
> "How to Be Happy Though Miserable"
> "Handling Your Handicaps"
> "Conquering Loneliness"
> "A Pastor Ponders Vietnam"
> "Good News for the Bored"
> "Will the Real God Please Step Forward"
> "The Best Things in the Worst Times"
> "Living with Your Imperfections"
> "The Extreme Middle"
> "Morticians of the Mind"
> "How to Sin and Enjoy It"
> "The Roar of a Lion, the Heart of a Rabbit"
> "Evil Spelled Backwards Is Live"
> "Is There a Bomb in Gilead?"
> "The Partly-Good Samaritan"
> "Too True to Be Good"

These titles, together with an analysis of sermon anthologies and the Saturday church page, suggest the variety of title types available to the preacher. Some of these are:

1. Biblical
   "The Wages of Sin Is Aaaughh!"
   "The Foolishness of Preaching"
   "Footwashers, Inc."
   "The Power of the Resurrection"
   "The Partly-Good Samaritan"
   "The Forgiveness of Sins"
2. Paradox
   "Hosanna! Crucify!" (Palm Sunday Sermon)
   "To Die Is to Live"

3. A New Twist on a Cliché.
   "Too True to Be Good"
   "What About Life After Birth?"
   "How to Succeed Without Being Trying"
4. Mystery.
   "On Catching the Wrong Bus"
   "The Roar of a Lion, the Heart of a Rabbit"
   "Pillbox in a Meadow"
5. Psychological or Existential
   "When Life Tumbles In, What Then?"
   "Handling Life's Second Best"
   "Conquering Loneliness"
6. Current Events
   "A Pastor Ponders Vietnam"
   "The Ballot or the Bullet"
   "Selma and the Saints"

Given an imagination, you can doubtless add other categories and titles of equal usefulness.

1. Marks of Effective Titles

(1) **Stimulate interest.** Seek to stir the reader's imagination by setting his curiosity in motion. Remember, many a reader has never darkened the door of your church. Will the title you have chosen give the impression you are worth hearing? If you were outside the church, would you be curious enough to attend church based on this initial exposure? A sermon titled "Seven Ducks in a Muddy Pond" (a sermon on Naaman who was instructed to dip seven times in the Jordan River in order to be healed) may have the needed intrigue to interest a nonchurched passerby.

(2) **Succinct.** It has to catch people on the move passing the church. Hence it is unwise to use the title which one preacher chose: "The Width, the Height, and the Depth of God's Love." Use a lean style.

(3) **Contemporary.** The title should be a vote for the relevance of the church and its message, not a reminder out of the ancient past. Use today's language if you want to communicate with today's people. Speak to the issues that concern modern man. For example, "Handling Your Handicaps," "Believing Something When You Can't Believe Everything," "The Way of Nonviolence, Christ's Style" are appropriate because they address issues of current concern.

2. Common Weaknesses in Titles

(1) **Overstatement.** Titles should be humble. Any title that suggests a satisfying answer to a knotty, age-old question that has plagued Christians of every generation is overly optimistic. It should promise

no more than it can deliver. A title "Why God Permits Evil" is of such a nature. It is better to pose a question that promises less but is more realistic; for example: "Doesn't God Care?"

(2) **Sensationalism.** Some fail to develop a keen sense of propriety. What about the pastor who labeled his sermon on the virgin birth, "Sex and the Single Girl"? It certainly creates interest, but at too high a price. Striving after catchy, gimmicky titles may only cheapen the gospel. Brown, Clinard, and Northcutt mention some other sensational titles: "Why Every Preacher Should Go to Hell," "A Nudist in a Graveyard," "The Baptist Preacher Who Lost His Head at a Dance," and "Drive Like Hell and You Will Soon Get There."[16]

(3) **Vague.** Little direction is given by such titles as "What Are the Covenants of Promise?" "The Principle of Purpose," "A Beautiful Thing," "The Days of Our Years." Nothing in particular is communicated by such bland titles. They should be avoided.

4. **Remote.** By this we mean not necessarily remote to the realities of life, but remote to the outsider in his frame of reference. It is the interest of the outsider we are seeking to evoke. The others have already come or will plan to come without the title. Examples are to be found everywhere: "The Messiah," "His Blood," "The Kingdom of God," "Corinth: The Moral Conflict," "The Appetite for Righteousness," and "The Key to the Cross."

(5) **Trite.** These titles are treated to a "ho-hum" by outsiders: "The Power of Temptation," "No Man Is an Island," and "Love Your Neighbor."

The preacher will do well to recognize the relative value of titles. Hours spent in the selection of some "cute" title is a fallacious stewardship of time. If it comes, fine. If it doesn't, move on to other things. Don't labor excessively for a world stopper. Better to spend that valuable time in developing the sermon which is behind the title. Only a *few* have come to church through the scintillating character of a title, whereas *many* have had their lives changed through a well-prepared sermon.

When should the title be prepared? Ideally it is prepared when the sermon is completed so that the preacher knows what he is advertising. Often, of course, titles emerge before or during the early stages of sermon preparation. In some respects this is not only admissible, but essential. Titles placed on the bulletin board early in the week have more time to serve their purpose. It is hardly worth the effort to change them on Friday or Saturday. Newspapers also impose a deadline. Information for Saturday's page generally needs to be on the religious editor's desk by the middle of the week.

NOTES

1. *Webster's New Collegiate Dictionary* (Springfield, Mass.: G. & C. Merriam Co. Publishers, 1949).

2. John E. Baird, *Preparing for Platform and Pulpit* (New York: Abingdon Press, 1968), p. 51.

3. Henry Grady Davis, *Design for Preaching* (Philadelphia: Fortress Press, 1958), p. 43.

4. Baird, p. 51.

5. Davis, p. 43.

6. W. E. Sangster, *The Draft of the Sermon* (Philadelphia: The Westminster Press, 1961), pp. 122-123.

7. Davis, p. 26.

8. Charles W. Koller, *Expository Preaching Without Notes* (Grand Rapids: Baker Book House, 1962), p. 72.

9. John Henry Jowett, *The Preacher, His Life and Work* (New York: Doran, 1912), p. 133.

10. Davis, p. 35.

11. Baird, p. 56.

12. Helmut Thielicke, *The Trouble with the Church: A Call for Renewal*, trans. John W. Doberstein (New York: Harper & Row, Publishers, 1965), pp. 54, 55.

13. Glen E. Mills, *Message Preparation: Analyses and Structure* (Indianapolis: The Bobbs-Merrill Company, Inc., 1966), p. 14.

14. Thomas Chalmers, "The Expulsive Power of a New Affection" cited in Henry Grady Davis, *Design for Preaching* (Fortress Press, 1958), p. 32.

15. H. C. Brown, Jr., H. Gordon Clinard, and Jesse J. Northcutt, *Steps to the Sermon* (Nashville: Broadman Press, 1963), p. 96.

16. Brown, Clinard, Northcutt, p. 98.

CHAPTER NINE • INTRODUCTIONS AND CONCLUSIONS

INTRODUCTIONS AND CONCLUSIONS

Life, as we know it, is time bound. There is a start and stop for everything and everyone. Animate and inanimate things alike have a point of commencement and termination. So the sermon: it begins somewhere and ends somewhere. No sermon is eternal (though it may seem that way to the listener after thirty-five minutes). Effectiveness in the pulpit is dependent on many factors, including the introduction and conclusion of a sermon. Let us view these sermonic elements in order.

SERMON INTRODUCTIONS

It hardly seems necessary to argue for the validity of an introduction for a sermon. As J. A. Broadus says:

> Men have a natural aversion to abruptness and delight in a somewhat gradual approach. A building is rarely pleasing in appearance without a porch or some sort of inviting entrance. An elaborate piece of music will always have a prelude of at least a few introductory notes. And so any composition or address which has no introduction is apt to seem incomplete.[1]

Few would disagree. Formal oral communication should, or so it seems, provide a natural means whereby the gap between the speaker's purpose and the listener's condition (act or attitude) is bridged. An introduction begins the task of spanning that gulf. Karl Barth asks, "Is an introduction necessary?" Then he responds: "Not unless it is a Biblical introduction; any other kind is to be ruled out for several reasons, two of which may be noted: (1) Why do we go to church? To hear the Word of God, thus the successive acts of worship are sufficient introduction to the sermon—which is their culmination. A few opening words will suffice: any other sort of introduction is a waste of time—and a sermon should not be too long. (2) Only too often an introduction diverts the thoughts from the Word of God."[2]

All must concede the possibility of an occasional sermon that needs no introduction. "The idea of some preachers that all sermons must have an introduction is nonsense. If the subject demands it, it must have it, but be glad when it is quite unnecessary and you can step swiftly in."[3] Such is the exception, not the rule. Most sermons need an introduction. Why is this so?

1. Purpose of Introductions

(1) **To secure attention and arouse interest.** Henry Grady Davis contends that "the preacher's peril is not that attention is hard to win. His greatest peril is that attention and interest are too easy to win from the people who come to church."[4] Unfortunately, people have ears and hear not, eyes and see not. Years of practice have perfected feigned attention. We do not automatically win a hearing the moment we step behind the pulpit. It is fallacious, as well as presumptuous, to assume that people want very much to hear what we have to say. "Nobody is automatically interested in our message. . . . Regardless of how important, sacred, or controversial our content, we must begin beckoningly."[5]

As Sue Nichols puts it, "Today's communicator must ensnare dippers."[6] For the preacher every stimulus is a form of competition; whether it be outside noise, itching skin, the hat of a woman parishioner, the wiggling of a nearby child, the hum of an insect, the siren of a passing ambulance—all are potential enemies of interest and attention. James A. Winans, speaking in the early part of the twentieth century, maintained that "persuasion is the process of inducing others to give fair, favorable, or undivided attention to propositions."[7] His book instructed the speaker on how to get and hold audience attention. To his mind, attention was almost synonymous with persuasion and was certainly the ultimate goal of persuasion. In Monroe's "motivated sequence," to which we alluded earlier, attention is the first step in a persuasive speech. An introduction is successful, at least in part, if it creates interest, arouses attention, and serves to focus the concern of the audience on the speaker and his message. W. E. Sangster illustrates an interest-creating introduction by relating a humorous incident.

> They still tell at Princeton University of the visit of Sparhawk Jones to their chapel and his announcement of the text: "Is thy servant a dog, that he should do this thing?" (II Kings 8:13 KJV). After a moment's pause, he began crisply: "Dog or no dog, he did it!"[8]

His audience was obviously with him.

(2) **Establish the direction of thought.** The first moments of the sermon may answer one of two questions: What is he going to talk about? What in general is he going to say about it? Quite simply, the introduction should introduce. It may, in the process, provide background information, define terms, or clarify concepts. In so doing, the preacher is equipping the listener to follow the sermonic journey without conceptual or terminological stumbling blocks. A narrowing of focus will also be noted in the introduction. How much of a topic

will be covered? Limitations are acknowledged and the direction of thought is established.

(3) **Make the transition from the natural to the spiritual.** The well-known law of apperception—namely, moving from "the known to the unknown"—is an established practice of pedagogy. Jesus, the master teacher and preacher, practiced this law. When He spoke with the woman of Samaria He did not begin referring to spiritual truths and theology. He began rather with a discussion of water, and then inquired if she would provide a drink for Him. Then, He moved from a discussion of water to a consideration of that which could provide permanent satisfaction. His movement was from things natural to things spiritual. He moved from that which she knew to that which she ought to know. Jesus used the well known to teach profound spiritual truths—a fig tree, children, birds, bread, wine, the wind, shepherds, and so forth. He started where people were and took them where He wanted them. A carefully prepared introduction is a bridge builder into the world of the Spirit.

(4) **Show the pertinence of the message.** Every listener, consciously or unconsciously, asks, "Why should I listen?" For the preacher this is a heavy burden. His introduction will either gain a hearing or induce a self-imposed deafness on the part of the auditor. When the introduction has succeeded, the listener can give an appropriate, satisfactory answer to the question of *why* he should listen. Pertinence has then been established.

2. Requisites of Good Introductions

(1) **Brief.** According to Henry Grady Davis, it should be one or two minutes in length. Whitesell and Perry say 5 to 15 percent of the speaking time. It is reported that an old lady once told John Owen, the Puritan preacher, that he was so long spreading the table that she lost her appetite for the meal. If we remember that the introduction is to introduce and simply introduce, we are less likely to drag and more likely to move quickly into the body of the sermon. Most sermons need only a few words. Some will need a rather extensive introduction, but these are the exception. In some cases it occurs because of the audience's lack of knowledge or misunderstanding of the topic being considered. Clarification and definition of misunderstood concepts and ideas will then be necessary.

(2) **Appropriate.** Introductions should not be interchangeable between sermons. Each should be custom tailored to the exact sermon development which follows it. Davis states it hyperbolically, "If the introduction could possibly be used for any other sermon than this, it is not a good introduction to this sermon."[9] There must be an indigenous character to every introduction, with each word pointing toward the basic idea. Extraneous thought is likely to be a false lead.

An introduction is either an asset or a liability. Misdirected interest may keep the preacher scrambling all the way to the benediction. The introduction must, of necessity, fit *that* sermon.

(3) **Modest.** An introduction should promise no more than you can deliver. To say that you will answer the problem of race in an introduction is egotistical. To say, for instance, that your purpose this morning is to settle the question of eschatology is also highly presumptuous.

A layman criticized his pastor thus: "You started out by laying the foundation for a skyscraper, but you built a chicken coop upon it." Another layman, referring to his pastor, said, "His introductions are masterpieces of interest, carefully worded and memorized. But the rest of the sermon seems inferior by contrast." An impressive introduction followed by an innocuous sermon is a serious letdown. It is better to begin modestly and build a rhetorical structure consistent with the promises made in the introduction.

(4) **Interesting.** Dullness and holiness are not synonymous. The gospel is essentially a vital and exciting message. It is good news, not bad news. It is a sin to be dull at any point in the sermon. The introduction should reveal the inherent interest resident in the gospel.

A sermon is like a golf game. The introduction is comparable to the tee shot, the body of the sermon to the fairway game, and the conclusion to the putting game. A good sermon, like a good golf game, can be destroyed at any of the three points. Unless the introduction immediately captures the interest of the congregation, the preacher will scramble (i.e., need to make some "excellent shots") in order to recover in appropriate style. Interest lost in the introduction is hard to recover in the developing sermon. It must be created and sustained from the outset.

(5) **Suggestive.** Inasmuch as the introduction is not the sermon in digest form, do not give everything in the beginning. This part of the sermon is preparatory and suggestive, not exhaustive. It is the porch, not the main building. Interest will lag if nothing fresh emerges as the sermon develops.

Modern theorists suggest that "it is especially ill-advised to state one's thesis and major arguments if the audience is known to be hostile."[10] The introduction should not specifically anticipate what is to follow if there is an inimical audience or if there is hostility toward the subject. In fact it appears that most audiences react most favorably to a message in which "the persuader does not state his purpose in the introduction, but rather uses that introduction to emphasize areas of agreement between himself and his audience—and then uses the conclusion to make an appeal for specific action."[11]

Experiments by Walster and Festinger (1961) and by Brock and

Becker (1965) suggest that a speaker might do well to hide his intent even when speaking to an audience somewhat favorable to his point of view. It was "found that when listeners were highly involved with the topic and when they were favorable toward the speaker's point of view they were more influenced when they felt they were accidentally overhearing the message than when they knew it was intended for them."[12]

3. Types of Introductions

(1) **Biblical.** The biblical introduction is commonly used in narrative sermons. For instance, a sermon on John 3 began with an imaginative restructure of the scene. It depicted a second floor apartment where Jesus was staying. Up the rickety stairs went the richly attired Jewish leader, Nicodemus, for his well-known encounter with the Master. A discussion ensued in which John 3 was woven into the fabric of the unfolding narrative sermon.

Other forms of sermonic presentation can use the biblical introduction. For example, James Stewart in his sermon "The Rending of the Veil" began with a description of the temple with the holy of holies. He then told how the veil was rent from top to bottom; "What God has torn asunder, let not man join together." From there he proceeded into a development of the theological implications for his audience.

Karl Barth overstates the case when he insists that every introduction be biblical. If it is biblical, it needs to be marked by intrigue, drama, or elements of identification with the audience. All too frequently the biblical introduction is dull, remote, and archaic in flavor. I seriously question the interest created by a sermon that begins, "Today let us consider the passage from Jeremiah that relates the return of the exiled Jews from their Babylonian captivity."[13] People in general are not interested in Babylon nor in the Book of Jeremiah; they are concerned about the here and now. Any legitimate use of Jeremiah and Babylonian captivity should enlist signs of identification, intrigue, and drama in such a way that the correlation to today's moderns is at once discernible.

(2) **Secular.** Some teachers of preaching counsel exclusive use of a secular introduction. The rationale is simple. People are living in today; hence the sermon should begin where they are. To start in the world of the Bible is to start where your people are not. Secular introductions stamp a message with contemporaneity. They must be handled in the light of the prevailing mood of the worship experience. If there is laughing and lightness in the service, one begins in a light vein and gradually turns the listeners to more serious thoughts. On the other hand, if the mood is sober and grave, the speech can

begin on a serious note. To change the mood abruptly by the introduction is to overlook the role that "preliminary tuning" plays in the communicative situation. Many forms of secular sermon introductions are available:

(a) *Personal experiences.* This popular form of introduction has much to commend it. It helps establish the preacher's credibility as well as giving opportunity for the congregation to identify with the life situations he has experienced. The one possible drawback of this introduction is that it may unnecessarily focus attention on the preacher rather than on his message.

An appropriate use of personal experience is found in a sermon by John R. Claypool titled "Strength Not to Faint" in which he described the illness of his nine-year-old daughter, Laura Lue. He discussed the months in which she had been stricken with acute leukemia, the times of prayer, the shattering of hope, the waiting, the disappointments, and the gathering darkness. Against this backdrop he discussed the nature of the church and the provision of God, using Isaiah 40:27-31 as his text.[14]

(b) *Startling statement.* A message delivered prior to the "God is Dead" movement began, "We don't believe in God. We just say we do." The impact on the congregation was instantaneous. The preacher then proceeded to tell the congregation that although they were theoretically theistic, they were in all likelihood practically atheistic. Such a statement commands an instant hearing.

(c) *A news item.* Harry Emerson Fosdick began his sermon "On Catching the Wrong Bus" by saying:

Recently the newspapers carried the story of a man who boarded a bus with the full intention and desire of going to Detroit, but when at the end of a long trip he alighted at the destination, he found himself not in Detroit but in Kansas City. He had caught the wrong bus. Something like that goes on habitually in human life. People on the whole desire good things—happiness, fine family life, competence in their work, the respect of their friends, an honorable old age. Nothing is more common in our consciously-held desires and intentions than such good goals, but after a long trip, how many, alighting at the destination, find themselves somewhere else altogether![15]

(d) *Statement of a problem.* Another sermon by Fosdick titled "How Believe in a Good God in a World Like This?" began:

We face an old question this morning: How can we believe in a good God in a world like this? Job confronted it ages ago, and

Sophocles wondered how the gods could look complacently down on so much suffering and pain. Our generation feels afresh what Keats called "the giant agony of the world." How shall we reconcile an all-good and all-powerful God with earthquakes and cyclones, cholera and cancer, the long ruthlessness of the evolutionary process, ills like insanity that fall on individuals even at their birth, and all the welter of lust, poverty, and war that human life involves? We come to church to sing the praises of the all-great and all-good God, but in how many hearts the question rises, How can he be all-good and all-great if he made a world like this?[16]

(e) *A quotation.* Overton Stephens, a medical doctor from Toronto, started a sermon in Boston by saying, "There are only three types of people in the world: committed Christians, committed Communists, and amiable nonentities." Very often a quotation is the quickest route to attention.

(f) *Reference to a book.* A sermon by Roger Lovette was introduced as follows:

In his novel, *A Mass for the Dead,* William Gibson writes of that time when he picked up his late mother's gold-rimmed spectacles and her faded, dog-eared prayer book. He sat in what was once her favorite chair. He opened the book and tried to see what she must have seen in that book. He reached—in desperation—for the slender thread of her faith, once so alive, so real, so meaningful. And William Gibson writes that he did not see what she had seen; he could not hear what she had heard. The man tried to stoke the fires of his dead mother's faith—but it never works that way. Every person must discover a faith of his own.[17]

(g) *Reference to the season.* An Eastertide sermon by Frank A. Nichols commenced,

Easter has lost its religious impact for many Christians. Not so on that first Easter morning! On that day the Resurrection answered the deepest questions that troubled mankind. Last Sunday we heard this basic New Testament message. Simply stated, it is this: the Resurrection of Jesus Christ signals God's victory over sin and death.[18]

(h) *A humorous incident.* Humor has a legitimate place in preaching when it is used with caution. Often the introduction is the most appropriate place for it. While "the recitation of one funny but unrelated story after another may give the congregation the impression it is observing a court jester of a king rather than a prophet of the Most High," it may also be an effective and appropriate instrument in the hands of the wise.[19] A reading of

Elton Trueblood's *The Humor of Christ* will assist the preacher in developing perspective. Humor need not be irreverent. It may, in fact, guarantee a hearing if properly geared to the content of the sermon and not tacked on for interest's sake only.

Other possibilities for introduction include the following: a question, vivid word pictures, a definition, a parable, a riddle, a prediction, poem, brief history of the problem or theme, a prayer, a proverb, and the like. The possibilities are almost unlimited.

Two introductory tendencies should be resisted. First, to refer to the last time you preached this particular sermon is a slap in the face. It is an insult to the congregation, for it implies that you did not care enough to make fresh preparation. A sermon may be used again and again, but it must always be updated, never preached as if it is simply one from "the barrel."

Second, the preacher ought to avoid apologies: "I didn't have much time to prepare"; "I am not happy with this message"; "I left my notes at home." Or, "I am not much of a preacher." Stand up, preach, let the people make their own evaluation.

SERMON CONCLUSIONS

Sermon conclusions are frequently considered the most difficult part of the sermon to prepare. It is no surprise, therefore, to discover that nothing is so consistently inadequate among the printed sermons as the conclusion. I am not certain just why this is true. It may be that too much time is given to development of ideas and introductory matters. Whatever the answer, the phenomenon is disconcerting. I wish I could turn your attention to twenty volumes of sermons that illustrate effective conclusions; unfortunately I cannot. Even the best of preachers (including the likes of Phillips Brooks, Henry Ward Beecher, Joseph Parker, Harry Emerson Fosdick, James Stewart, and Arthur Buttrick) fail us regularly. Many sermons just seem to end; they "grind to a halt." An impressive opening and a persuasive development often terminate with a bland conclusion. To return to our metaphor, the tee shot (introduction) is straight and true, the fairway game (body of the sermon) is skillfully played, but the preacher "blows" his putt (the conclusion).

These comments are not intended to counsel despair, but to encourage the sermon builder who knows the dilemma. Most of us need help at the point of the conclusion.

1. Marks of a Good Conclusion

(1) **Natural and appropriate.** The conclusion should be thematically consistent with what precedes it. It should have a continuity with the idea developed in the body. I once heard a sermon on "Nebuchadnezzar's Golden Image" from Daniel 3 which concluded with an

invitation for baptism. There was no correlation whatever between the body and conclusion.

(2) **Unmistakably personal in its theme.** Preaching is a personal encounter with God. James Stewart's sermons regularly conclude with a flourish of lofty, poignant, majestic language. There is emotion without emotionalism. The challenge only indirectly calls people to repent, believe, and serve; more obviously it calls people to worship. It does not ask people to stand and be counted so much as to kneel and adore. The expected response is one of praise to God. His sermons do not so much leave you in the midst of the world, as they leave you at the feet of Christ. The emphasis is on a personal encounter with God. Rather than a frantic call to get out and serve, there is a compelling call to bow before the Lord Almighty. Worship becomes the fount from which service naturally flows.

(3) **High point of the sermon.** The developing idea should increase in intensity so that the conclusion constitutes the emotional high point of the sermon.

One textbook on preaching says, "The crisis is at hand. The moment of decision has come . . . the conclusion is the time to bring all things to a harmonious and moving culmination . . . the message is now to come into sharpest focus, the conclusion is a time of suspense."[20] Preaching does not and cannot move along a horizontal line. There are peaks and valleys. The true graph of attention is never a straight line. It is more like a graph of the fluctuations of the stock market: a level, a peak, a valley, a plateau, a peak, a valley, and finally a peak.

It is wise and proper to occasionally rest an audience, to give them a breathing spell—not a time out for triviality, but a change of pace in the material or in the voice. A sermon is a series of climaxes. The preacher breaks through with intensification of emotion, the stepping up of animation, and finally he concludes at the time of the highest peak. When the emotional climax is reached, the sermon should terminate. All that follows is anticlimactic.

(4) **Brief.** Both the introduction and conclusion should be short in length, succinct in expression, and to the point. Long introductions and conclusions betray shaggy thinking and an inability to speak in lean and precise fashion. If the sermon has been adequately developed, the conclusion need be no more than two or three minutes out of a total of twenty-five or thirty.

2. Forms of Conclusion

(1) **Recapitulation.** Labored recapitulation is as unnecessary as it is tedious. It loses its effectiveness when it is more a matter of redundancy than review. The preacher will be well advised to learn the art

of synonym, of reflection, and of restatement without excessive dependence on the exact expressions used in the body of the sermon. Use equivalent words. In this way ideas can be recapped without becoming repetitious and boring. It should "draw the speech together into a unified, impelling impression that will aid in the accomplishment of the speech purpose. This is the place to consolidate all of the impressions for the final impact."[21]

A sermon by Gene W. Aulenbach concludes with recapitulation: "The unjust steward was clever enough to provide a second chance for himself. He was wise enough to provide for friendships and eternal habitations. Will you be as clever?"[22]

(2) **Application.** A graphic sermon by a seminary student portrayed the drama of the crucifixion—the trial, the walk to Golgotha, the nails driven into the hands and feet of Christ, the jarring of the Roman gibbet into the ground, and the excruciating pain which attended this event. He concluded simply with the familiar words of John 3:16, "For God so loved the world that he gave his only Son."

(3) **Exhortation.** This takes the form of a challenge. For example, a sermon could conclude with a phrase from Isaac Watts' hymn, "Love so amazing, so divine, demands my soul, my life, my all." It may ask a question: What is your response? or, What will you do?

(4) **Invitation or call.** This may be geared to either unbelievers or believers. It calls the congregation to do something about the sermon, privately and quietly or publicly and overtly. It may be to confess sin or to worship. It may be a call to come and stand in the front of the sanctuary, publicly declaring the intention to follow Christ. It may be an invitation to be baptized or join the church. Whatever the challenge, it advises the audience as to precisely what they ought to do, and do now.

Robert T. Oliver, from the perspective of secular speech, speaks eloquently to the preacher:

It is necessary not only to lay the basis for agreement, but actually to win it. The conclusion is the "sign on the dotted line" portion of the speech. The introduction has sown the seeds, the discussion has cultivated the crop, and the function of the conclusion is to reap the harvest. Generally the conclusion of a persuasive speech takes the form of an appeal for action.[23]

(5) **Benediction.** A sermon may conclude with a blessing pronounced on the people of God. John Chrysostom frequently ended his homilies with a combination of prayer and doxology.[24]

(6) **Encouragement.** This is particularly apropos in the therapeutic sermon. It may take the form of consolation, a final reminder of God's provision. P. T. Forsyth encouraged people by affirming that "your

faith . . . may fail Him, but you know . . . that He will not fail your faith."[25]

(7) **Poem.** When a poem is used, it should not be read but memorized. James S. Stewart's sermon "The Wind of the Spirit" concludes:

If only we would take Christ at His word today! If only the Church, if each of us, would allow the Holy Spirit to have His way with us! I know the difficulties. I know all too well the towering, formidable difficulties. But I also know that in the last resort it is as simple as this: will I take Jesus at His word? Now is the accepted time. Listen to the wind, Nicodemus. Listen to the wind!

> And so the shadows fall apart,
> And so the west winds play;
> And all the windows of my heart
> I open to Thy day.[26]

(8) **Shock or surprise.** Whereas the recapitulation is predictable, the surprise ending is just the opposite. That is its unique strength. Obviously it can only be used sparingly for greatest effectiveness. When anything is predictable—even surprise—it loses its power. Peter Marshall concluded a graphic sermon on Elijah by saying, "If God be God, worship Him. But if Baal be god, worship him and go to hell. Let us pray."

This list is only suggestive. With imagination and creativity many other forms can be enlisted and used with great benefit.

THINGS TO AVOID

Homiletical orthodoxy has always maintained that the conclusion is a recapitulation, restatement, exhortation, or invitation based on material already stated. If this is true, you should not introduce new material. If new material arises in the conclusion, it is an evidence of improper management of the sermon body. The conclusion should be a last word, a refocusing, a final look at what has preceded it—not a bearer of new information.

A second taboo is to say, "in conclusion" or "as we close" or "finally." It is best to conclude without announcing your intention. Sangster says, "It is amazing how many synonyms can be found for 'finally.' It is best to avoid all these stimulations of hope (!) and run right on to that clear conclusion that has been in your eye from the moment you set out."[27]

Generally, the conclusion is prepared before the introduction. The sermon should be nearly completed before the introduction can be properly developed in its final form. The logic is obvious. The introduction, if it is truly to introduce, must be built upon what follows. It should be clear that a lucid, interesting introduction and a forceful final note sounded in a succinct, challenging conclusion are imperatives in a good sermon.

NOTES

1. J. A. Broadus, *On the Preparation and Delivery of Sermons,* rev. Jesse Barton Weatherspoon (New York: Harper & Brothers, 1944), p. 101.

2. Karl Barth, *The Preaching of the Gospel,* trans. B. E. Hooke (Philadelphia: The Westminster Press, 1963), pp. 78, 79.

3. W. E. Sangster, *The Craft of the Sermon* (Philadelphia: The Westminster Press, 1951), p. 124.

4. Henry Grady Davis, *Design for Preaching* (Philadelphia: Fortress Press, 1958), p. 187.

5. Sue Nichols, *Words on Target* (Richmond: John Knox Press, 1963), p. 29.

6. Nichols, p. 19.

7. James A. Winans, *Public Speaking* (New York: The Century Company, 1921), p. 194.

8. Sangster, p. 135.

9. Davis, p. 188.

10. Gary Cronkhite, *Persuasion: Speech and Behavioral Change* (Indianapolis: The Bobbs-Merrill Company, Inc., 1969), p. 193.

11. Cronkhite, p. 195.

12. Cronkhite, pp. 193-194.

13. Harold W. Kaser, "When People Ask the Way to Zion," *Pulpit Digest* (April 1970), p. 45.

14. John R. Claypool, "Strength Not to Faint," *Pulpit Digest* (February 1970), pp. 46 ff.

15. Harry Emerson Fosdick, *Riverside Sermons* (New York: Harper & Brothers Publishers), p. 38.

16. Fosdick, p. 247.

17. Roger Lovette, "A Faith of Our Own," *Pulpit Digest* (April 1970), p. 15.

18. Frank A. Nichols, "Resurrection Postscript," *Pulpit Digest* (April 1970), p. 11.

19. H. C. Brown, Jr., H. Gordon Clinard, and Jesse J. Northcutt, *Steps to the Sermon* (Nashville: Broadman Press, 1963), p. 126.

20. Brown, Clinard, and Northcutt, p. 121.

21. Glen E. Mills, *Message Preparation: Analysis and Structure* (Indianapolis: The Bobbs-Merrill Company, Inc., 1966), p. 83.

22. Gene W. Aulenbach, "Get Thee Wisdom," *Pulpit Digest* (April 1970), p. 44.

23. Robert T. Oliver, *The Psychology of Persuasive Speech,* 2nd ed. (New York: Longmans, Green and Co., 1957), p. 339.

24. Davis, p. 199.

25. P. T. Forsyth, *Positive Preaching and the Modern Mind* (London: Independent Press, Ltd., 1960), p. 46.

26. James S. Stewart, *The Wind of the Spirit* (Nashville: Abingdon Press, 1968), p. 19.

27. Sangster, p. 149.

BIBLICAL TRUTH—UNFOLDING THE IDEA

OUTLINE

QUALITIES OF GOOD OUTLINES

SUPPORTING MATERIAL

1. Explanation
2. Exemplification
3. Accentuation

LOGIC AND EMOTION

1. Logic
2. Emotion

STYLE AND LANGUAGE

1. Strive for Precision
2. Do Not Fear the Short, Familiar Word
3. Cultivate the Friendship of Sensuous Words and Expressions
4. Resist the Temptation to Lapse into Clichés
5. Build Your Vocabulary

CHAPTER TEN • UNFOLDING THE IDEA

CHAPTER TEN / BIBLICAL TRUTH—UNFOLDING THE IDEA

A well-organized sermon unfolds in purposeful fashion. Traditionally, this process has incorporated an introduction, a body, and a conclusion. To speak of the body of a sermon involves a consideration of outline, supporting material, logic and emotion, style and language. These sermonic ingredients will be considered in order.

OUTLINE

Once the raw material is in hand you are ready to develop the skeleton (i.e., structure) upon which you will hang the flesh of the sermon. An outline will aid both the speaker and the listener. It prevents the preacher from rambling. It establishes an order, a direction for thought. Omissions, digressions, inconsistencies, misplaced emphases, and unsupported assertions will be sharply reduced. Sermons wander without the safeguards of a well thought out structure. Phillips Brooks said, "True liberty in writing comes by law, and the more thoroughly the outlines of your work are laid out the more freely your sermon will flow, like an unwasted stream between its well-built banks."[1]

Although many jokes have been told about homiletical orthodoxy, "three points and a poem," it is well to use an outline to minimize discursiveness. Little Mary's essay on "Pigs" will illustrate the problem.

> A pig is a funny animal, but it has some uses (the uses are not mentioned). Our dog don't like pigs—our dog's name is Nero. Our teacher read a piece one day about a wicked man called Nero. My Daddy is a good man. Men are very useful. Men are different than women and my Mom ain't like my Daddy. My Mom says that a ring around the sun means that a storm is coming. And that is all I know about pigs.[2]

Sad to say, there have indeed been sermons preached with a similar pattern.

Scaffolding in a sermon maintains order as well as reasonableness in the development of thought. Though out of favor and joked about in some circles, competent preachers tend to fear it less and less. Structure, if properly understood, is not an end, it is a means. The way to get rid of boniness in a sermon is not by leaving out the skeleton, but by clothing it with substantial flesh. Freedom in delivery, which usually implies freedom from manuscript or excessive dependence on notes, comes in part from a structure that is both logical and easily recalled at the moment of delivery. Some announce the heads or divisions of a sermon. Others hesitate because they feel it is stiff, formal, and old-fashioned. Although the preacher need not formally announce divisions, he ought to take great pains to let the audience recognize progression.

Congregations need an outline. Because the sermon is not a printed presentation, where the reader can see the divisions or reread a section to discover the connection, it needs verbalized guidelines. When they are lacking, confusion reigns and interest lags. It is safe to assume that most congregations welcome a clear, precise statement of the course that a particular sermon is going to pursue. A sermon is not like a picture that once painted stands completed before the eye. A sermon which has an orderly, consistent progress aids the listener's memory. The points of the sermon serve as memory hooks to assist him in the recall process, once the sermon has been completed.

The development of a sermon is admittedly a painstaking labor; it takes time. Some preachers, for instance, spend hours on structure. This practice is questionable. It is inordinate; a misguided use of time. However, a proportionate amount of time in careful thought and concerted effort ought to be given to establish a meaningful, clear, helpful structure that will assist preacher and listener alike.

QUALITIES OF GOOD OUTLINES

1. **Succinct statements.** Avoid involved phrases or cumbersome sentences which are not only difficult to remember, but tend to confuse the auditors. F. W. Robertson, though an exemplary preacher in many respects, broke this rule. His pulpit strength lay, however, not in his structure but in the rich thought which laced his sermons. Good outlines state the point in clear, crisp style. John Wesley's sermon on stewardship with its three points, "Earn all you can, Save all you can, Give all you can," is a noteworthy example.

2. **Parallel statements.** Parishioners have witnessed much straining after alliteration or bending of the text to derive a "neat" outline. Rather than being helpful, it degenerates into forced categories, sometimes to the point of being ludicrous. A student gave me the following poem, an obvious parody on pulpit alliteration.[3]

Melody in F (The Prodigal Son)

Feeling Footloose and Frisky, a Feather-brained Fellow
Forced his Fond Father to Fork over the Farthings,
And Flew Far to Foreign Fields
And Frittered his Fortune Feasting Fabulously with Faithless
   Friends.

Fleeced by his Fellows in Folly, and Facing Famine,
He Found himself a Feed-Flinger in a Filthy Farmyard.

Fairly Famishing, he Fain would've Filled his Frame
With Foraged Food From Fodder Fragments.
"Fooey, my Father's Flunkies Fare Far Finer,"

The Frazzled Fugitive Forlornly Fumbled, Frankly
    Facing Facts.
Frustrated by Failure, and Filled with Foreboding,
He Fled Forthwith to his Family.
Falling at his Father's Feet, he Forlornly Fumbled
"Father, I've Flunked,
And Fruitlessly Forfeited Family Favor."

Alliteration can be helpful; often it is not. It often reveals the ingenuity of the preacher rather than being an accurate representation of the biblical passage under consideration. If alliteration is natural, fine. If not, avoid it. Parallelism, however, is to be developed. If two points are short and the third is long, if two state truths with adjectives and one does not, we have evidences of shoddy thinking. Parallelism is a means of assisting both the parishioner and the preacher.

3. **Proportioned statements**. As the outline unfolds, it ought to have a sense of balance. A sermon that gives half time to one point and the rest of the time to two or three additional points lacks proportion. Donald G. Miller says, "Lack of balance is a homiletical as well as a nautical danger. Many a sermon has been the victim of shifted cargo. To overweight truth on one side may not show up as dramatically as a capsized boat, but both homiletically and theologically it is equally disastrous."[4] Any point that needs excessive consideration within the sermon should either be further divided into additional points or should serve by itself as a single sermon. An ill-proportioned sermon needs to be recast for balance.

4. **Mutually exclusive statements**. Each major point within the outline ought to be a distinct idea, worthy of separate attention. Discreteness, in which each point is a separate and distinctive idea, eliminates overlapping.

5. **Contemporary statements**. Outlining is done in the present tense for purposes of audience identification. A sermon with three or four points relating directly to Peter or Paul or Moses may be invitation enough for the congregation to affect an early closure. The truth of Scripture must be restated in the contemporary idiom to underline its universal application. For example, a sermon on John 4 could be developed: (1) The woman of Samaria needed acceptance. (2) Jesus accepted the woman of Samaria. A better rendering of the passage would be: (1) We need to be accepted. (2) We are accepted by Jesus.

Some outlines come very easily. David H. C. Read, in a sermon titled "Labor, Leisure, and Worship," unfolds his thought in three points: (1) Labor, (2) Leisure, and (3) Worship.[5] Most sermons do not unfold that readily.

A sermon on Psalm 3, describing the inner turmoil of David as he was fleeing from his avaricious son Absalom may be developed in the following fashion: (1) Man's complaint, vv. 1-2; (2) God's comfort, vv. 3-4; (3) Man's contentment, vv. 5-6.

Two-point sermons may be developed with the first point referring to the past, the second referring to the present. A sermon on Genesis 28:10-22 titled "Making Bargains with God" can be developed: (1) The ancient bargain table (Jacob and Rebecca cheat Esau) and (2) The modern bargain table (Modern man continues to bargain with God).

A Thanksgiving sermon titled "The Thankful Heart" on Ephesians 5:18-20 unfolds in telescopic fashion: (1) Giving thanks to God, (2) Giving thanks to God always, (3) Giving thanks to God always for all things. Although this outline may not be in parallel statements, it is nevertheless succinct, mutually exclusive, contemporary, and very biblical. Not every outline will have all the qualities we have noted in respect to good outlines. No rule is unbreakable. Rules serve only as helpful guidelines, to deprive us of thoughtless development.

SUPPORTING MATERIAL

Just as a healthy man is a combination of healthy skeleton and healthy flesh, so is the sermon a combination of healthy structure and substantial supporting material. Supporting material is divisible into three categories: explanation, exemplification, and accentuation.[6]

1. Explanation

Definition is one means of clarifying ideas, words, or concepts that are fuzzy, unknown, or misunderstood. It may be a theological word like "justification" which needs clarification for the parishioner. Or, the preacher may define a concept like "sin" as it relates to the modern scene. The idea may be further clarified by division: an isolating of the parts of a concept is followed by analysis of each part. A concept like "justification" may be broken down into its God-ward and its man-ward dimensions and then clarified by further analysis.

2. Exemplification

Persuasive speeches in particular need this form of supporting material. It may be an example or illustration which is factual or hypothetical. If factual it takes a real-life situation and uses it in the sermon as typical. If hypothetical it develops a situation that could be typical. Speakers may give numerous examples to prove a statement or a single example in which the typicality of that incident or instance is ascertained.

Certain shortcuts to the example such as a list of names, places, or events in which parallel situations are noted can be used successfully. Examples may be tested for their appropriateness by asking whether or not they are relevant to the idea being developed, appropriate to the audience, and typical, therefore applicable to others as well as to the one who is being discussed.

Analogies may be used to show typicality. The greater the number of similarities, the greater the likelihood that the typicality will be accepted.

Analogies may be either literal or figurative. In a literal analogy two or more phenomena are essentially alike—two political parties compared, two schools of theology compared, two doctrines compared. In a figurative analogy the comparison "deals with phenomena that are essentially different, but which nonetheless contain a critical common element."[7]

Some analogies may be used simply for insight in which case the demands for similarity are not as exacting. A sermon on heaven included the comment, "Heaven is a place without Mondays or mornings." A sermon on hell included the statement, "Hell is an endless train ride without a club car."

Statistics also serve as a form of exemplification. Statistics are "codified and classified examples"[8] which must be handled with care. The same raw data can be juggled by two different groups according to their distinct purposes. The task is accomplished by selection and interpretation of statistics. If statistics are used, they must be dependable and clear, from a reputable source, and interesting as well. When statistics are related to the listener's frame of reference, they take on significance. For instance, a missions message might appeal to the congregation to support orphans. The preacher might mention that it takes only $10 to support an orphan in Korea. This could be made more interesting by noting that this would be only about 30c a day; then asking the question, "How much could you do with 30c a day?" Such an investment in the life of a Korean orphan would be easy to make at the same time that it would make an extraordinary contribution to a needy child. A sermon on poverty might note that 20 percent of America is in a state of poverty, living at under $4,000 annual income. "How much can you buy with $4,000?"

3. Accentuation

Explanation is an attempt to clarify, exemplification is an attempt to prove, and accentuation is an attempt to clinch the idea. It is a form of oral underlining. When you read a book you can reread it until it is understood. In speech this is not possible. The wise speaker, therefore, uses repetition, recapitulation, and restatement. Quantitative research suggests that "the reinforcement of major ideas may strengthen retention."[9] The thoughtful preacher will be advised to develop the art of internal review before moving on to another point. This serves to clinch ideas.

Quotation is another form of accentuation. It adds vividness but should be used sparingly. Unfortunately some sermons "are only a tissue of quotation." Such sermons have degenerated into a cut and patch job. It is better to have a few short quotations than one long one. It is perfectly ethical to shorten a quotation if one can do so without seriously changing the intended meaning. When using this form of testimony, it is well to ask if the person quoted is known and respected. If he is not, make certain the idea is worthy. If it is sufficiently unique, use it without citing the person's name. Simply suggest that "it has been written," or "someone said," or "a recent volume notes"; then give the quote. The inclusion of the man's name should add credibility, not create confusion. If the speaker is Martin Luther, it should be noted. If, on the other hand, it is some obscure sixteenth century Catholic cardinal, it is useless to note him specifically.

A well-respected preacher who has established his credentials as a man of high ethos will only hurt himself by excessive citing of the testimony of others, since others may not have the high ethos that he does and hence may only distract. "A low-ethos speaker is well-advised to cite the testimony of others, assuming those others have greater ethos than his own."[10]

Supporting material must be used in the light of its attention-securing character. According to the behavioral scientists, a single stimulus has a duration of only five to eight seconds in terms of attention.[11] Interest is secured by appealing to the vital interests of the audience, appealing to what is concrete and vivid, to suspense (without being corny or melodramatic), the use of conflict, appealing to the familiar or to the novel, appealing to what is vital (whatever affects life, health, reputation, property, or employment), and by using humor, if tastefully done. In addition to these content elements, variation in pitch, rate, or volume, along with activity or movement of the speaker, will also assist in securing attention of the listener.

Supporting materials, to be useful, must be believable. If the congregation is to be moved, it must grant credence to the preacher. People believe in a number of ways. They believe because they sense it—they can see it, they can smell it, they can feel it, they can hear it. This may be through a direct experience of forgiveness, answer to prayer, loneliness, heartache, grief, joy, or love. If they have felt it, if they have experienced it, they will believe you when you talk about it.

Vicarious experience is second best, although it also is a powerful means of encouraging belief. Vicarious experience occurs when direct experience is made so vivid that the listener can enter into it as if he was actually having a direct experience. This draws forth from the speaker imagination, insight, and concrete imagery in language. People believe that which comes to them on good authority. The testimony of a leading political figure, of their doctor, of a university professor, or of a trusted pastor is generally believable. The preacher will be well advised, therefore, to make certain that the sources to which he alludes and from which he derives support are authoritative for the people who hear him.

A further reason why people believe anything at all is that they are convinced of its validity. Ministerial addiction to easy answers and shoddy thinking undercuts the logical expectation of listeners. A good speaker, therefore, tests his facts, the various supporting materials, quotations, statistics, and illustrations that are coupled with the biblical text in the sermon he is preparing.

LOGIC AND EMOTION

Aristotle said that there are three modes of persuasion furnished by the spoken word: ethos, pathos, and logos. "The first kind depends on the personal character of the speaker; the second on putting the audience into a certain frame of mind; the third on the proof, or apparent proof, provided by the words of the speech itself."[12] In referring to pathos he says, "Persuasion may come through the hearers, when the speech stirs their emotions."[13] Of logos he says, "Persuasion is effected through the speech itself when we have proved a truth or an apparent truth by means of the persuasive arguments suitable to the case in question."[14]

The terms "ethos," "pathos," and "logos" have remained intact over the succeeding 2,300 years. Slight modifications in meaning and importance of these categories have taken place. Perhaps the most significant variation in the Aristotelian construct is the discrediting of a logical-emotional dichotomy. The absence of a significant difference between logical and emotional proof is perhaps attributable to the falseness of the dichotomy enunciated by faculty psychology which is now discredited. Martin Scheerer says, "In principle, then, behavior may be conceptualized as being embedded in a cognitive-emotional-motivational matrix in which no true separation is possible. No matter how we slice behavior, the ingredients of motivation-emotion-cognition are present in one order or another."[15]

An increase in the logic of a speech need not imply a decrease in its emotionality or vice versa. "The best persuasive speech is probably one which is both logical and as emotional as possible."[16] Experimental evidence suggests that logical arguments are no more influential than emotional appeals or general impressions.[17] It is not a question of either logic or emotion but of both logic and emotion. The concepts must be hyphenated, not distinguished.

For purposes of analysis, recognizing that certain messages are weighted heavier in one than in the other, let us distinguish them.

1. Logic

Bertrand Russell, who placed great emphasis upon the reasoning power of man, maintained that "the truly rational individual cultivates a habit of taking account of all relevant evidence in arriving at a belief. When certainty is unattainable, a rational man will give most weight to the most probable opinion, while retaining others which have an appreciable probability in his mind as hypotheses which subsequent evidence may show to be prefer-able."[18] Such a goal is not only to be commended, it is a goal toward which every preacher ought to aspire. To affirm one's faith in the rationality of man is to affirm faith in man as a logical creature. We want to be as rational as possible, recognizing that our ability is weak and there is no expectation of consistent success.

Textbooks which discuss persuasion generally argue for either a logical *or* a psychological pattern of organization. Research evidence gives very little support to either position. "There is evidence, however, which indicates that communicators would exercise good judgment if their messages and the arguments within the messages are made to appear logical, even if they cannot be easily tested."[19] As might be expected, persons with high intelli-gence tend to be more influenced by logical presentations because of their ability to draw valid inferences. Those with lesser intelligence seem to find less influence because of their lower intellectual ability.[20] In this respect, Hovland, Janis, and Kelley counsel that "climax order will be favored on issues with which the audience is familiar and where deep concern is felt, but that anti-climax order will be favored on unfamiliar topics and with uninter-ested audiences."[21] This means essentially that the major arguments will be spelled out early in the speech when the idea is unfamiliar or the audience is uninterested in the topic. The minor arguments can remain for the latter part of the message when the audience is favorable and where the issue is already sensed.

Logical presentations, as already noted, take either a deductive or an inductive form. Deduction is a process of reasoning by which an interpreter proceeds from a general thought and then develops this theme in its particu-lars. In induction the preacher moves from particular ideas to a general principle by way of conclusion.

In life-situation or problem centered preaching, a three-step logical format may start with diagnosis, move to etiology, and conclude with prescription. Diagnosis is the description of the facts or symptoms of a condition. Etiology is a search for causes, leading to a judgment or opinion. Prescription is the recommendation of treatment, antidote for disease, and program for health which responds to the question, "What should I do about the problem?"[22]

Much superficial preaching is heavy in prescription and weak in diag-nosis. Thoughtful preaching, on the other hand, in an unconscious attempt to overcompensate has sometimes been guilty of "the paralysis of analysis," which gives inadequate attention to prescription. Peter's sermon on the Day of Pentecost evoked the question, "What should we do?" from his listeners. That is always a pertinent question which the preacher must painstakingly address, sometimes directly, sometimes indirectly.

Logical sermons, it has been argued, should have a presentation of the options; namely, the recommended position as well as the alternates. One-sided messages, researchers inform us, "are more effective when the receiver is already in agreement with the source, *provided* that the receiver is not likely to be exposed to later opposing messages."[23] The role of a two-sided message is to immunize receivers against contradictory information in later situations.

Logical methods include the following: arguing from statistics, from circumstantial detail, from comparison, by analogy, by generalization, from authority, from condition, by alteration, and by categorization or what some have called syllogistic reasoning. A careful analysis of the audience by the preacher will determine which method or methods should be enlisted in the arguments being developed.

2. Emotion

> "I don't know enough," replied the Scarecrow cheerfully. "My head is stuffed with straw, you know, and that is why I am going to Oz to ask him for some brains."
> "Oh, I see," said the Tin Woodman.
> "But, after all, brains are not the best things in the world."
> "Have you any?" inquired the Scarecrow.
> "Now, my head is quite empty," answered the Woodman, "but once I had brains, and a heart also; so having tried them both, I should much rather have a heart."[24]

So men have argued since the days of Aristotle. The argument is no longer tenable because the choice does not need to be made. It is emotion *and* logic, not either/or. Logic appeals to knowing, emotion to feeling. The two are intertwined and interdependent. James Hillman defines emotion as "a response to a stimulus involving the individual as a whole, comprising a reaction that is visceral, conscious, and tending toward a definite behavior."[25] Emotions are of two primary types, pleasurable and distressing. Included in the pleasurable would be delight, joy, elation, hope, gratitude, affection, love, pride, and so forth. Distressing emotions would include anger, fear, blame, shame, terror, hatred, remorse, envy, sorrow, grief, rage, anxiety, sympathy, pity, and the like.[26]

Aristotle adds three additional distressing emotions: indignation, emulation, and pugnacity.[27] Criticisms of emotionalism in speech are well known. Any exposure to the movie industry, television, novelists, dramatists, or some communication theorists is enough to underscore the problem. Arthur N. Kruger, in his critique of emotional modes of proof, says, "It belittles rational processes, shows little faith in man's ability to govern himself, extols the techniques of the confidence man, presumes that the end justifies the means, ignores the consequences of social manipulations." He adds:

> Many writers try to justify emotional proof by arguing that these are times when certain worthwhile proposals should be adopted and that the best means to this end are emotional appeals. . . . This argument, of course, assumes that the advocate alone knows what is worthwhile

and that those being appealed to cannot be depended on to reach the same conclusion by means of reason.[28]

Kruger overstates his case. His hyperbole is well intended but if accepted literally, it is an impossible scheme to maintain. It is true that if one places no limits on emotional appeals, he would reduce men to the behavior of lower animals. But "to object to all emotional proofs is to attempt to deny one's humanity."[29] Kruger fails to note how emotional his own statement is when he rejects emotionalism. To be rational is not to say that you cannot be emotional. Rationality has never implied an elimination of the emotional component in human thought and action. The goal is not to remove emotion from reason, but "to stimulate the appropriate emotion."[30]

A wise preacher makes careful selection, use, and application of emotional material to accomplish this end. I suggest the use of the following questions as a fitting criterion for the selection of pathetic or emotional proofs. (1) Is the evidence or information true? (2) Is it appropriate? (3) Is its use ethical? Listen to the testimony of two well-known teacher-preachers. Arndt L. Halvorson says, "Sermons without passion, which don't stir the inner man, which don't sing or lament, which neither shout in victory nor beg for mercy, which neither exult in faith nor grope for meaning, can hardly . . . be called sermons."[31] W. E. Sangster speaks in similar terms:

> To imagine that guilty sinners on their way to the cross must be forbidden all expression of emotion or that forgiven sinners returning from the cross must be denied a vent to the rapture in their souls, is to ask the impossible and to make nonsense of life in so doing. It leaves one wondering if the people who fear, and forbid it, have ever been forgiven themselves, or know the longing for a thousand tongues to sing the great Redeemer's praise.[32]

It is tragic if in an age known for its emotional extreme, when tears flow in the theaters, when people sob in front of their television sets, when people unburden their hearts while reading a novel, that these same people cannot be allowed such an expression in the framework of worship. The gospel, which addresses the most probing, essential, life-character questions, is geared to man at his depths. When the gospel touches man at these central issues of life, of meaning, of alienation, of guilt, of purpose, of fulfillment, who is to say that proper emotion cannot or should not be expressed? Sermons which speak to the great, vital issues of love, grace, salvation, and human destiny should, in the direct presentation of these truths, enlist legitimate emotional ingredients. To eliminate feeling and visceralness from a sermon is a caricature of life and its complexity. The church does not need to remove emotion, it needs to encourage its proper use. Extremes in emotion are questionable. The absence of emotion is equally questionable. Churches that have replaced emotion with a logic through some form of frozen liturgy are just as much at fault as the most extreme religious groups that thrive on emotional abandon.

Bettinghaus shows how even a metaphor can carry a highly intense emotional reaction. Some examples: (1) Draft laws are legalizing *murder;* (2) Passing this bill means the *rape* of our woodlands; (3) Legalized gambling is legalized *sin.*[33] A study in 1962 by Robbins reports that fear-arousing communications produce an instigation to aggression; therefore high fear appeals may be especially useful when the speaker is urging some form of aggression. Cronkhite says, "The speaker, then, is well advised to present a specific plan of action and to demonstrate its feasibility and effectiveness *whenever* he uses a strong fear appeal."[34]

STYLE AND LANGUAGE

The final step in developing a biblical sermon after the outline and supporting material have been determined, is to shape it in some stylistic fashion. It is at this point that the artisans are separated from the artists. Aristotle said, "Style to be good must be clear, as is proved by the fact that speech which fails to convey a plain meaning will fail to do just what speech has to do. It must also be appropriate, avoiding both meanness and undue elevation; poetical language is certainly free from meanness, but it is not appropriate to prose."[35]

Good style exists when language is so skillfully used that the beliefs and emotional experience of the speaker are shared by the listener. It has generally been assumed that those who have developed an effective style have either written out their sermons in entirety or have found some equally effective substitute for manuscript writing. Henry Grady Davis expresses the goal poetically:

> A sermon should be like a tree.
> It should be a living organism:
> > With one sturdy thought like a single stem
> > With natural limbs reaching up into the light.
> It should have deep roots:
> > As much unseen as above the surface
> > Roots spreading as widely as its branches spread
> > Roots deep underground
> > > In the soil of life's struggle
> > > In the subsoil of the eternal Word. . . .
>
> Illustrations like blossoms opening from inside these very twigs
> Not brightly colored kites
> > Pulled from the wind of somebody else's thought
> > > Entangled in these branches. . . .[36]

Style is essentially language and language is dependent on the alphabet. John Culkin, S.J., obviously influenced by Marshall McLuhan, says:

> Reality is squeezed through the funnel of the alphabet. Reality comes

out one drop at a time; it is segmented; sequential; it is fragmented along a straight line; it is analytical; it is abridged; it is reduced to one sense; it becomes susceptible to perspective and point of view; it becomes uniform and repeatable.[37]

Perhaps the purpose of language is to elicit a picture in the mind of the receiver comparable to that in the mind of the sender. Communication is successful when the meaning received is equivalent to the meaning sent. "Words, like maps, become reliable when they adequately express the experiences and evaluations they represent. When words do not accurately designate their referents, the likelihood of confusion, misunderstanding, and sometimes even danger exists."[38]

One of the primary functions of language is to assign labels (words) to experiences. These labels then become the means of meaningful communication between sender and receiver. Meanings are not in words. Meanings are learned; they are not God given. When people have similar meanings for words it is because their learning experiences have been similar.[39] When we set out to describe God within the limitations of language, we find how difficult the task really is. As a result some theologians assume that nothing can be said at all about God, and others think that anything and everything can be said about God. William Hordern reminds us,

> In Christian faith a way can be found between these two errors. Because Christian faith recognizes the transcendence of God, it can never suppose that its words capture the mystery of God. But, because it believes that God has revealed himself, it is convinced that it has a base of knowledge from which it can speak.[40]

Limitations, yes. Hopelessness, no. Communication faces some grave problems. No word has a particular meaning. Dictionary definitions simply point out conventional usages in terms of broad areas of meaning. It is necessary anytime a word is used in a sentence to discover both the context of the word and the background of the reader or hearer to ascertain any exactness in meaning.

S. I. Hayakawa describes it graphically. "Your 'Mississippi River' can never be identical with my 'Mississippi River.' The fact that we can communicate with each other about the 'Mississippi River' often conceals the fact that we are talking about two different sets of memories and experiences." Once this limitation is acknowledged there is enough shared information to make communication not only possible but very, very meaningful. Hayakawa continues:

> Korzybskis' simple but powerful suggestion is to add "index numbers" to all terms, according to the formula: A_1 is not A_2; it can be translated as follows: Cow$_1$ is not cow$_2$; cow$_2$ is not cow$_3$; politician$_1$ is not politician$_2$; ham and eggs (Plaza Hotel) are not ham and eggs (Smitty's Cafe); socialism (Russia) is not socialism (England); private

enterprise (Joe's Shoe Repair Shop) is not private enterprise (AT&T).[41]

Illustrations of this sort are not intended to counsel skepticism and confusion, but suggest the limitations inherent within the use of the English language. Language does have great power. Words can help, hinder, encourage, inspire, deceive, enslave, divide. The task is therefore to use words in such a way that they serve good purposes and accomplish good ends. A sloppy use of language involves us in grave problems. Easy answers or quick categories such as "the black man is lazy," or "Jews are greedy," or "Germans are bullheaded" only reveal our misunderstanding of language. In so doing, we fall prey to an error that no respectable anthropologist today regards as proven; namely, that there is a single character difference between races.[42]

Due to the ambiguous nature of language which lends itself to readily acknowledged misunderstanding, it is well to consider ways in which desired meanings can be obtained: *relearning* is an educational process of teaching people what words really mean; *classification* points up a term's position within a category when a category already known by the listener will give insight into that particular item; *negation* tells the receiver what he is not referring to; *operational definition* says if you do such and such, the term will be identified.

Rudolf Flesch has a practical method of simplifying language. That is, write and speak as if you were talking to a foreigner—to someone who may be just as smart as you are but who has grown up in another language and hasn't had a chance yet to make himself fully at home in English.[43]

Sue Nichols isolates three marks of appealing material: (1) it produces economy, (2) it has energy, and (3) it has subtlety.[44] Fowler offers some practical rules:

> Prefer the familiar word to the far-fetched.
> Prefer the concrete word to the abstract.
> Prefer the single word to the circumlocution.
> Prefer the short word to the long.
> Prefer the Saxon word to the Romance.
> These rules are given roughly in order of merit;
> the last is also the least.[45]

A few guidelines may be helpful as we consider the subject of vocabulary.

1. Strive for Precision

Succinctness and economy are correlative ideas. Many words are fuzzy in meaning—fast travel, expensive meal, good book, bad weather. Choose words that express the exact shade of meaning you intend to convey; if necessary, consult the dictionary or a book of synonyms. Edward John Carnell, who served for some time as president and later as professor at Fuller Theological Seminary in Pasadena, California, sensed the need for precision in his own personal vocabulary. He devoured one or two pages of a small pocket dictionary every day, taking cognizance of words that were not presently in his own working vocabulary. That day he would use the new word in his conversation, in his writings, and in his teaching, thereby assimilating it into his own vocabulary. As a result he seemed to have just the right word for every situation. He never seemed obscure; instead, he chose the word with the exact shade of meaning he wanted to convey.

Economy is the task of achieving the maximum effect with the fewest number of syllables. A lean style puts words through the wringer to squeeze out unnecessary words in sentences. Lean style tends to keep listeners more alert. They appreciate the fact that every word has value and counts in the total message. The task of the communicator is to be understood, not to confuse or mislead. In order to make that which we say understandable, to rivet it in the listeners' minds, it is necessary to develop a vocabulary that is exact and crystal clear. As you study Scripture you discover the Bible's sublime economy of words. Take, for example, the story of Ruth and Naomi. There is no striving after literary effect. The entire story is told in short, quiet, almost staccato sentences. The goal is not simply to cut down syllable length which may lessen effectiveness, but to choose words with the fewest number of syllables which accomplish the maximum effect toward which we are gearing our message.

Aristotle said you should describe a thing instead of naming it. For example, "Do not say 'circle,' but 'that surface which extends equally from the middle every way.' "[46] It is hoped that modern communicators will not take Aristotle seriously. Modern language practice demands preciseness as well as description. It is generally necessary only to name an item or an object. Circumlocution or padding is an unacceptable written or spoken pattern. The verboseness of Karl Barth is not fitting for pulpit fare.

Rudolf Flesch approaches the subject differently. He suggests that you enlist filler words which provide excelsior for your conversation. It is not difficult ideas expressed in easy language; it is rather abstractions embedded in small talk. "It is heavy stuff packed with excelsior. If you want to be better understood you don't have to leave out or change your important ideas; you must use more excelsior. It's as simple as that."[47] This padded approach may have some attractiveness, but it may lead us up a dark alley. It is more important that a difficult word be placed in a context where the idea is readily understood. To develop a style that is verbose—that is, padded, that has excelsior in it—may be less than helpful.

2. Do Not Fear the Short, Familiar Word

A common vice among preachers is love of the long word. Profundity and incomprehensibility are not synonymous. This is pedantic. It has little to do with the communication of anything other than the speaker's intellectuality. Men who are intoxicated with big words, who enjoy polysyllabics when single syllable words would more adequately accomplish the task need to check their motivation as well as the response of listeners. A seminary professor once confessed, "It takes three years to get through seminary and ten years to get over it." The problem is that much theological jargon needs to be popularized before it can be shared in public from the Christian pulpit. Oral language and written language are not the same. We write for the eye and not for the ear. Written language contains greater idea density and greater numbers of different words, difficult words, and complex sentences. [48]

As we might expect, quantitative research supports the conclusion that "familiarity with the words increases intelligibility."[49] Jules Laurence Moreau reminds us, "As God in Christ entered concretely into a specific culture at a given time and place, so the message of his revelatory-redemptive act must become incarnate in and for each generation by entering the culture of that generation and redeeming it."[50] The truths of the gospel must be expressed in present-tense language, in the language of our day; it is a sermon for today, not a lecture on yesterday. The dynamic language in the sermon must be that with which the congregation is familiar. Some feel it is necessary to use religious language in preaching. This, at best, is a small asset. It is not necessary to express religious truths by using esoteric language. In the final analysis there are no essentially religious truths: there are only truths which are religious or Christian. It is necessary for the preacher to speak the language of the people in order to express the eternal truths of the Christian faith. However, there are times when theological concepts cast in biblical terms can be retained. And the way this is done is not to eliminate the words but to put them in a setting surrounded by one-syllable or two-syllable words so that the word itself is understood by its context.

Almost everyone is able to understand an unfamiliar word or concept if the context makes clear what it means. A child once said to his mother regarding her pastor, "He can't be too smart, Mommy; I can understand him." This is the tradition of the master preacher, Jesus. His language was plain, familiar, suggestive, and colorful. And we are told, "the common people heard him gladly." Profound ideas can be and ought to be clothed in simple language. James S. Stewart says, "Every man at Pentecost heard the Gospel, we are told, in his own tongue. And that is the basic condition of effective preaching still."[51]

At the same time that we give our attention to short, familiar words, we ought also to strive for short sentences. Rudolf Flesch suggests a seventeen-word standard. If sentences are longer, we should look for joints in their construction and break them into smaller pieces until they are of the right average length.[52]

3. Cultivate the Friendship of Sensuous Words and Expressions

Compare the following two lists from Grady Davis' book, *Design for Preaching*.

Abstract	*Sensuous*
The alarm	The roar of the siren
He criticized them severely	He blistered them with words
	(Fulton Sheen)
We avoid thinking of death	We disguise death with flowers
	(Peter Marshall)
Young people enjoy life	Life is sweet on the tongue of youth
The spot where Jesus lay	The cold stone slab (Marshall)
The odors in Jesus' tomb	Strange scents of linen and
	bandages, and spices, and close
	air and blood (Marshall)[53]

For most of us this friendship with sensuous words and rich imagery does not come automatically; it is not an innate ability or an inherent gift. It comes as a result of discipline, of hearing, of touching, of tasting, of becoming aware of all that is around us, a practice of looking at life for poignancy. It may be necessary to record your impressions, for impressions without expressions are often nil and lost forever. Learn to paint pictures with words. Jesus said, "A city set on a hill," "the wings of the morning." Dean Walter Muelder of Boston University School of Theology once prayed, "Take the tender tissue of our fear and make it into the strong muscle of courageous witness." Bruce Thielemann, pastor of Glendale Presbyterian Church, in an Easter sermon said, "The clouds were bumper to bumper from horizon to horizon. Then the sky cleared its throat with thunder." If at length you see at any given situation only what everybody else can see, you are not so much a representative of a culture as a victim of it. The development of poignancy requires a disciplined mind and life.

Ours is a picture age, television and movies being the most popular form of entertainment. Illustrated magazines and visual aids have become the handmaid of education. By the skillful use of word pictures the preacher can become a part of this common taste which characterizes contemporary listeners. Modern man has his thought patterns in a mainly visual setting. He may be reached only in thought forms with which he is familiar. "Imagery makes the shadowy real and the supernatural as visible as possible."[54]

The novelists are excellent teachers. Flannery O'Connor's book *Wise Blood* depicts the ignorant hillbilly and his fight with Jesus. Her language is "always of life, of nerve ends, of hot blood, of passion, of need. None of this cumbersome, translated German theology which is being dished out today!"[55]

4. Resist the Temptation to Lapse into Clichés

This is a sure sign of a sleepy mind. It is a guaranteed shortcut to dull preaching. Bob Newhart, in one of his comedy routines, describes the employer's speech at a farewell ceremony recognizing years of faithful service by a retiring employee. The language of the speech was hackneyed and dog-eared. Newhart referred to the speaker as "Mr. Trite." His name is Legion; his relatives frequent the pulpit.

Examples of this kind of language are all too familiar. "Dead as a doornail," "pretty as a picture," "the patience of Job." To gain a hearing you need to help your audience see the common things with new eyes, that it may burst in upon them with freshness and new vitality. Old truth in old dog-eared language is deadening. Find, for example, synonyms for the verb "to be." Choose words like "animates," "poses," "constitutes," "displays," "embraces," "enfolds," "enhances," "enlivens," "formulates," "generates," "instills," "looms," "promotes," "pulses," "replaces," "savors," "substitutes," "succeeds," "undergirds," and the like. It may even be well to be unorthodox. Use prepositions at the end of sentences. Split infinitives. We are not on display like an English essay. Our task is to communicate and make truth impressive by using language that is fresh and unencumbered by the old or the common. Read the masters: Shakespeare, Milton; and contemporary writers and preachers like Joseph Parker, T. S. Eliot, Peter Marshall, George Buttrick, Ralph Sockman. All are masters of expression. Let the spark jump from their life to yours. Let their imagination strike fire in yours. Let their means of expression begin to color yours and then write, write, and rewrite. Write everything. Evaluate carefully. Strike out the dead, lazy, sleepy words. Replace them with fresh and vital and picturesque language.

5. Build Your Vocabulary

Every time you run across a new word jot it down. Look it up and use it in your conversation. When you assimilate new words into your vocabulary, don't use them for purposes of display. Help people understand what you are saying by simplifying the context and then placing the word in the well-known setting. In this way, understanding is encouraged.

Particular attention should be given to strong nouns and verbs. It is the verb that gives life to any sentence. It literally makes the sentence go. Adjectives are not as important, although studies reveal that adjectives do affect their nouns and that the association of an adjective with a noun does rub off onto the meaning contained within the noun.[56]

In this chapter we have discussed the unfolding of the idea contained in the body of the sermon. We began with an outline which served as the structure upon which the supporting material will serve as the flesh. We spoke of explanation, exemplification, accentuation, maintaining attention, along with the use of logical arguments and emotional material. We have concluded by underlining the importance of style, where the ideas are expressed in clear, appropriate, understandable language. We must say it and say it well. Our goal is accurate communication of truth, the truth about God.

NOTES

1. Phillips Brooks, *Lectures on Preaching*. Reprint. (Grand Rapids: Baker Book House, 1969), p. 178

2. Martin R. DeHaan in his devotional booklet, *Daily Bread.*

3. Unknown.

4. Donald G. Miller, *The Way to Biblical Preaching* (New York: Abingdon Press, 1957), p. 76.

5. David H. C. Read, "Labor, Leisure, and Worship," *Pulpit Digest* (September 1969), pp. 13-17.

6. Charles W. Lomas and Ralph Richardson, *Speech: Idea and Delivery* (Boston: Houghton Mifflin Company, 1956), for a development of these categories.

7. Otis M. Walter and Robert L. Scott, *Thinking and Speaking: A Guide to Intelligent Oral Communication*, 2nd edition (New York: The Macmillan Company, 1968), p. 48.

8. Lomas and Richardson, p. 98.

9. Wayne N. Thompson, *Quantitative Research in Public Address Communication* (New York: Random House, Inc., 1967), p. 63.

10. Gary Cronkhite, *Persuasion: Speech and Behavioral Change* (Indianapolis: The Bobbs-Merrill Company, Inc., 1969), p. 188.

11. Dale Leathers, Class lecture, UCLA, Winter 1969.

12. Aristotle *The Rhetoric*, trans. W. Rhys Roberts (New York: The Modern Library, 1954), pp. 24-25.

13. Aristotle, p. 25.

14. Aristotle, p. 25.

15. Martin Scheerer, "Cognitive Theory," *Handbook of Social Psychology*, ed. Gardner Lindzey (Cambridge: Addison-Wesley Publishing Company, Inc., 1954), p. 38.

16. Cronkhite, p. 42.

17. Thompson, pp. 50-51.

18. Bertrand Russell, *Sceptical Essays* (London: George Allen and Unwin, Ltd.; New York: Barnes and Noble, Inc., 1962), p. 32.

19. Erwin P. Bettinghaus, *Persuasive Communication* (New York: Holt, Rinehart and Winston, Inc., 1968), p. 160.

20. Carl I. Hovland, Irving L. Janis, and Harold H. Kelley, *Communications and Persuasion* (New Haven: Yale University Press, 1964), p. 183.

21. Hovland, Janis, and Kelley, p. 120.

22. Henry Grady Davis, *Design for Preaching* (Philadelphia: Fortress Press, 1958), p. 223.

23. Bettinghaus, pp. 156-157.

24. L. Frank Baum, "The Wizard of Oz," quoted by Don Fabun, *The Dynamics of Change* (Englewood Cliffs, N.J.: Prentice-Hall, Inc., 1967), p. 28.

25. James Hillman, *Emotion* (Evanston: Northwestern University Press, 1961), p. 8.

26. Raymond W. McLaughlin, *Syllabus: Preaching to Persuade* (Denver: Conservative Baptist Seminary), p. 17.

27. Aristotle, p. 217.

28. Arthur N. Kruger, "The Ethics of Persuasion: A Re-Examination," *The Speech Teacher*, XVI (November 1967), pp. 296, 303.

29. Alfred A. Funk, "Logical and Emotional Proofs: A Counter-View," *The Speech Teacher*, XVII (September 1968), p. 215.

30. Thomas R. Nilsen, *Ethics of Speech Communication* (Indianapolis: The Bobbs-Merrill Company, Inc., 1966), p. 49.

31. Arndt L. Halvorson, "Preaching Is for People," *Lutheran Quarterly* XX (November 1968), p. 359.

32. W. E. Sangster, *The Craft of Sermon Construction* (Philadelphia: The Westminster Press, 1951), p. 55.

33. Bettinghaus, pp. 139-141.

34. Cronkhite, p. 184.

35. Aristotle, p. 167.

36. Davis, p. 15.

37. John Culkin, S.J., "The New World of Marshall McLuhan," *McLuhan: Hot and Cool*, ed. Gerald Emanuel Stearn (New York: Signet Books, 1969), p. 56.

38. Raymond W. McLaughlin, *Communication for the Church* (Grand Rapids: Zondervan Publishing House, 1968), p. 28.

39. Bettinghaus, p. 135.

40. William Hordern, *Speaking of God: The Nature and Purpose of Theological Language* (New York: The Macmillan Company, 1964), p. 131.

41. S. I. Hayakawa, *Symbol, Status, and Personality* (New York: Harcourt, Brace and World, Inc., 1963), pp. 8, 17.

42. Hayakawa, p. 23.

43. Rudolf Flesch, *The Art of Plain Talk* (New York: Collier Books, 1951), p. 195.

44. Sue Nichols, *Words on Target: For Better Christian Communication* (Richmond: John Knox Press, 1963), pp. 45, 61, 64.

45. Fowler's *The King's English*, quoted by Rudolf Flesch, *The Art of Plain Talk* (New York: Collier Books, 1951), p. 58.

46. Aristotle, p. 176.

47. Flesch, p. 47.

48. Joseph A. DeVito, "The Encoding of Speech and Writing," *Speech Teacher*, XV (January 1966), pp. 55-60.

49. Thompson, p. 128.

50. Jules Laurence Moreau, *Language and Religious Language: A Study in the Dynamics of Translation* (Philadelphia: The Westminster Press, 1961), p. 194.

51. James S. Stewart, *Heralds of God.* Reprint. (Grand Rapids: Baker Book House, 1972), pp. 130-131.

52. Flesch, p. 57.

53. Davis, p. 272.

54. Prentice Meador, "Toward an Understanding of Today's Listener," *Preaching*, II (September-October 1967), p. 41.

55. Arndt L. Halvorson, "Preaching Is for People," *Lutheran Quarterly*, XX (November 1968), p. 361.

56. Bettinghaus, pp. 142-143.

CHAPTER ELEVEN • ILLUSTRATIONS

CHAPTER ELEVEN / BIBLICAL TRUTH—ILLUSTRATIONS

The mark which most often distinguishes average preaching from excellent preaching is the use of illustrations. Reflect for a moment. What sermons stick with you? What made them particularly meaningful? Very likely it was an illustration (or illustrations) that made them memorable. The experience is common.

There are three basic reasons for using illustrations: the logical, the psychological, and the emotional.

1. **Logical reason.** Illustrations serve as bridge builders. An appropriate illustration spans the chasm between the biblical period and the twentieth century. For example, a biblical concept such as that of "atonement" can best be understood against the backdrop of a twentieth century incident in which one person is sinned against by another person. A third party enters the scene, brings the two together, and accomplishes atonement. This we understand; a bridge of understanding links the two distinct periods of history.

The chasm between the world of the spirit and the world of the flesh may also be spanned by the use of illustrations. Jesus, the master teacher, used a parable to show a man with the question who his neighbor was. A man, probably a Jew, was beaten and left to die. A priest and a Levite passed, whereas a member of the hated Samaritan tribe looked over the scene, ministered to the wounds of the needy man, took him to an inn, and paid for his care. Jesus then asked the question, "Who is my neighbor?" Grady Davis says, "An illustration to be effective must be an example clarifying or supporting some definite point that is being made. *Illustrate* is a transitive verb. We do not simply illustrate; we illustrate something."[1] It moves us from the known to the unknown; from what we understand to what we do not understand. Illustrations which need explaining are hardly illustrations at all, for the purpose of an illustration is to help explain and should not itself need explaining.

Illustrations are a form of mental replay. Truth stated propositionally is replayed by way of an illustration. It makes repetition possible without weariness. The wise preacher will limit his deliberations to a few trenchant concepts. How then can this be accomplished without becoming redundant and dull? The illustration does this through replay, rethinking, and restating, while simultaneously sustaining interest. Recapitulation, even duplication, may be effected through this form of supporting material. There is some sense in the rustic preacher who said, "First I tells them what I am going to tell them, then I tells them, then I tells them what I told them." The illustration is a skillfully disguised restatement of the preacher's thesis. If handled appropriately, the listener comes to a clear understanding of the truth(s).

Because anecdotes and other forms of illustrations tend to linger longer in the mind than bald concepts, the preacher is aiding the memory of his listeners when he uses the device. This makes it imperative that he select appropriate illustrations, ones that are directly on target.

Keith Miller, in *A Taste of New Wine,* talks about honesty in prayer. He once prayed, "Gracious Lord, forgive me for being the kind of man I am in business. I don't want to be this kind of man. Forgive me. Amen." He said, "I no longer pray that way. I now pray, 'Gracious Lord, forgive me for being the kind of man I am in business. I have to be this way. I have to cut down colleagues if I am to get ahead. Forgive me, because this is the kind of man I am. Amen.' " People remember this. It lingers in the memory. The illustration drives people back to the illuminated truth. Thus, it is critical that the illustration be accurate.

2. **Psychological reason.** Much good preaching can be graphed. It has climaxes throughout the sermon, usually concluding on a high note or peak. Preaching with sustained intensity overtaxes a congregation. Mental breathing spells, periodic mental rests, or humor will satisfy a psychological need. Illustrations do this in spite of Grady Davis' argument to the contrary. He says that "twenty-five minutes of concentrated listening, following the uninterrupted progress of a compelling thought, is not an insupportable ordeal."[2] If every sermon was twenty-five minutes of "compelling thought," we might concur. However, it is generally fallacious to assume that modern man can maintain interest, at a high level of intensity, for extended periods. Modern theorists say it just is not true. We need points of relaxation in order to "catch our breath." The amount of time that the average congregation can listen to any sustained argument is strictly limited. It must rest for a moment or two before moving on again to new concepts. Relaxing the congregation can be risky since there is always the danger of sidetracking thought. Nevertheless, such relaxation would appear necessary for thought retention.

3. **Emotional reason.** We need to identify with truth to feel that it is related to our world. The gospel is logical; it is also visceral. The Christian faith is not only known, but felt; it is properly experienced at the "gut level." One layman, pained by sermonic remoteness, said, "I'm sick and tired of being talked to as if I were a Corinthian."[3]

The humanization of concepts through proper emotion is an imperative dimension to preaching. People want to enter into the vital, emotionally healthy quality of life the gospel promises. Many successful preachers have known how to reach people at this level. D. L. Moody, in spite of his limited education and his sometimes naive theology, knew how to touch the heart of his listeners through illustrations. So have Spurgeon, Phillips Brooks, and Billy Graham.

Years ago Louis Evans served as pastor of the First Presbyterian Church in Hollywood. In his congregation was a gifted surgeon. As a sensitive

Christian he was alert to the working of God in his life. Repeatedly he sensed that God was calling him to the mission field. After much inner struggle, he finally surrendered to the voice of God. He went to Korea, little known at that time though well known to us today, to set up a medical missionary practice. His pastor, Dr. Evans, stopped off to visit him during a world tour. On the day he arrived, his doctor friend was preparing himself for surgery on an eight-year-old child. Dr. Evans observed through a window in the small hut where the operation took place. The minutes turned into half hours, and the half hours turned into a total of almost three hours. Finally he stepped back from the operating table of the makeshift surgery room and said, "She will be all right now," leaving the child in the care of the national helpers. He went outside and joined his pastor. As they walked along Evans asked, "How much would you have received for that operation back in the States?" "Oh, $500 to $750 is the going rate, I guess." As they talked, his pastor observed that his lips were purple from the strain and his hands were shaking from the exacting labor and tension related to this delicate surgery. He said, "How much for this one?" "Oh, a few cents—a few cents and the smile of God." And then the surgeon put his hand on Pastor Evans' shoulder, shook it slightly, and added, "But man, this is living!"

That is the kind of truth that people need to see and feel. When God says people can have abundant life, they want to know how it works out—not only in theory, but in practice.

USING ILLUSTRATIVE MATERIAL

1. Types

A great deal of confusion exists regarding what a sermon illustration is. In popular use an illustration is anecdotal. The fact is that an illustration is much more. It is a concrete example in support of a general assertion. Let us look at a few of the types.

1. Ejaculatory examples. These are short, undeveloped examples, shared generally in multiples. Buttrick frequently does this. Two examples of this from his sermon "The Sound of Silence" may be helpful.

> Catastrophe has little power to cure. That fact our generation must confront. Miami was once almost leveled by a tempest, but Miami is not a mecca of saints. San Francisco was shaken and broken by an earthquake, but San Francisco is not the "Golden Gate" to heaven. Chicago was partly demolished by fire, but not purified of dross.[4]

Again,

> Tell what has deeply moved you. Not some earthquake, but seemingly trivial events. You saw in the face of an elevator man looking upward the type of all human longing. You heard Roland Hayes sing, "Were you there when they crucified my Lord?" You saw a dog run over,

watched a child hug the dog in its death spasms, and thought of men being killed across a world of war. You heard great music, and one phrase haunted you for a week.[5]

2. **Figures of speech.** Word pictures—similes. Phillips Brooks, in a sermon titled "The Fire and the Calf," uses a striking simile: "Every man's personality . . . is like a tree in the open field from which every bird carries away some fruit."[6] John Henry Jowett said, "I once saw the track of a bleeding hare across the snow; that was Paul's track across Europe."[7]

3. **Analogy.** According to Lomas, an analogy is a "method of reasoning based on *compared examples.*"[8] Joseph Parker enlisted this form of illustration with regularity. On one occasion he said, "Without enthusiasm, what is the church? It is Vesuvius without fire, it is Niagara without water, it is the firmament without the sun!"[9]

4. **Allegory.** Bunyan's *Pilgrim's Progress* with Mr. Greatheart, Mr. Obstinate, and friends is an example of this form—where virtue or vice is personified in a sermon. A biblical example is found in John 15 with its reference to the vine and its branches.

5. **Fable.** The best known are by Aesop. These are fictitious stories which relate some significant fact about life.

6. **Parable.** Stories that enshrine spiritual truth and reveal the relations of God to man. Approximately one-third of Jesus' ministry involved the use of parables. Among the best-known parables are the lost coin, ninety-nine sheep, dragnet, leaven, prodigal son, and the good Samaritan.

7. **Historical allusion.** This draws from the barbarian world, the Greek world, the Roman world, the Renaissance, the Reformation, the medieval period in a historical fashion. Roland Bainton's *Here I Stand* is a graphic history of Martin Luther and his period which has significant illustrative value. James S. Stewart regularly alludes to historical events in his sermons. In a sermon titled "He Is Able" he says:

> "At Augsburg are the powers of hell," said the German princes to Martin Luther, seeking to dissuade him from his perilous venture. But the reformer would have none of that craven capitulation. "And at Augsburg," he shouted, "Jesus reigns!"[10]

In another place he says:

> There are indeed myriads of facts in this world you can disregard, multitudes of events you do not need to come to terms with. They lay no compelling hands upon you. The politics of Julius Caesar, the origins of the sonnet, the tactics of Waterloo, the internal motions of the planetary nebulae—such things do not enter directly into the structure of my everyday experience. I can ignore them. I can disregard them. But there are other facts that will not thus be disregarded.[11]

8. **Anecdotes.** This, the most popular form of illustrative material for

beginning preachers, is a very useful type, if not carried to excess. Some preachers are guilty of making their anecdotes too long or too developed. When this occurs the stories become an end rather than a means of illustrating. They become an object of attention rather than focusing attention on something else.

Anecdotes are generally autobiographical, biographical, or drawn from current events. While we must be cautioned against excessive self-exposure which deflects interest from the One to whom it belongs, there is value in the judicious use of personal illustrations. Preaching is, after all, partly testimonial. One layman said, "The sermons which get my attention are the ones in which they relate a story of everyday living and use it to tell us about Christian living."[12]

The popularity of Keith Miller's books plus the insights of Reuel Howe and Clyde Reid give compelling support to the thesis that most people prefer life situation illustrations to historical or literary illustrations. There is much support for the claim that effective preaching is predicated upon an identification with the audience. Hence, the value of contemporary, life situation illustrations becomes apparent.

COLLECTING ILLUSTRATIVE MATERIAL

Every preacher needs to develop an alertness toward life in order to think illustratively. As you read, as you feel, and as you act and react, all of life becomes a reservoir from which you can draw illustrative material. Secure your own illustrations. They are always fresh, a quality that does not apply to those bound in illustration books. These volumes are replete with old, trite, unbelievable stories far removed from life in the present day. James S. Stewart counsels, "Omnibus volumes of sermon anecdotes are the last refuge of a bankrupt intelligence. The best illustrations are those which come to you as the harvest of your own reading and observation. . . .Be your own anthologist."[13]

1. Sources

The **Bible** is the prime source for sermon illustrations. It is not true that people know this book as they may once have known it. People do not read the Bible as they should; they are illiterate regarding its contents. It contains much fresh truth that people do not know and should be confronted with illustratively. Many of the Old Testament stories of Abraham, Joseph, Samson, Ruth, Samuel, David, Goliath, Naaman, Gehazi, and Absalom still throb with vitality and interest. Clovis Chappell used a biblical story in a sermon titled "The Forks of the Road—Moses."

For Moses to make this decision was to bring bitter disappointment to one who loved him, and to whom he was under very great obligations.

> I think we have never given sufficient credit to this Egyptian princess who was Moses' foster mother. The fact that she was a heathen did not prevent her from being a good woman. It did not rob her of a mother heart. When that strange craft afloat on the Nile was found, and when its lone occupant pelted this Egyptian princess with his weakness and cannonaded her with his tears, she had the grace and the tenderness to capitulate. She took this little waif to her heart and protected him. It was to her that he owed his life. It was to her that he owed the fact that he had been educated in the royal universities. It was by no means easy, therefore, for a big-souled man like Moses to disappoint one who had thus helped him and who tenderly loved him.[14]

Another source is **biographies** and **autobiographies**. Noteworthy examples are the autobiography of C. S. Lewis, *Surprised by Joy*, and the biography of Martin Luther King. Harry Emerson Fosdick recounts an incident from the biography of Phillips Brooks which is useful for illustrative purposes.

> In the old days when Phillips Brooks held consultation hours at Harvard University, one student came to his office and said with an anxious air: "Dr. Brooks, I would like to talk over some of my doubts; but I don't want to disturb your faith." And Brooks broke out into uncontrollable laughter. Disturb his faith, he who knew the deep experiences of the soul that only God can adequately explain![15]

Novels are also helpful. Classics like *The Scarlet Letter, Crime and Punishment,* and *Adam Bede* abound in timeless insight. In Harry Emerson Fosdick's sermon "Forgiveness of Sins" he says,

> Recall George Eliot's story of Adam Bede—Hetty Sorrel, pretty, vain, and superficial; Adam Bede, the stalwart carpenter; Arthur Donnithorne, careless, impulsive, well-meaning, rich. You remember Adam Bede's honest love for Hetty and his wish to marry her, Hetty's ruin at the hands of Donnithorne, her hapless child, her frenzied wanderings. You remember the scene where Donnithorne, having tried desperately to make amends for what never could be mended, goes to Adam Bede and asks forgiveness. Well, Adam gives it, but it is not easy. "There's a sort o' damage, sir," says Adam, "that can't be made up for." Aye, you whose sin hurts other folk, remember that![16]

Fables should not be overlooked. You may recall the story of Chicken Little, who frantically darted around the farmyard after being hit by a leaf. He found Turkey Lurkey and told him the sky was falling. He talked also to Duckey Luckey and Henny Penny about the impending doom. Finally, along came Foxy Loxy who recognized the problem immediately, "Ah, yes, Chicken Little, I have just the place for such a time as this." And then he invited Chicken Little, Turkey Lurkey, Duckey Luckey, and Henny Penny to his cave. Then, Foxy Loxy ate very, very well. The truth of the story is basic to all of life: fear is contagious; if we yield to it, we yield to our own destruction.

General reading will provide additional illustrative resources. Robert L. Short, who penned *The Parables of Peanuts* and *The Gospel According to Peanuts,* shows how an astute theologian like Charles Schulz portrays truth graphically via cartoons. He depicts foibles through Good Ol' Charlie Brown, the need for security through Linus and his blanket, and hostility through Lucy. Much of the renewal literature such as *Journey Inward; Journey Outward* by Elizabeth O'Connor, *The Incendiary Fellowship* by Elton Trueblood, *Dare to Live Now* by Bruce Larson, *The Taste of New Wine* and *A Second Touch* and *Habitation of Dragons* by Keith Miller is still useful. Books by Harry Golden such as *Enjoy, Enjoy, Only in America,* and *For 2c Plain* are delightful reading which lend themselves to illustrative use. For example, at one point Golden recounted that there is no recorded case of anyone having seasickness during the sinking of a ship. Such an idea just aches for a sermon home. Another book, *Malcolm X Speaks,* is the kind of source from which to illustrate the significant revolution that has been taking place in the Black community. You hear it from their own lips, read it from their own pen.

Books of sermons are a perennial source of illustrations. George Buttrick, Frank Boreham, Ralph W. Sockman, David H. C. Read are among the best illustrators when a man needs to uncover useful material.

Magazines will also be helpful. Religious magazines such as *Eternity, Christianity Today, Christian Century,* and *Pulpit Digest* can be consulted with profit. "The Starting Line" by Bishop Gerald Kennedy in *Pulpit Digest* has been particularly useful to preachers who needed fresh illustrations. Secular magazines such as *National Geographic, Saturday Review, Atlantic, Time, Newsweek,* and even *Reader's Digest* have proved their worth to preachers.

Newspapers. If you have a choice, get the best local newspaper, even if it is rather bland reading. Be aware of life in your community. Read the human interest stories and the columnists.

Observation. Observe nature; be sensitive to life around you. Put up your antenna to pick up the signals. Children in particular are a source of fascinating illustrative material. My own children have frequently provided material for sermons. Steve, at the age of six, was praying at bedtime. "Lord, thank you for this world; bless Mom and Dad, and Lynn, bless Kevin, and Billy, Jimmy, Stuart, Joel, Glenn, Papa and Nana Baumann, Papa and Nana Jones," and then he started praying for the same items a second time, and then a third time. I said quietly, "Amen." Steve opened his eyes and they were aflame. He looked me straight in the eyes and said, "Daddy, I wasn't finished yet; besides, I wasn't talking to you." He had caught something that many of us overlook: prayer is to God.

Personal experiences. Much caution must be practiced lest you tell information shared in confidence which might destroy that relationship as well as further pastoral opportunities. Be discriminating. Do not reveal the personal needs of individuals in your congregation. On the other hand, Brown, Clinard, and Northcutt say, "Regardless of the theme in the mind of the preacher, he can by concentration call out of the past the choicest experiences of his life. These do not smell of books and research, but of joy, sorrow, happiness—of life itself."[17] George Whitefield, in a sermon "The Burning Bush," says:

> Our suffering times will be our best times. I know I had more comfort in Moorfields, on Kennington Common, and especially when the rotten eggs, the cats and dogs were thrown upon me, and my gown was filled with clods of dirt that I could scarce move it; I have had more comfort in this burning bush than when I have been at ease.[18]

Personal experiences are legitimate in the pulpit because preaching is partially testimony to what God has done in your life. Be careful, however, lest your family be paraded so regularly through the pulpit that anyone in your congregation could write your biography. Excessive attention on the preacher distracts people from proper focus on the Saviour. When personal experiences are recounted they ought to include both positive and negative concepts, otherwise the preacher appears victorious over every temptation, the conqueror of every evil, and one whose prayers are always answered in a positive manner.

Imagination is another sermon resource. Illustrations may be created. If an illustration cannot be found that adequately expresses the desires of that sermon, one can be created out of the preacher's own imagination. This is absolutely acceptable if the preacher does not "pretend that the illustrations actually occurred and if the truth which it illustrates is not dependent on the fact that it did occur."[19]

2. Collection Processes

Be alert. Save for future reference. This will assist faulty memories. The process includes tearing out material from newspapers, magazines, brochures, and printed sermons. Anything that belongs to you, which will be destroyed, may be legitimately ransacked, torn out, and saved. At other times it will be necessary to copy something down, that which you hear or that which you want from someone else's material. It is obviously unethical to tear out material from someone else's magazine, book, or journal; therefore I suggest that you carry a 4x6 card in your pocket to record impressions that may be useful at a later date. It is also well to index your books and periodicals. You may want to make notes in the margins. In the back of each book it is useful to make your own index, pointing out pages and ideas of particular interest that may be discovered at a moment's notice when you return to that volume.

SELECTING ILLUSTRATIVE MATERIAL

A file system ought to be developed. *How* you do it is a matter of preference; *that* you do it is absolutely essential.

A pastor in Wisconsin showed me his illustration filing system when I was just beginning theological training. It was a flexible, simple, and inexpensive system which I have used ever since. You start with a single manila folder. In it you place twenty illustrations, marking each one from 1 to 20. Then you mark the folder "A-1," the items within it are "1A-1," "2A-1," "3A-1," and so forth, up to "20A-1." Next, you purchase a multi-ring notebook which has ten to twenty categories observable at a glance on overlapping cards. Every new illustration is recorded in this book, which is the key to the system. If, for example, your first illustration is about children, you would place it alphabetically in a category you label as "Children." Then on this card you write "1A-1," followed by a single sentence description of the illustration. If you wanted to cross reference it under "Honesty" you would label another card "Honesty," place it in alphabetical order, write "1A-1" and add the single sentence description. The cross referencing can be done as many times as you choose; simply add new categories and note the number and description of the illustration on each. When the first folder is filled you would then add a second and call it "A-2," and a third, "A-3." You can go as high as you choose ("A-10," "A-100," etc.). Then you may want to start "B-1," "B-2," "B-3," and so forth. With a multi-ring notebook it is always possible to add new categories by simply dropping the cards down a notch in order to make room for the additional category. You need only as many folders as you have illustrations and a notebook which serves as the key.

If you have a filing system, use it. Of course, you should do your Bible study first. The exegetical and expository task precedes any dependence on a filing system. Once that is accomplished you should selectively choose illustrative materials. Trace the subjects you need. It must fit. Be cruel. It may be a beautiful illustration that really speaks to you, full of interest, a vital expression of truth, worthy of a sermon home. If, however, it is thematically inappropriate it must be set aside for later use. The danger is "that the anecdote is too often used for its own sake, for its intrinsic interest, and it claims attention for itself and not for the point it ought to illustrate."[20]

FINAL SUGGESTIONS

1. **Illustrate every major point.** Charles W. Koller counseled, "One good illustration to each main point would be about right."[21] John E. Baird adds, "The illustration is so important that you are urged to adopt the following rule for all of your speaking: Any point worth talking about is worth a

detailed illustration."[22] They are both right if they define an illustration exclusively as an anecdote. However, if they are referring to illustrations in general, the point they make is irrelevant. If you mean analogy, example, historical allusions, or ejaculatory examples of one sort or another, many may be used. If we are speaking of a long, detailed anecdote, no more than one per major point would be in order. One preacher counseled, "Too many illustrations is like a woman with too much jewelry—it detracts from rather than enhances beauty." We have all heard sermons in which illustrations were illustrated, where one illustration followed another illustration, *ad nauseam*.

2. **Commit them to memory.** A good illustration demands eye contact and total involvement. To read an illustration is to destroy it. To tell it with feeling is to make it live.

3. **Keep them short.** Illustrations are a means to an end, not the end. They are windows, as Spurgeon said, not the house. One sermon delivered by a Chicago preacher had an illustration that lasted twenty minutes. The preacher discussed a tree which blew down in his back yard. The sermon never got much beyond that illustration, although it was a peripheral point in the total development. The sermon served the illustration, instead of vice versa. Illustrations should be kept short.

4. **Keep them to the point.** A good illustration out of context is a bad illustration. It is not always necessary that there be a positive illustration. A negative illustration will serve as well. If the speaker cannot give an actual case, positive or negative, he may invent a hypothetical illustration. The point is that it must be an illustration of his proposition, not simply an illustration.

5. **Keep them practical.** Illustrations must be real. Many are guilty of idealism which frustrates the serious Christian. We talk about living the life of faith and whom do we discuss? A man like George Mueller, who brought thousands and thousands of dollars into the orphanage in Bristol through simple faith, is established—though quite inadvertently—as a norm for Christians to follow. We talk about prayer by relating the experiences of a man like Praying Hyde, who spent twenty-four consecutive hours on his knees. The difference between Praying Hyde and ourselves is unbearable. When we talk about the "committed Christian" we remind the listeners of Hudson Taylor or C. T. Studd. What happens? These great ideals, so removed from our life experience, produce frustration and despair. An illustration should help a person answer the question, "How do I take the next step?" This is where preaching ought to begin. What is the next step that I can take by the grace of God? Illustrations should help people see tangible, realistic steps they can take in the pilgrimage of faith right now.

NOTES

1. Henry Grady Davis, *Design for Preaching* (Philadelphia: Fortress Press, 1958), p. 255.

2. Davis, p. 257.

3. Reuel L. Howe, *Partners in Preaching* (New York: The Seabury Press, 1967), p. 32.

4. Andrew W. Blackwood, *The Protestant Pulpit* (Nashville: Abingdon Press, 1947), p. 181.

5. Blackwood, p. 181.

6. Blackwood, p. 135.

7. W. E. Sangster, *The Craft of Sermon Illustration* (Philadelphia: The Westminster Press, 1950), p. 27.

8. Charles W. Lomas and Ralph Richardson, *Speech: Idea and Delivery* (Boston: Houghton Mifflin Company, 1956), p. 95.

9. James S. Stewart, *The Wind of the Spirit* (Nashville: Abingdon Press, 1968), p. 190.

10. Stewart, p. 165.

11. Stewart, p. 177.

12. Howe, p. 31.

13. James S. Stewart, *Preaching* (London: The English Universities Press, Ltd., 1955), p. 126.

14. Blackwood, p. 187.

15. Harry Emerson Fosdick, *Riverside Sermons* (New York: Harper and Brothers, 1958), p. 155.

16. Fosdick, p. 297.

17. H. C. Brown, Jr., H. Gordon Clinard, Jesse J. Northcutt, *Steps to the Sermon* (Nashville: Broadman Press, 1963), p. 89.

18. Blackwood, p. 38.

19. Brown, Clinard, Northcutt, p. 77.

20. Davis, p. 256.

21. Charles W. Koller, *Expository Preaching Without Notes* (Grand Rapids: Baker Book House, 1962), p. 82.

22. John E. Baird, *Preparing for Platform and Pulpit* (New York: Abingdon Press, 1968), p. 114.

BIBLICAL TRUTH—THE DELIVERY

NONVERBAL DELIVERY

1. Dress and Appearance
2. Posture and Body Movement
3. Gestures
4. Eye Contact

VERBAL DELIVERY

1. Rate
2. Volume
3. Tone
4. Emphasis

METHOD OF DELIVERY

1. Without Notes
2. With a Manuscript
3. With Notes

LENGTH OF SERMON

FEAR IN THE PULPIT

CHAPTER TWELVE • THE DELIVERY

CHAPTER TWELVE / BIBLICAL TRUTH—DELIVERY

The gospel of Jesus Christ is a proclaimed gospel. A sermon is never really a sermon until it is shared with the congregation. A minister is never a preacher until he communicates his message to others. The most polished sermon manuscript is never a sermon—it is only preparation. The sermon itself is a creative interchange of thought between a preacher and his people. Phillips Brooks reminds us that preaching is both truth *and* personality.[1] Truth may be contained in the manuscript, but it is a sermon only when mixed with the personality of the preacher and communicated to his listeners.

Unanimity of thought is unusual within the behavioral sciences. The complexity of variables and test situations makes conflicting findings rather common. It is interesting therefore that "every study of the relation of delivery or of any of its aspects to some desirable outcome arrives at the same conclusion: good delivery does matter."[2]

Strangely enough, in spite of the importance of delivery, it is often the most neglected area of sermon preparation. Pastors who diligently give hours to sermon construction, seldom give serious attention to self-improvement in delivery. Yet it must be affirmed that "there are two phases to every true sermon—creation and resurrection. It has first to be created in the study; then it has to be raised from the dead on the first day of the week."[3] Many rationalizations are offered by men who soft-pedal self-improvement. They frequently maintain that you must be yourself in the pulpit; practice at delivery becomes mechanical and theatrical. While it is true that a man must be himself, he is nevertheless obligated to be his best self.

Writing and speech are two different matters. The first is marked by permanence, the second by immediacy. The test of good speech is not the same as the test of good writing. Immediacy of apprehension and response is necessary if a speech is to pass the test.[4] Public speakers are at a disadvantage. The listener cannot see visible markings such as commas, capitals, or periods. He can only go by the sounds that he hears, the expressions that he sees, and the movements of the preacher. He has nothing else whatever to guide him in interpretation and understanding. The listener must immediately grasp the truth being shared. There is no opportunity for going back and rereading. What is said must be said well, expressed well, and delivered effectively or it will fail.

NONVERBAL DELIVERY

Communication is nonverbal as well as verbal. Frequently the nonverbal actions are random and incidental. McLuhan affirms the importance of nonverbal dimensions when he states that "the medium *is* the massage." Although the truth is cast in hyperbole, the point is clear. A noted anthropologist, Edward T. Hall, says, "In addition to what we say with our verbal language we are constantly communicating our real feelings in our silent language—the language of behavior."[5] Note the following list of nonverbal forms typically observed in interpersonal communication: "vocal intonation, selectively exaggerated articulation, throat-clearing, yawning, laughing, crying, decreasing and increasing volume, gesturing with arms and hands, facial expressions and changes of expression, bodily posture, speed of movement, and movement pattern."[6]

Nonverbal clues play an important role in the message the listener interprets. "If some of these messages are in opposition to the verbal message we are delivering, then our listener must choose which meaning he will accept as being the true intent of our communication."[7] For example, we are all acquainted with the games that lovers play with each other. A young man may ask for a kiss, and the young woman may say "no," but she may do it in such a provocative fashion, with certain intonations and with an expression in her eyes to suggest that the real answer is "maybe." What about the preacher who intones about love and the need for love between people and yet says it in an unloving fashion, in tones that suggest something quite contrary to the very thing he is suggesting? Which message is the congregation going to believe? Is it possible to preach faith in a listless and indifferent manner? One may say, "No, he's preaching disbelief." Do his words say anything about disbelief? "Oh, no, they are perfectly orthodox, but his manner preaches disbelief."[8]

Thomas M. Scheidel says that "a speaker's words may show strength, whereas his posture reveals weakness; the unsteady hand and the lack of eye contact may say more than the sentences spoken."[9] Americans tend to develop gestures, movements, and intonations which are distinctly part of the American idiom. The use of the eyes and eyebrows, the hands, the face, and the body generates meaning for the listener to observe, just as much as the heard content of the communicative situation. Nonverbal elements frequently express the emotional side of the message. Not exactly what he said, but the way he said it is what really matters. Psychologist Albert Mehrabian has devised this formula: "Total impact of a message = 7 per cent verbal plus 38 per cent vocal plus 55 per cent facial."[10]

While the speaker is involved in both verbal and nonverbal communication with his auditors, the persons before him are communicating with him in nonverbal ways. Sometimes these are understood, frequently they are not. Feedback is not an infallible science. While generally the clues are understood, occasionally clues are misunderstood and become deviate clues regarding the effectiveness of the communicative process. It may be necessary for the minister to seek out persons who send misunderstood nonverbal messages. He could go to them and say, "Your nonverbal signals are affecting me. What do they mean?"

It may be unnecessary to hear another person's opinion when it really is beyond the speaker's control. A member of the congregation may be fighting sleep during the sermon, which may not be indicative of the quality of the communication but rather an indication of the listener's long hours in the office. On the other hand, the communicator can have control over the temperature of the building or the staleness of the air in the sanctuary, environmental factors which adversely affect audience feedback. In short the preacher does well to minimize the possibilities for negative nonverbal feedback.

Let us consider some of the nonverbal elements in delivery:

1. Dress and Appearance

A man's appearance does matter. Communicators should be concerned about their appearance because it can enhance communicative success. For example, either carelessness regarding fashion or excessive concern for fashion may focus undue attention upon appearances and thus distract attention from the message. When listeners are drawn to the appearance of the preacher for one reason or another, his attire is very likely inappropriate. The problem is quite simple for the man who wears a robe or liturgical attire. For those within the free church tradition, clothing is a matter of legitimate concern. How should a man dress when he preaches?

It is well to be conservative, dignified, and "normal." Take note of the clothes worn by thoughtful businessmen. Avoid faddism on the one hand and complete disregard for appearance on the other. It is not necessary to wear black in the pulpit. By the same token it is probably unwise to wear bright reds or yellows. A suit, rather than sporting attire, is recommended. Suits should be kept clean and unwrinkled. It may be necessary to have clothes cleaned and pressed every week. It is a worthy expenditure.

Among the potential distractions for listeners are pockets bulging with pens, pencils, and datebooks; a crooked or loosely tied tie; a flimsy handkerchief; or jewelry that glitters. My pet peeve is to see a preacher who wears socks that droop, revealing bare legs. One layman told me, "I have difficulty listening to my pastor, because of his disregard for minimal standards of style. I can't stand to see his big old hairy leg hanging out." One magazine carried an ad where it depicted a man and a woman looking into each other's eyes. Both were well dressed with one exception: the man was wearing short socks and pants which did not hide his ankles. The ad said, "Oh, those ugly, shiny, hairy shins. They're a fashion disaster. All because you didn't care enough to buy socks that won't creep down the calf to the ankle."[11] I suggest over-the-calf socks to wear when conducting a worship service.

Dress and appearance should be in harmony with the situation, the listeners, the message, and the personality and physique of the speaker. The hair should be kept attractive, combed and washed frequently to avoid dandruff and a greasy look. Because of changing hair fashion standards, the style chosen should be appropriate to the community. It used to be suggested that a man be cleanly shaven. Here again standards are in constant flux. Moustache, long sideburns, and beards are acceptable, even recommended for certain collegiate-type settings. In most urban, suburban, and rural areas parishioners prefer the "clean-cut look." A man should be sensitive to community standards in order to do nothing that unnecessarily hinders the communicative process.

Of course a man should keep clean. A bath Sunday morning and the use of a deodorant may be crucial to communication. And how about a man's breath? While a preacher with a twinkle in his eye said, "Halitosis is better than no breath at all," it is clear that clean, fresh breath is a must. Toothpaste, gargle, and a breath mint will be helpful. Counselors at Billy Graham crusade meetings are advised to use a breath mint around the time when the invitation begins. In short, avoid any offense created by poor hygiene, garlic, onions, or other odoriferous delicacies. It may taste good, but smell very bad. Anyone who greets the public, whether in homes, at the front of the sanctuary, or at the door of the church should avoid the social offense created by bad breath.

2. Posture and Body Movement

At the risk of perpetrating the excesses of the old elocutionist school, let me suggest what appropriate posture means: shoulders should be back, relaxed and dropped, level with each other, the head not pushed too far forward or backward or tilted sideward. The chest should be erect, without strain, and the hips not too far forward, backward, or tilted sideward. Special hindrances such as leaning on the lectern or slouching on the pulpit must therefore be avoided. Though this posture promotes "folksiness," it is a hindrance to proper breathing and gives the impression that the preacher is lazy.

Mechanical features, such as microphone placement and lectern height, can be conducive to good posture. Every church should have a pulpit with an adjustable lectern. Lecterns, unfortunately, are frequently constructed with only the present pastor in mind. If he is short, his successor may strain to see his notes. If the present pastor is tall, the successor may have to stand on a hassock. Building committees should be reminded of this important matter.

When a man begins to preach, he ought to go to the pulpit, then pause a few seconds after arriving at the lectern in order to rivet the attention of the congregation upon the sermon. He should take a normal, easy breath, situate his feet so that the weight is distributed equally, establish eye contact, and then start with a crisp, well-prepared opening sentence.

If there is an adequate public address system, there is nothing wrong with moving the whole body forward or backward or to the side. However, one should avoid twisting, shuffling, bouncing, swaying, or wiggling. Random, meaningless motion is very distracting. To be too stiff or rigid is equally offensive. The only rule is, if you move, move decisively. Take full steps, pivots, and turns. Do not shuffle, lean, or slide. The movement should be consistent with the verbal message. If you move out of habit, rather than because it is natural to the message being shared, stand still. If the movement arises naturally out of the verbal content, feel free to express it.

3. Gestures

The language of gesture is important. Many distinct and meaningful signals may be sent via the gesture. Generally, they should be omitted during the opening moments of the sermon because people are not yet prepared. They must first warm to the message and the messenger. Once the preacher and parishioner are involved in the sermon, gestures are very appropriate within the total communicative process. One textbook on preaching says:

> There are four conventional gestures, so-called because they are the basic hand and arm movements from which all other gestures are derived. The index-finger gesture is one of location and mild emphasis. The clenched fist denotes dramatic and strong emphasis. The palm-up gesture reflects affirmative and even pleading emotion. The palm-down gesture displays disapproval, rejection, or contempt. Descriptive gestures, which are variations and combinations of the conventional actions, are as infinite as the moods they communicate.[12]

Gestures are very easy for some, and very difficult for others. Whatever you do, make certain that your gestures are natural. Avoid the stilted extremes of elocutionism. There is no place in a manuscript to record the appropriate gesture. If it comes, fine. If it does not come, well and good. They should not be tacked on. They should flow very naturally from a wholehearted involvement with the message being shared.

What are the qualities of good gestures? They certainly ought to be *definite*. Either make a gesture or do not make it. There is no value to a half gesture. It should be a definite, meaningful movement. Random fidgeting with the hands or flailing of the arms is always distracting. This kind of perpetual motion is simply a nervous churning of the air. Those who practice such gymnastics are advised to put their hands on the pulpit until they learn control. Parishioners are also disturbed by the "face fondlers," "tie tighteners," and "pants hikers."

Gestures should be *characterized by variety*. It is very easy to fall into some comfortable pattern in which you use the same gesture again and again. A thoughtful critic, wife, church officer, or faithful friend should be regularly consulted to discover if there is anything that needs attention. I once heard of an eccentric professor who, when his lecture approached a high point, would make a circular gesture in the air. And once he hit that point, he would puncture the circle with his pointed finger. Rather than being helpful, this move was looked upon by the class as a rather humorous diversion from the otherwise dull lectures. Variety, not predictability, is essential.

Gestures ought also to be *properly timed.* A gesture that is either premature or late confounds rather than confirms truth. Gestures, in summary, must flow naturally from the material as an indigenous part of the preacher's total expression of truth.

4. Eye Contact

Preaching is a form of conversation. It necessitates an awareness of the listener who is being addressed. When the congregation is viewed simply as a blurred mass, the preacher is too wrapped up in his own thoughts and manuscript. The capable communicator is aware of the reaction of his listeners. Stevenson and Diehl say:

> When you talk with people look at them, one by one, and see what they are saying back to you pantomimically. Keep yourself in dialogue with your listeners. Some ministers address their small congregations as though they were vast concourses of two thousand people. The late Charles H. Spurgeon is said to have addressed two thousand people as though he were speaking personally to one man.[13]

Because preachers are not carrying on a soliloquy, they are to look people in the eye, not simply staring but seeing them so as to discover what their reactions are. The goal is more mental directness than mere physical directness, a relationship with the listener which makes him feel that the speaker is thinking of him and talking personally to him. This goal is difficult to achieve for the manuscript-bound preacher. According to one study, as would be expected, audiences do prefer maintenance of good eye contact in a face-to-face-situation.[14]

Speakers ought to gaze adequately toward each listener successively or toward well-spread representative listeners when the audience is too large for contact with each individual. One should avoid looking downward, out the windows, or over the listeners' heads. Too much concentration on certain sections, or individuals, while ignoring others should be avoided. One man, whose messages are thoughtfully prepared and generally well delivered, gazes over the listeners' heads to the back of the sanctuary. Although the truth he shares is important, one senses a remoteness in the interchange. The electric spark which should leap between pulpit and pew never occurs when no eye contact is effected. The speaker should strive for a balance between blankness of expression and an intensity of eye contact created by staring. Adequately pause for a second or two with a listener, and then move to others. On the other hand, rapid eye movement, which is shifty and darting, which does not stay long enough on any individual, gives an impression of anxiety.

Certain mechanical hindrances to eye contact should be cared for. Eyeglasses sometimes glare, especially when lighting is at a bad angle. Unbalanced or otherwise inadequate lighting, a difficult angle between the pulpit and the pews, or placement of the speaker at too great a distance from the audience—all these contribute to the problem. When there is a lack of eye contact a barrier is created. People should inspire us; look at them in order that they may do it. Eye contact gives the speaker an opportunity to interpret the effect of what he says. Sensitivity needs to be developed—it will serve you well. Give *everyone* the impression that he is important and that you are interested in communicating with him.

VERBAL DELIVERY

Previously we spoke about the language used in sermons; now let us talk about the voice itself. Spurgeon once lamented,

> There are brethren in the ministry whose speech is intolerable; either they rouse you to wrath, or else they send you to sleep. No narcotic can ever equal some discourses in sleep-giving properties; no human being, unless gifted with infinite patience, could long endure to listen to them, and nature does well to give the victim deliverance through sleep.[15]

This, sad to note, frequently occurs. A few vocal concerns deserve our attention:

1. Rate

The normal speaking rate is between 125 and 190 words per minute. A reduction in listenability begins somewhere above 200 words per minute.[16] Speakers should strive to be rapid enough to show vitality and yet slow enough to be certain there is distinct articulation and comprehensibility. A proper rate is one that is both varied and sufficiently rapid to insure interest in the sermonic movement. As a congregation increases in number and the acoustics become more difficult, the rate should be slowed down to accommodate that particular situation.

2. Volume

Some speakers prefer to shout in an attempt to add emphasis. However, when a sermon is simply an extended shouting session, there is no emphasis at all. Sometimes a decrease in volume will give the desired emphasis. Unfortunately, it is too seldom used. Any change in pace or pattern will help a speaker achieve a measure of emphasis. And of course we should not confuse volume with unction.

3. Tone

A frequent fault of pulpit men is the so-called preacher's tone or ministerial melody. This stained-glass voice is characterized by a habitual pitch tone; that is, it "makes statements sound like questions;...the preacher gives a rising inflection at the end of indicative sentences just as he would with interrogative sentences."[17]

4. Emphasis

There is a verbal form of underlining known as emphasis through which we stress important words and subdue those that are less important.[18] Nedra Newkirk Lamar's very helpful book, *How to Speak the Written Word,* says that able communicators have generally avoided two pitfalls common to public speakers: overdramatic speech and colorless speech. One, they have discovered, is as bad as the other. Trumped-up enthusiasm is readily detected. Audiences feel embarrassed in the presence of such speakers. They are troubled by the experience so much that they frequently feel contempt for the charlatan. When this occurs in the pulpit it is especially heinous. Preachers, people are conditioned to believe, should be an incarnation of the truth they proclaim. Falseness in delivery marks the sermon with questionableness. Frequently, falseness arises out of noble intentions. The preacher wants the people to be enthusiastic about his message, but when he finds no natural enthusiasm within him he resorts to fabrication. The results are reciprocally disastrous. On the other hand, the preacher may simply have had one drama course too many. He becomes an actor (of the method school variety) instead of a person whose method is an indigenous whole characterized by verbal and nonverbal naturalness.

Surely it must be a mortal sin to preach the gospel in lackluster fashion. Truth of the earth-shaking variety shared in "multiple choice" style is an anomaly. How a preacher who gushes enthusiasm over the exploits of a pro basketball team, baseball team, or hockey team can become so lifeless in the pulpit is a mystery. We should not blame the gospel. It addresses man regarding life and death issues. We dare not blame the congregation. They want to hear something worth getting enthusiastic about. We must blame the preacher. He is either excessively self-conscious, afraid to be real and vulnerable, doubtful of congregational expectations, has not allowed the gospel to sufficiently transform his life, or—dare we pose it?—he is inadequate for the task.

Ideally, the gospel that changes people will be allowed to change the preacher, liberating him to be a reservoir of spiritual integrity and vitality. His natural (though supernaturally changed) self is neither dramatic and affected nor colorless and bland. He is a man whose encounter with God matters and who seriously desires meaningful, life-changing encounters for his people. When this occurs the preacher is true to himself, the gospel, and his congregation. People know it when they see it. Preachers know it when it is absent. As James S. Stewart says,

> Through the risen Christ there has been let loose into the world a force which can transform life beyond recognition—this is the most momentous message human lips were ever charged to speak. It dwarfs all other truths into insignificance. It is electrifying in its power, shattering in its wonder. Surely it is desperately unreal to talk of themes like these in a voice deadened by routine.[19]

METHOD OF DELIVERY

The homiletical tradition has isolated three methods of delivery: without notes, with a manuscript, or with notes. Let us look at these in order.

1. Without Notes

The sermon, viewed from this perspective, is an animated conversation on a Christian theme shared without dependence on any written materials, manuscript, or notes.

Noteless preaching may be practiced without any written preparation. Instead, thoughts and ideas are turned over and organized in the preacher's mind. For most preachers some notes or a manuscript have been prepared and then left in the study. If it is extemporaneous, he is not dependent on the manuscript for exact wording. The manuscript, in this instance, is an attempt to perfect expression or impress the ideas firmly on his mind. It is not memorized. In addition, there is a form of noteless preaching which is a recitation of the manuscript in animated fashion from the pulpit. Impromptu speaking, though often confused with extemporaneous speaking, is another matter. Impromptu speech is done without preparation. Extemporaneous speech is done with preparation, though without dependence on exact wording.

Gerald Kennedy represents many people when he suggests that there is no equal to noteless preaching. "It is worth all it costs, and many a fine preacher has surrendered a large percentage of his power to manuscripts and notes."[20]

After showing the advantages and disadvantages of manuscript preaching, John A. Broadus concludes that extemporaneous (noteless) preaching alone allows "free play for his [the preacher's] powers."[21] Charles W. Koller adds,

> There are, as there always have been, ministers who preach effectively from manuscript or copious notes in the pulpit, as well as some who read their sermons in full; but the same preachers would be even more effective if they could stand note-free in the pulpit. This seems clearly to be the verdict of history.[22]

His verdict does not, however, have empirical verification. Although preaching without notes is enthusiastically commended by many theorists, it does not find much acceptance on the part of practitioners. A recent study of preaching within one denomination revealed that less than one in twenty uses this method.[23]

Proponents of note-free preaching underscore three factors in preparation for noteless sermons: (1) *Saturation.* The preacher needs to be thoroughly familiar with his material. Cicero said, "No man can be eloquent on a subject that he does not understand." (2) *Organization.* It should be simple, obvious, natural, and orderly. A rambling discourse is difficult to recall. The structure should be very obvious. Stewart says, "Freedom of delivery will tend to vary in direct proportion to accuracy of construction. If you can fashion a sermon which stands out clearly in all its parts before your own mind, the tyranny of the manuscript is broken."[24] (3) *Memorization.* A good memory is largely the result of cultivation. One well-known preacher spends two hours for every sermon simply mastering his manuscript. Koller says there is "no escape from a certain amount of pure memorization."[25] He says that saturation is 50 percent, organization is 40 percent, and memorization is only 10 percent of the process. Noteless preachers, although genuinely committed to the preparation of a manuscript or extensive notes, should feel free to deviate at any point from their prepared message in order to address the needs that surface at the time of delivery.

2. With a Manuscript

Many competent preachers have depended on a sermon manuscript. Some are surprised to discover, for example, that Jonathan Edwards' well-known sermon "Sinners in the Hands of an Angry God" was delivered from a manuscript which he painstakingly read. Henry Sloan Coffin commented, "I know that many prefer me to preach without the manuscript; but I also know that I say more in a given number of minutes, say it with greater precision and in defter sentences than when I let myself go without it."[26] Whether or not a man preaches from a manuscript, it is worthwhile for him to write a manuscript on a regular basis. I am assuming that he recognizes the wisdom of John Baird who says, "Your oral style should be quite distinct from your written style. You should never attempt to write a speech until your oral style has become fixed as a result of a great deal of practice in speaking."[27] This is good advice. Too frequently preachers develop a written style which is transported into the pulpit. This is fine for books and articles, but not for sermons. A sermon is *not* an oral essay. It is a message shared in a distinctively oral manner. Oral styles ought to be developed; and once this has been accomplished, the written manuscript becomes a healthy discipline.

3. With Notes

The most common practice of preachers is to use notes. In the study to which we earlier referred, eight out of ten preachers used some form of notes in the pulpit.[28] A Presbyterian minister says:

> For many years I boasted of "preaching without notes," but there came a time when I realized I was using more mental energy trying to remember what came next than in giving convincing voice to the thoughts I wanted to communicate. Indeed, there were times when, weary of mind, I found that I was preaching not only without notes but also without ideas. With notes that can be used inconspicuously, I am more relaxed and maintain better contact with the congregation. After all, according to the Chinese proverb, "The weakest ink is stronger than the strongest memory."[29]

How does one resolve the personal dilemma—noteless, with notes, or with a manuscript? Reuel Howe, coming out of his experience with the Institute for Advanced Pastoral Studies, feels that people would rather have a direct address from their preacher, a real face-to-face encounter, even though it might be stylistically less perfect than having a finished product read from a manuscript. He feels that a man should be as unencumbered as possible. This does not mean that he should speak without a manuscript, but he should experiment and preach in a way that will lead to the most free relationship possible between himself and his congregation. "The relationship is more important than the manuscript, because the Gospel is a relational matter. . . . I believe that preaching is the homiletical encounter. Not the delivery of a manuscript."[30]

Perhaps we have too frequently focused upon the form and not upon the fact of communication. Preachers who have been infected by a form-delivery virus may have weakened the simple, straightforward communication of the gospel. Congregations are neither impressed nor concerned with *how* it is done. In the final analysis, it really does not matter whether the sermon is delivered from a manuscript, from notes, is read, or is delivered without notes. These questions are quite beside the point. Any method that permits a man to be relaxed and free, while retaining effective contact with his congregation, is worthy. C. John L. Bates, senior pastor of Westminster Church in Minneapolis, preaches from an entire manuscript of up to thirty pages, yet he communicates admirably. Professor Howard Hendricks of Dallas Theological Seminary frequently speaks from a manuscript without any adverse effect. On the other hand, certain noteless preachers lack precision, tend to meander, and communicate with questionable effectiveness.

John Knox is correct: "Which method a particular preacher adopts does not really matter so long as the nature of preaching as personal communication is not violated; that is, so long as the sense of personal contact between preacher and hearers is maintained on both sides."[31] If a man makes contact with his audience, then the method is secondary. Communication is the important matter. Each man must discover the method that will accomplish that end in his own ministry.

LENGTH OF SERMON

Sermon lengths vary. Robert G. Lee, the eloquent Southern Baptist, frequently preached an hour or more. He once commented, "Sermonettes are preached by preacherettes and they produce Christianettes." Professor Robert Smith of Bethel College, St. Paul, Minnesota, generally preaches over an hour, yet people feel that he is worth hearing. Others, serving large churches, with multiple Sunday worship services, deliver twelve- to fifteen-minute sermons. Perhaps most common is a sermon that runs anywhere from twenty to thirty minutes, although one study revealed that the typical preacher spends thirty to forty minutes delivering his Sunday morning sermon.[32]

An infallible way to insure fidgety, inattentive, restless, and even resentful congregations is to let your sermon do like Tennyson's babbling brook: "run on and on and on." Bishop William Stubbs of Oxford responded to the curate who asked him what to preach about, "Preach about God and preach about twenty minutes."[33] There is an old adage which says, "Stand up to be seen, speak up to be heard, shut up to be appreciated."

A radio preacher, concerned about the impact of the electronic age, says, "Pulpits must speak to man as he is today, not as he was yesterday. His life span is longer, but his listening span is shorter. So we shall have to talk to him in shorter sentences and shorter sermons."[34] The best advice is for a man to watch people, not the clock. People's attention span is not long. Do not exaggerate the interest of your sermon nor the attention of your congregation. Leave them with the feeling that they would like to hear more, not that you should have quit earlier.

FEAR IN THE PULPIT

A frequent malady of preachers is anxiety. How can one cope with this problem? When I was a teen-ager I spoke in a small church. The pastor, noting my trepidation, hesitancy of speech, and wobbling knees, rebuked me. "You are afraid of people and that is a sin. You are depending upon yourself rather than God." I have frequently reflected upon that advice in the intervening years. It was well intended but wrong. A little nervousness is not only necessary, it is absolutely imperative. Without some sweating of the palms, without some fear, the preacher can go to the pulpit without the necessary adrenalin shooting through his system and the resultant excitement which allows his message to have the contagious quality necessary in all effective communication. When the minister goes to the pulpit completely relaxed, it may be that he is not so dependent on God, but that he is overly confident in his own ability.

To my limited knowledge, most competent preachers experience some presermon anxiety. It could be an upset stomach, a headache, sweating of the palms, or some other expression of finitude. Yet to see these men in the pulpit, one would never guess this was so.

I would not want to discount the place of some necessary apprehension, but we must seriously deal with the problem of excessive fear or excessive anxiety. John Baird suggests that enthusiasm for the message and the choice of a subject that means much to you allows you to open your mouth and throw yourself into the message. He says, "Think in terms of your audience. Remember how important your ideas are for them, how vital to their lives. Lose yourself in your message."[35] A more mechanical approach is to

> Breathe deeply
> Loosen tongue and jaw
> Maintain good posture
> Relax hands and wrists
> Settle shoulders in proper position
> Relax head and neck
> Yawn[36]

Use whatever methods are personally helpful. Some find that a certain diet helps them relax prior to the message. Others run a mile. Some play the piano. Some sing. If necessary, find some way to burn off excess energy, so that when you ascend to the pulpit you are your best self. To my mind, there is nothing as helpful as thorough preparation, saturation in the message, and then a dependence on God that having done what you could, you can trust the Holy Spirit to speak through you.

NOTES

1. Phillips Brooks, *Lectures on Preaching.* Reprint. (Grand Rapids: Baker Book House, 1969), p. 5.

2. Wayne N. Thompson, *Quantitative Research in Public Address and Communication* (New York: Random House, Inc., 1967), p. 83.

3. Dwight E. Stevenson and Charles F. Diehl, *Reaching People from the Pulpit* (New York: Harper and Row, Publishers, 1958), p. 57.

4. Henry Grady Davis, *Design for Preaching* (Philadelphia: Fortress Press, 1958), p. 265.

5. Edward T. Hall, *The Silent Language!* (Greenwich, Conn.: Fawcett Publications, Inc., 1969, copyright 1959), p. 10.

6. George A. Borden, Richard B. Gregg, Theodore G. Grove, *Speech Behavior and Human Interaction* (Englewood Cliffs, N.J.: Prentice-Hall, Inc., 1969), p. 84.

7. Borden, p. 62.

8. Anthony Schillaci, O.P., "The Use of Motion Pictures in Preaching," *Preaching*, II (March-April 1967), 18.

9. Thomas M. Scheidel, *Persuasive Speaking* (Glenview, Ill.: Scott, Foresman and Company, 1967), p. 54.

10. Flora Davis, "How to Read Body Language," condensed from *Glamour*, in *Reader's Digest* (December 1969), p. 128.

11. Advertisement in *McCall's* magazine, May 1970.

12. H. C. Brown, Jr., H. Gordon Clinard, Jesse J. Northcutt, *Steps to the Sermon* (Nashville: Broadman Press, 1963), p. 184.

13. Stevenson and Diehl, p. 59.

14. Martin Cobin, "Response to Eye-Contact," *Quarterly Journal of Speech* XLVIII (December 1962), 418.

15. *Spurgeon's Lectures to His Students*, p. 199.

16. Thompson, p. 88.

17. John E. Baird, *Preparing for Platform and Pulpit* (New York: Abingdon Press, 1968), p. 132.

18. Note Nedra Newkirk Lamar's book, *How to Speak the Written Word*, which discusses this in thorough fashion.

19. James S. Stewart, *Preaching* (London: The English Universities Press, Ltd., 1955), p. 38.

20. Gerald Kennedy, *His Word Through Preaching* (New York: Harper and Brothers Publishers, 1947), p. 88.

21. John A. Broadus, *On the Preparation and Delivery of Sermons* (New York: Harper and Brothers, 1944), p. 334.

22. Charles W. Koller, *Expository Preaching Without Notes* (Grand Rapids: Baker Book House, 1962), p. 34.

23. J. Daniel Baumann, *Preaching Within the Evangelical Free Church of America*, unpublished Th.D. dissertation, Boston University School of Theology, 1967, p. 142.

24. Stewart, pp. 158-159.

25. Koller, pp. 85-97.

26. Henry Sloan Coffin, *Here Is My Method*, ed. Donald MacLeod, p. 58.

27. Baird, p. 22.

28. Baumann, p. 142.

29. Irvin Shortness Yeaworth, "The Minister's Workshop: Preach Biblical Themes," *Christianity Today* (April 1, 1966), p. 35.

30. Reuel Howe, "The Responsibility of the Preaching Task," *Preaching*, IV (November-December 1969), 16, 17.

31. John Knox, *The Integrity of Preaching* (New York: Abingdon Press, 1957), p. 63.

32. Baumann, p. 143.

33. As cited in W. E. Sangster, *The Craft of Sermon Construction* (Philadelphia: The Westminster Press, 1959), p. 179.

34. Peter H. Eldersveld, "The Pulpit and Our World," *Christianity Today*, VII (June 7, 1963), 4.

35. Baird, p. 168.

36. Jean DeSales Pertram-Cox, "Relaxation: An Approach to Platform Poise," *The Speech Teacher*, XIV (September 1965), 235-236.

BEHAVIORAL CHANGE

PART THREE

BEHAVIORAL CHANGE—PURPOSE OF PREACHING

KERYGMATIC PREACHING

DIDACTIC PREACHING

THERAPEUTIC PREACHING

SOCIAL-PROPHETIC PREACHING

CHAPTER THIRTEEN / BEHAVIORAL CHANGE—
PURPOSE OF PREACHING

If a sermon is to accomplish anything, it has to accomplish something. The question is: what? One Saturday night early in his ministry, Benjamin R. Lacy read one of his sermons to his wife. She replied, "Ben, *why* are you going to preach that sermon?" He returned crestfallen to his study because he had no answer for her question. After throwing the message into the wastebasket he burned the midnight oil to prepare a new sermon that could answer that question.[1]

The question of purpose should haunt the preacher at the beginning of his preparation and not leave him until he has found a satisfactory answer. R. W. Dale once remarked that "many young preachers, when they sit down to prepare a sermon, start like Abraham, who 'went out, not knowing whither he went.' "[2] The problem is simply this—if you aim at nothing, you are liable to hit it. The wise homiletical traveler determines his destination before he embarks on the journey. Harry Emerson Fosdick has correctly noted that the difference between a sermon and a lecture lies in the fact that while a lecture is chiefly concerned with a subject to be elucidated, a sermon is chiefly concerned with an object to be achieved.[3]

Earlier in this volume we noted that a sermon has the explicit purpose of eliciting behavioral change. That is to say that preaching worthy of the name calls persons to a decision, to a confrontation which hopefully issues in modification of behavior. This behavioral change may take any number of directions including salvation, vocation, adoration, praise, confession, baptism, church membership, service within the life of the community, or wholeness regarding psychological and emotional health. Explicit preaching is directed toward life-style changes. Preaching fails when it allows the listener to be neutral or indifferent.

It was once fashionable to delineate the purposes of general speaking as follows:

> In many circumstances the speaker will seek only *to inform* his listeners by explaining a subject to them. In some instances he will wish *to entertain* his listeners by pleasing and amusing them. On ceremonial occasions he will endeavor *to impress* his listeners by paying tribute to the attainments or merit of an individual or a group. Concerning controversial matters, he will seek *to convince* his audience by trying to establish or to change beliefs. When action is to be taken, he will seek *to persuade* by trying to induce his listeners to do what he thinks is desirable.[4]

This scheme, in large measure dependent on faculty psychology, has fallen into disrepute. Some maintain, for example, that there is no speech that is not persuasive speech. In a certain sense this may be true. In Chapter 14 we will examine "persuasion" in greater detail. For now we can list four distinct purposes for contemporary preaching.

Forms	Audience	Function
1. Kerygmatic	Unbelievers	to redeem
2. Didactic	Believers	to teach
3. Therapeutic	Believers	to heal (personally)
4. Prophetic	Believers	to heal (socially)

Technically, only *kerygma,* that is, "proclamation of the gospel," is called preaching in the New Testament. Therefore, some have implied that "no preaching is legitimate in the church's public ministry in our day except that which meets the New Testament test of *Kerygma,* both in content and in form."[5]

Modern theorists have noted that the ministry of the Word has other purposes in addition to that of converting unbelievers.[6] There are Christians who need to be nourished in their faith, and there are problems which must be solved in the lives of believers and society at large.

Ronald A. Knox, after reviewing departures from orthodox teaching which were branded as heretical in the history of the church, says:

> In all ages, the tendency of the heretic is to single out one aspect of Christian life or doctrine, and treat it as if it were the whole: bodily healing, if you are a Christian Scientist; survival after death, if you are a Spiritualist. Donatists chose martyrdom for their special devotion; and enriched the annals of Christian abnormality with a unique record of misguided heroisms.[7]

This is a most trenchant insight. Ministers of the gospel have frequently taken a part of the truth and treated it as if it were the whole truth. If the task of the Christian preacher is to preach the whole gospel, then there is a need for balance between the available sermon types. Just as the pastor called and endowed with the gift of evangelism is not allowed the luxury of social indifference, so the pastor-prophet who alerts society to its ills is not excused from the demands of evangelism. A balanced ministry is geared to the needs of the whole man—personally and socially, redemptively and therapeutically. Currently, there is a trend toward specialization, a trend which creates local churches where gospel medicine is dispensed for only a limited number of "spiritual" ills. Because men's needs are multiple, the Christian church needs men who are willing to be general practitioners, who will strive for a balance between evangelistic, doctrinal, therapeutic, and prophetic preaching. All of these needs are resident in a contemporary congregation. It is "heresy" for a pastor to isolate one dimension and shun the others. All the patients need help.

KERYGMATIC PREACHING

Kerygmatic preaching is also called proclamation or evangelistic preaching. Peter's sermon on Pentecost contains the basic ingredients of the kerygma (Acts 2:14-38):

1. A proclamation of the death, resurrection, and exaltation of Jesus, seen as the fulfillment of prophecy and involving man's responsibility.
2. The resultant evaluation of Jesus as both Lord and Christ.
3. A summons to repent and receive forgiveness of sins.

Proclamation declares that "God was in Christ reconciling the world to himself" (II Cor. 5:19). It announces "good news" for people caught in the web of sin and incapable of extricating themselves. It offers divine forgiveness to those who will repent and believe. The history of the Christian church is eloquent testimony to the fact that it works. Proclamation is unashamed evangelistic preaching that calls men to make a personal decision regarding Jesus Christ as Saviour and Lord. Taking a clue from Jesus who said, "Follow me, and I will make you fishers of men" (Matt. 4:19), let us elaborate upon the possible directions evangelistic preaching may move:

(1) **Drawing the net.** Billy Graham's ministry is primarily one of drawing the net, of giving an opportunity for people to respond. It includes a distinct call for decision. This form of preaching asks pointedly, "Will you come now?" Because many churches have fallen prey to the subtle pressures of institutionalism it is appropriate to remind ourselves that a prior place must be allotted to a form of intelligent, compassionate, parish centered evangelism which calls people to take a distinct stand for Christ.

(2) **Luring the fish.** This is preparatory work. Much evangelistic work is foundational and preliminary to a later decision which will crystallize the step for a new believer. It finds precedence in what occurred in the Corinthian situation where Paul said, "I planted, Apollos watered. . ." (I Cor. 3:6).

(3) **Training the fisherman.** Lay evangelism is not, nor ever should have been, a luxury; it is a necessity. Enlistment of lay witnesses demands prayerful, careful teaching from the pulpit as well as time-consuming practice. People generally are hesitant and fearful regarding any sharing of their faith. The pastor's own enthusiasm and example are crucial. The minister who wishes to lead others in evangelism must himself be an evangelist. A noteworthy example is D. James Ken-

nedy, pastor of the Coral Ridge Presbyterian Church in Fort Lauder-
dale, Florida, who has led his congregation in an aggressive program
of church centered evangelism.[8]

It is currently necessary to defend evangelistic preaching as a worthy
form of parish ministry. This is true in part because evangelism has developed a bad name. Mention the possibility of a special evangelistic series to
leading laymen in your church and it is very possible that you will discover
some areas of resistance. Some evangelists are viewed with suspicion as
high-powered economists, who profess to follow the Master's example but
have never taken Matthew 6:33 literally. Laymen become uneasy when
evangelists demand a large financial guarantee. Others have been guilty of
"show biz." That is to say that too much of Hollywood has crept in with an
emphasis on personalities or dependence on gimmicks. Manipulation has also
been evident in the campaigns of certain evangelists. Helmut Thielicke calls
them "salvation engineers."[9] In addition, people simply do not come as they
once did to special evangelistic meetings. There are too many demands upon
time and too many competitive forces to contend with. Because of these,
and other problems or excesses, pastors have steered away from legitimate
parish evangelism.

"Why," some ask, "should evangelistic sermons be preached at all?" The
answer is quite simple. Luke 24:46, 47 says, "Thus it is written, that the
Christ should suffer and on the third day rise from the dead, and that
repentance and forgiveness of sins should be preached in his name to all
nations." The basic spiritual need of men appeals to the conscience of the
pulpit. Sophistication may dull us, but persons ultimately stand before God
the righteous Judge and their eternal destiny is established. Only two
distinctions are recognized by God—those who are His children and those
who are not. The pulpit cannot gloss over this. Evangelistic preaching is
necessary because Christ has commanded it and people need it.

Worthy evangelistic preaching has certain hallmarks:

(1) **It proclaims God's holiness.** Isaiah 6, although not generally regarded
in this light, is peculiarly evangelistic. A missing element in much of
Protestantism is that man stands before a holy God. God loves us,
but He demands justice because He is holy.

(2) **It magnifies the grace of God.** Ephesians 2:8, 9 teaches the initiative
of God. He *is* the evangelist. Men do not, contrary to their own
testimony, "find the Lord." Jesus Christ came to seek and to save
the lost (Luke 19:10).

When we magnify the grace of God we underscore the futility of
self-salvation. Boot-strap theology, human merit, good works, and
ceremonialism are discounted. God never offered a pound of salvation for a pound of good works. This cash-register view of salvation is
unbiblical. Christ alone is sufficient for man's needs.

(3) **It is kerygmatic.** Acts 2:14-42 has established the centrality of Christ, His cross, and resurrection, with the concomitant call to repentance and faith. The Bible has no truck with a Christless Christianity. There is no place for "cheap grace" or an "easy believism." The way of faith is through repentance.

(4) **It appeals to the whole man.** There is no premium on ignorance. God has, we readily acknowledge, saved some, in spite of (not because of) certain evangelistic sermons which were replete with shoddy exegesis and strained typology. This is a tribute to the sovereignty of the Holy Spirit, not to man and his foolishness. Evangelistic preaching needs to be intellectually respectable. George Buttrick says, "The church door should be high enough that a man can bring his head inside."[10] Evangelistic preaching also provides a legitimate outlet for emotion. In an age that is emotionally drained, and often fatigued, emotion needs to be put in its proper place. The gospel offers man something worth getting emotional about. The gospel is also a volitional matter. Christianity calls for an act of the will; it cannot be a matter of indifference.

(5) **It is bifocal.** There is not simply a hell to shun and a heaven to gain. While these facts are true, it is equally true that "He who has the Son *has* life" (I John 5:12). Salvation is future, to be sure; it is also a here-and-now reality.

(6) **It provides an occasion for response.** That is, some form of invitation is offered. Clifton J. Allen says it well: "The invitation is not a gimmick to catch souls. It is not a fetish to insure results. It is not a ritual to confirm orthodoxy. It is simply the call of Christ to confront persons with the offer of his redemption, the demands of his lordship, and the privilege of his service."[11]

Some churches have made it a practice to give an invitation at every service. This may be appropriate if the congregation regularly includes persons who are outside of the faith, but in many cases it is quite unnecessary. There ought to be a thematic appropriateness to the invitation. It should not simply be tacked onto the sermon without relationship to the text, theme, or purpose of the sermon. The ethics of persuasion demands that tricks or manipulation be avoided. It is unethical to ask people to raise their hands when all heads are bowed and eyes are closed, then later ask them to step forward to show their sincerity. All questionable techniques which sweep people to the altar, quite apart from the work of the Holy Spirit, are to be discounted.

A variety of invitations are available to the concerned pastor. An altar call, the most common invitation of all, is an appropriate means of confirming a decision. When used it ought to be consistent with the sermon and its theme, be prepared in advance, and given simply, clearly, and compassionately. People should know exactly what they are responding to. John Stott, pastor of All Soul's Church in London, has an after-service where inquirers may come to be confronted with the simplicity of the gospel invitation and dealt with according to their individual needs. The pastor's study is an excellent place to invite people to come and discuss a decision. This method recognizes that Nicodemus' name is Legion. On occasion the pastor will want to leave the door of the church and go immediately to his study to wait for inquirers. Another possibility is to have people sign a card which is dropped in the offering plate or given to the pastor at the door. Appointments can then be made with the pastor for him to follow up during the week.[12]

(7) **It depends on the Holy Spirit.** If it is of God, it does not require the questionable techniques of hypersensationalism, mood music, emotional illustrations, or will manipulation. God the Spirit will draw men to Christ.

(8) **It gives due regard to follow-up.** This is a very difficult but essential matter if we intend to conserve decisions. Two options seem popular: to assign new converts to one person who meets with him on a weekly study basis, or to enroll new Christians in a small class with others who are beginning the fresh adventure of being God's children.

(9) **It depends in large measure on the burden of the preacher.** Immersion in the task seems to be the needed behavior that changes a man's attitude. People grow cold. Preachers grow cold. They need to catch a sense of the fire of evangelism. It may be that a pastor will need to get next to another pastor whose life has this concern in order to catch the spark from his life. He can then pass the spark to his people.

DIDACTIC PREACHING

It is common to find lay antipathy for so-called doctrinal sermons. Because of this less than enthusiastic response from some congregations, certain preachers have turned to more acceptable types—life-situation, in particular. Why the distaste? Much of what is pawned off on congregations as doctrinal preaching is theological abstraction, "word castles" with minimal cash value in the marketplace of life. They have low translation possibility and are in desperate need of concretion.

Some doctrinal sermons are rehashed seminary lectures—theological treatises replete with scientific analysis, elaborate logic, and the specialized vocabulary of the theologian. Little, if any, thought is given to the mind-set, needs, and interests of the congregation. There is too much talk about existentialism, too little about life; too much about soteriology and too little about salvation.

Doctrinal sermons are often rather dull. It is not that doctrinal preaching is necessarily dry, but some men, as W. E. Sangster notes, "could make any subject dry! Their capacity in dehydration is unlimited. But doctrine is not dry of itself."[13] Sermons of this type are drab discourses because the preacher has never come alive to their possibilities. His own lack of enthusiasm is contagious. He does it simply because some book or homiletics teacher gave him a guilt complex on the subject.

Why is doctrinal preaching necessary? J. A. Broadus says, "Doctrine, i.e., teaching, is the preacher's chief business."[14] Gross ignorance exists in the Christian church. Basic concepts are misunderstood. Entering exams given in Christian liberal arts colleges reveal a tragic ignorance among churched young people, who have spent their childhood in youth groups, Sunday schools, and churches where the Bible was supposedly taught. People do not know their faith. At the same time that there is ignorance of basic biblical teaching, there is a desire for significant wrestling with doctrinal truth on the part of many thoughtful people. They are not satisfied with the "homilies on happiness."

Doctrinal preaching can be defined as "the systematic pulpit exposition of the 'truth-about-God-in-relation-to-man.' " It takes seriously the here-and-now concern of Bultmann without maintaining his priority of anthropology. In a purist sense there is no such thing as nondoctrinal preaching, for all Christian proclamation must have some theological content if it is a genuine unfolding of the divine revelation.[15] For example, even sermons on the wanderings of Israel are indirect testimonies to the doctrine of sin or the doctrine of judgment or grace. A message on Abraham can never get far from the doctrine of faith. And a message on creation can never get far from God's redemptive concern.

The characteristics of a doctrinal sermon may be outlined as follows:

It is didactic in nature. It is the development of a biblical idea or gospel concept in the light of sound exegesis and ecclesiastical tradition. Essentially it is a teaching sermon. It answers the question, What does the Bible teach on this subject? Those who follow C. H. Dodd literally make a sharp distinction between preaching and teaching in the primitive church.[16]

I concur with John Knox, who questions "whether the distinction between 'preaching' and 'teaching' was as sharp as Dodd implies and, more particularly, that the functions of the preacher and teacher were ever actually separated in the life of the primitive community."[17] The doctrinal preacher blends what Dodd unfortunately distinguishes. As opposed to inspirational, therapeutic, or impressionistic sermons which make you feel, these are more informational. The emphasis is upon knowledge and understanding.

It is necessarily practical. The antipathy for doctrinal preaching is only heightened, and correctly so, when this dimension is shunned or not seriously considered. Brunner's preface to his sermon series on the Apostles' Creed notes: "It is the intention of these twelve sermons to show in what sense faith in Jesus Christ includes the facts to which the creed refers and to show what this belief means in our life, both individually and socially."[18]

H. H. Farmer says that doctrinal preaching has to "teach the Christian interpretation of life in all its fullness. Yet it has to do this, without any loss of that concreteness, that thrusting relevance, that direct I-thou relationship, of which we have spoken so much."[19]

Common to these men and all good doctrinal preachers is the demand that theological truth be related to the basic needs of twentieth century man. Relevance must be there, without diluting the doctrine to make it appear contemporary—when in fact it may not be. The contemporaneity must be indigenous to the truth enunciated.

One purpose of doctrinal preaching is to awaken faith. Good evangelistic preaching is frequently good doctrinal preaching, although not always. Phillips Brooks commented, "Preach doctrine . . . preach all the doctrine that you know, and learn forever more and more; but preach it always, not that men may believe it, but that men may be saved by believing it."[20] A faith in Christ as Saviour needs to be built upon substantial doctrinal preaching, rather than upon the intrigue of the sermon, the ability of the preacher, or the emotional climate of the service. Doctrinal preaching is the finest form of evangelistic confrontation. It is also helpful in confirming faith. It is through definition, clarification, and careful exposition of Scripture that the church is intellectually equipped to be the light of the world and the salt of the earth. The goal of doctrinal preaching is the maturity of Christians, who are thereby enabled to give an answer for the faith that is within them.

Doctrinal preaching must be focused on content. It is inadvisable to embrace the whole of a doctrine in a single sermon, in spite of the fact that as a beginning preacher this breadth may guarantee that you will have enough to say. Take a facet of a doctrine, no more. A logical focusing may be done; for example, taking the doctrine of repentance. A single sermon may look at the nature of repentance. Additional sermons could be preached on the results of repentance, the motivation of repentance, or the obligations of repentance. Focus may also be accomplished by considering simply what one text says about the doctrine. The text imposes its own limitations.

Doctrinal sermons should usually include: (1) an intensification of a need, which awakens interest; (2) definition, exegesis, exposition, illustration; and (3) application of the doctrine to modern life.

Do not fear the great doctrines. You need not search after the obscure or the unique. Preach the basics. The situation of the hearers is the crucial matter. If there is a problem of immaturity in the faith, your auditors may need the kind of milk that was offered to the church at Corinth (I Cor. 3:2).

For inspirational purposes you are encouraged to read some of the exemplars of the art of doctrinal preaching. I would at least include *God Was in Christ,* by Donald Baillie; *A Faith to Proclaim,* by James Stewart; and *How the World Began,* by Helmut Thielicke. Note also the sermons of Paul Rees, William Barclay, H. H. Farmer, and David H. C. Read.

In the final analysis, doctrinal preaching will evoke interest when it is seen as a solution to contemporary needs. Abstract truth will not garner a hearing; relate the teaching of Scripture to modern needs and it will be heard—gladly!

THERAPEUTIC PREACHING

Many Christians are sick—some are neurotic—all have needs. One pulpit master contended that "there is a broken heart in every pew." Therapeutic preaching was never more necessary than today. Whether you choose to call it "pastoral preaching," "life-situation preaching," or "therapeutic preaching," is inconsequential. Most important of all is that you preach to heal personal ills.

All such preaching needs to be grounded in an understanding of human nature and its behavior. It is set against the background of a sound psychology. This does not mean that psychological terms should be included in the sermon. In fact, it is preferable if most technical terms are avoided. A knowledge of psychology is imperative; however, the language of the sermon should be the language of the people.[21]

Therapeutic preaching generally does the following:

It recognizes a problem or difficulty. It may be anxiety, bitterness, hate, envy, or the like. In the words of Harry Emerson Fosdick, the acknowledged high priest of life-situation preaching,

> Every sermon should have for its main business the solving of some problem—a vital, important problem puzzling minds, burdening consciences, distracting lives—and any sermon which thus does tackle a real problem, throw even a little light on it, and help some individuals practically to find their way through it cannot be altogether uninteresting.

He adds, "There is nothing that people are so interested in as themselves, their own problems, and the way to solve them. That fact is basic. No preaching that neglects it can raise a ripple on a congregation." Again, "Preaching is wrestling with individuals over questions of life and death, and until that idea of it commands a preacher's mind and method, eloquence will avail him little and theology not at all."[22]

It defines and locates the difficulty.
It reveals the possible inadequate solutions.

It brings the truth of Scripture to bear upon the problem. That is, it concludes with the provision or enablement provided by God.

As would be expected, this type of preaching does have its share of problems. Some argue that it creates problems that do not exist. This can happen when pseudopsychologists, in the description of certain maladies, create them among their listeners. This phenomenon is common during the training of nurses. While studying all the symptoms of a disease, some begin to sense similar maladies in themselves; thus they wonder if they do not have the disease that the professor discussed. Some therapeutic preaching also errs by blending much psychology with inadequate theology. A sensitive pastor will recognize his own limitations, speak without the aura of omniscience, and humbly observe that he may be misleading.

Life-situation preaching often opens doors for counseling. It will tell people that you are human, approachable, and understanding. Listeners will seek you out. Howard J. Clinebell, Jr., feels that one test of a good sermon is how many people seek you out for counseling as a result of the sermon. [23] Although there are other indicators, this is a significant one.

Life-situation preaching is dependent on a great deal of counseling and visitation. Unless a person is acquainted with people, with human nature in general, his preaching will be superficial. People are a source for sermons. As you live among them, hear their voices, feel their pulses, and enter into their crises, you can empathize with them. Only then can you preach therapeutically. The preacher's concern is primarily persons, not subjects or even texts. Initial concern is with an object, not with a subject. As Harry Emerson Fosdick has said, "It is personal counseling on a group level."[24] Gerald Kennedy writes that "our message becomes one of healing the brokenhearted, restoring confidence to the fearful, making each man feel important and proclaiming how man may find life."[25]

SOCIAL-PROPHETIC PREACHING

At a time when America is experiencing unprecedented social revolution, many churches, strangely enough, refuse to accept a prophetic role. Some of these churches, located like islands in the midst of racially mixed communities, remain silent on the subject of racism. Communities heaving under the weight of labor difficulties often have churches that fear to address the labor-management question with any perception or prescription. A nation caught up in the spasms of war and international unrest all too frequently has within its borders churches where the subject is seldom broached and only occasionally acknowledged. Mass media relate one set of national and international problems while large sectors of the church tackle a separate set. Members enter the church with one cluster of questions and leave the church with answers to another "churchy" set of questions. Why is it that many preachers, and particularly evangelicals, fail to tackle social-prophetic preaching? The following list is suggestive, though not necessarily exhaustive:

(1) **Detachment.** Absorption in church related activities, meetings, calling, counseling, and sermon preparation often denies the pastor any form of significant involvement with his community.

(2) **Inadequate academic training.** Until recently seminaries have done precious little with social ethics, social problems, and the role of sociology in the training of its clergymen.

(3) **Equating of theological liberalism with social concern.** While in our day it is true that most social reformers are liberals, it is also true that not all liberal ministers are concerned with social reform and not all ministerial social reformers are liberals. The question most frequently raised by evangelicals is whether such an emphasis could lead to a social gospel emphasis in the wrong sense. The old social gospel hang-up short-circuits a confrontation with social issues.

(4) **Societal skepticism.** Many modern churches are convinced that it is futile to attempt the correction of social problems inasmuch as conditions will only get worse. They feel social redemption is an inviable option; it is impossible. Personal evangelism is the dominant task assigned to the contemporary church. Sociological involvement is both foolish and futile.

(5) **Eschatological concern.** An eye to the future has distracted some from necessary involvement in the here-and-now. Sociologist David O. Moberg says, "All too often, waiting for his coming has taken the place of working until his coming."[26]

(6) **A deep-seated feeling that politics is dirty.** Church purity is threatened by social involvement. Church leaders wonder if it is wise for a church to make pronouncements with respect to social issues that tend to become political in nature.

(7) **Fear of position.** Social issues are ambiguous. A wise position according to some is one of silence. Why divide a church over such matters? The prophet may speak bravely, but a pastor could lose his job if he did so. It is safest for him "to preach the gospel."

For thoughtful Christians social-prophetic preaching is no mere option for the contemporary "gospel preacher." It is absolutely essential for a number of reasons:

(1) **Biblical teaching demands it.** Jesus counseled, "Love . . . your neighbor as yourself" (Luke 10:27). According to the apostle John, one serves God when he serves his fellow men (I John 2:10–3:18). The judgment recorded in Matthew 25 is in terms of food for the hungry, drink for the thirsty, lodging for the stranger, clothes for the naked, and visiting of the sick and imprisoned. In Ephesians 2:10 the apostle Paul declares that we are saved "for good works." James 1:27 says that "religion that is pure . . . is this: to visit orphans and widows in their affliction. . . ." Jesus went about healing the sick, the blind, the crippled, and raising the dead. His was a ministry of compassion. This

pattern remains normative for any ministry that claims to be Christ-like.

(2) **Our history demands it.** Traditionally, conservatives have been concerned about social problems: alcohol, tobacco, sex, divorce, gambling, literature, orphans, and the elderly. Timothy L. Smith in his study of mid-nineteenth century America points out the intimate correlation between evangelical theology and social action.[27] It is inconsistent for us to now withdraw. Christian interest should presently extend to such problems as poverty, unemployment, nuclear warfare, mental illness, population explosion, ecology, racial conflicts, and crime.

(3) **Our humanity involves us.** To be a person is to be socially involved. Life cannot be lived in a vacuum. David Moberg says that "social problems are personal."[28] We are dependent upon others for employment, housing, transportation, and food. To glean from, but not to minister to the world is selfish. The story of the good Samaritan makes it clear that our neighbor is anyone in need. Neutrality is impossible because inactivity conveys implicitly an endorsement of the status quo. If we do not do it, then it will be done by others or not done at all.

We must recognize, of course, that prophets are unpopular. Resistance often comes from the religious establishment. Vested interests are at stake. Preach a sermon on race, suggest the advisability of integration and people will inevitably query you about the potential devaluation of real estate. How, they ask, would you feel if your son or your daughter married a Black?

Preachers are not itinerants. Therefore it is necessary to recognize that while the prophet could speak his message and move on, the preacher must speak and remain. Therefore the pastor-prophet in the local church must earn his right to be heard. He must preach in such a way that his credentials are established with a deep, firm commitment to biblical truth and to the doctrines of the Christian church. He must be careful lest he alienate the very ones who need this message. For those who agree, they will still agree after you have spoken. But those who need to be changed will need to be won very carefully and cautiously, recognizing that you speak out of a concern for the Christian faith and their own well-being.

The preacher-prophet's spirit may be the critical issue. No pastor should stand in the pulpit as if he were untouched by prejudice and bigotry. A confession of failure is the place where all of us must begin. Such preaching must be done in a healthy fashion, not as a pathological venting of hostilities. David Belgum says:

> If your motivation for preaching hellfire and brimstone down upon sinners stems from the fact that your church council did not approve your purchase of an IBM Selectric typewriter, your people will know

it. They will know that your prophetic preaching has nothing whatso-
ever to do with righteousness and that you are using the pulpit for the
kind of therapy you should have had on the tennis court. On the other
hand, if you grasp the devastation of sin and the personal tragedy
wrought in the lives of many of our people by the moral decay in our
society, you will be able both to weep over Jerusalem and to drive the
money changers out of the Temple.[29]

Let us consider some directives for social-prophetic preaching:

(1) **Know the issues**. Do not shoot the homiletical gun without proper
ammunition. Read the literature. Much has come from the presses
written by psychologists, sociologists, noted theologians, and careful
analysts of the contemporary scene. All such literature helps to
provide the informational reservoir from which a man can draw in
order to be properly prepared to address these issues in the pulpit.
Both sides of an issue must be investigated before a preacher com-
mits himself to one of the options. He must know an opponent's
stance so well that he can represent it faithfully and even defend it.
For example, it is well for a dove to recognize that not all hawks are
blood-shedding, hateful persons without an ounce of love in their
system. And it is well also for the hawks to recognize that not all
doves are irresponsible or non-Christian. With respect to the racial
demonstrations, it is well to recognize that not all the leaders are in
favor of militant anarchy, bent on destruction of property, nor are
they motivated by a communistic conspiracy. In every age the
preacher-prophet is called upon to take the pulse of his society to
discover the idols, to challenge the idols, and then call men to turn
from these idols and serve the living God.

It might be the issue of human rights or the racial question. One
of the anomalies of traditional Christianity is that we can fully
support the Apostles' Creed and hate Blacks at the same time. Our
creeds are often deficient at the point of application to life. What are
we to do in such a society? Certainly there ought to be freedom to
choose with equal opportunity in education, housing, and employment. We need to encourage minorities in the direction of entre-
preneurship. Decisions must be faced courageously by the preacher.
When he speaks it should be out of genuine Christian concern, not
out of wrath.

It may be the question of war and peace. When is war really
right? How does one decide? Is pacifism a possibility? We should
teach that there are at least three possible motivations for pacifism:
one which is based upon fear; another which arises out of a high
regard for life and a distaste for violence and suffering; and a third
which arises out of genuine Christian commitment and concern.

It may be the problem of affluence or poverty. The materialistic, "gold-in-God" cult has dulled the conscience of many Christians. Sacrifice is an obsolete category for many churchmen. Cherished values are often identified as Christian and a prosperous man feels he has a corner on God. History has taught us, however, that there is no correlation between holiness and wealth, or between poverty and unrighteousness. In fact, the contrary is often true.

A man must do his homework in order to be concretely helpful and thus avoid the creation of pious fog. Specifics rather than generalities are essential to this kind of preaching. Mark it down as axiomatic—once you become specific, you are open to criticism.

(2) **Preach a whole gospel.** Avoid the impression that personal, individualistic concerns (salvation, consecration, purity of life and motive) and social-prophetic concerns (race, poverty, war, affluence, labor, ecology, etc.) represent two gospels. There is only one gospel, with both social and personal implications. Liberals have often erred by neglecting the foundation of social action—namely, personal redemption through Jesus Christ. Conservatives, on the other hand, have just as often neglected their responsibility for the totality of man's need. They have sometimes given the impression that they have performed all that is required by introducing a person to Jesus Christ the Saviour.

(3) **Confess personal inadequacy.** Technical details cannot be mastered. Time and training will inevitably limit what a man can say and what he is capable of controlling by way of preparation. Ambiguity is often involved. Principles will be shared but people of necessity will be compelled to make their own decisions; and all such preaching must be done humbly, recognizing the possible distortion of truth.

(4) **Call Christians to action.** Mental assent is inadequate. You must, as a good pastor, show your concern by personal social involvement. A shepherd leads. Teach your people that risk and misunderstanding are to be expected. Don't have your people "tarry" for proper motives. Improper motives which issue in good action are better than passivity without proper motives, which accomplishes nothing.

Two possible approaches to social preaching are open. The first is *direct,* where a frontal attack on social issues is made. The issues are named and addressed forthrightly. Or, it may take an *indirect* route, where principles are taught and the people are trusted to make applications. No attempt is made to be specific. Rather than insulting the congregation you let them feel they made the decision. You are suggestive rather than exhaustive. Above all else, support your thought with biblical truth. Let your people know the difference that the Christian faith makes. Read again the prophetic utterings of Hosea, Amos, Isaiah, Jeremiah, or Jesus Christ. Social preaching without biblical support is not preaching at all.

What is the purpose of preaching? The purpose of preaching is to address the whole man—a man who first of all needs to be redeemed by the power of Jesus Christ, a man who makes a personal decision to let Jesus Christ come into his life as Saviour and Lord. He needs also to be taught regarding the Christian faith. Then he needs the encouragement that the "Balm in Gilead" can soothe his aches and heal his hurts. Finally, he needs to know that God has a word for him regarding his society and his place in it as a Christian.

The church needs preachers who are willing to handle all four sermonic areas. A myopic ministry that makes an unnecessary, ill-defined focus upon one and skirts the others is unfair to the complexity of the human situation.

Seek as best you can, with the Spirit's enabling, to preach "the whole counsel of God."

NOTES

1. Donald G. Miller, *The Way to Biblical Preaching* (New York: Abingdon Press, 1957), p. 112.

2. Miller, p. 123.

3. Harry Emerson Fosdick, *The Living of These Days* (New York: Harper and Brothers, 1956), p. 99.

4. Dorothy Mulgrave, *Speech: A Handbook of Voice Training, Diction, and Public Speaking* (New York: Barnes and Noble, Inc., 1954), p. 21.

5. Henry Grady Davis, *Design for Preaching* (Philadelphia: Fortress Press, 1958), p. 106.

6. John Knox, *Integrity of Preaching* (New York: Abingdon Press, 1957); Robert Mounce, *The Essential Nature of New Testament Preaching* (Grand Rapids: Wm. B. Eerdmans Publishing Co., 1960); and Robert C. Worley, *Preaching and Teaching in the Earliest Church* (Philadelphia: Westminster Press, 1967).

7. Ronald A. Knox, *Enthusiasm* (New York: Oxford University Press, 1950).

8. See D. James Kennedy, *Evangelism Explosion* (Wheaton, Ill.: Tyndale, 1969).

9. Helmut Thielicke, *Encounter with Spurgeon* (Philadelphia: Fortress Press, 1963), p. 1.

10. George Buttrick, *Jesus Came Preaching* (New York: Charles Scribner's Sons, 1931), p. 73.

11. Clifton J. Allen, *Church Administration* (February 1964), p. 12.

12. Note the article by LeRoy Patterson titled "Is the Altar Call a Sacred Cow?", *Eternity* (December 1967), pp. 15 ff.

13. W. E. Sangster, *The Craft of Sermon Construction* (Philadelphia: The Westminster Press, 1951), p. 43.

14. J. A. Broadus, *On the Preparation and Delivery of Sermons,* revised by Jesse Burton Weatherspoon (New York: Harper and Brothers, 1944), p. 60.

15. Frank Colquhoun, "The Priority of Preaching," *Christian Foundations,* 2 (Philadelphia: The Westminster Press, 1965), 52-53.

16. C. H. Dodd, *The Apostolic Preaching* (New York: Harper and Brothers, 1950).

17. John Knox, *The Integrity of Preaching* (New York: Abingdon Press, 1957), p. 49.

18. Emil Brunner, *I Believe in the Living God* (Philadelphia: The Westminster Press, 1961), p. 13.

19. H. H. Farmer, *The Servant of the Word* (New York: Charles Scribner's Sons, 1942), p. 143.

20. Phillips Brooks, *Lectures on Preaching.* Reprint. (Grand Rapids: Baker Book House, 1969), pp. 128-129.

21. See Charles F. Kemp, *Life-Situation Preaching* (St. Louis: The Bethany Press, 1956), pp. 11-27, for a helpful introduction to life-situation preaching.

22. Harry Emerson Fosdick, "What Is the Matter with Preaching?", *Harper's Magazine*, 157 (July 1928), 134, 139, 141.

23. Howard J. Clinebell, Jr., *Mental Health Through Christian Community* (New York: Abingdon Press, 1965), p. 86.

24. Harry Emerson Fosdick, *The Living of These Days*, p. 94.

25. Gerald Kennedy, *His Word Through Preaching* (New York: Harper and Brothers Publishers, 1947), p. 185.

26. David O. Moberg, *Inasmuch* (Grand Rapids: Wm. B. Eerdmans Publishing Company, 1965), p. 19.

27. Timothy L. Smith, *Revivalism and Social Reform* (New York: Abingdon Press, 1957).

28. Moberg, p. 62.

29. David Belgum, "Preaching and the Stresses of Life," *Lutheran Quarterly* XX (November 1968), p. 358.

BEHAVIORAL CHANGE—THE DYNAMICS OF CHANGE

THEORIES OF CHANGE

1. Festinger's Cognitive Dissonance
2. Boulding's Image
3. Burke's Consubstantiality

TYPES OF CHANGE

INFLUENCES EFFECTING CHANGE

1. Need
2. Data
3. Motives
4. Frame of Reference
5. Participation
6. Ego Involvement
7. Mass Media

RATE AND DURATION OF CHANGE

CHANGE THROUGH PREACHING

ETHICS OF CHANGE

CHAPTER FOURTEEN • THE DYNAMICS OF CHANGE

Change has always been part of the human drama. Individuals, societies, and institutions have been in constant flux. What differs in contemporary life is the pace of change and the prospect that such change will come faster and faster in every arena of life. Concerned persons ask, What changes are occurring? Are they beneficial? Are they good? Do they affirm or deny life? What can we do? It is important that we begin understanding the dynamics of change if we are to become participants in this process.

Persuasion. Persuasion is the term used by rhetoricians to describe the art of changing people. Persuasion is evident in the earliest of biblical accounts. The Genesis story depicts the serpent attempting to make Eve include the forbidden fruit in her diet. Abraham sought to persuade God to save Sodom. Moses sought to persuade Pharaoh to release Israel. Jonah, Isaiah, and Jeremiah were some of the other biblical persuaders. The persuasive process continues unabated in the present day. The entire advertising industry is caught up in a persuasive task. Parents, teachers, lawyers, clergymen—all are involved in a day by day process of persuasion which attempts to move people toward predetermined ends.

Persuasion, from the perspective of the behavioral scientist, is an "activity in which speaker and listener are conjoined and in which the speaker consciously attempts to influence the behavior of the listener by transmitting audible and visible symbolic cues."[1] Another definition of persuasion says that it is "the conscious attempt to modify thought and action by manipulating the motives of men toward predetermined ends."[2] For our purposes, "persuasion is a conscious attempt by one person to change the behavior of another person or persons toward some predetermined end through the transmission of some message." You will note that this definition identifies it as a "conscious" attempt: it is not chance. Freedom is inherent within this kind of situation. That is to say, persuasion is not compliance behavior; persuasion is the giving of a message and the reception of that message by another or others who can respond in freedom. It also assumes that these "others" have the ability to act and change. In addition it assumes people will actually attempt to change their behavior patterns.

Communication as the "meeting of the meanings" implies an understanding of what is being said. It does not necessarily involve any change of attitude, opinion, or behavior. Persuasion, on the other hand, necessitates some alteration if it is to succeed. This alteration or change is established in the mind of the persuader so that it may be accomplished in the life of the persuadee. Some maintain that all speech is persuasive. It seeks some change.

This is perhaps true. Even an inspiring address is persuasive in that it modifies attitudes, although the modification may simply be reinforcement. In many situations there is little disagreement to reduce.

All preaching, however, is persuasive by its very nature. It confronts people with options. It calls them to decision. It does not grant the freedom of neutrality. Eric Hoffer discusses change and notes the quasi-religious nature which that change involves.

> It would be legitimate . . . to assume that there is in man's nature a built-in resistance to change. We are not only afraid of the new, but convinced that we cannot really change, that we can adapt ourselves to the new only by getting out of our skin and assuming a new identity. In other words, drastic change generates a need for a new birth and a new identity.[3]

THEORIES OF CHANGE

1. Festinger's Cognitive Dissonance

Cognitive dissonance, a term coined by Leon Festinger, is a balance theory. Three statements by the author will help to put the theory into perspective.

(1) If two cognitive elements are relevant, the relation between them is either dissonant or consonant.

(2) The magnitude of the dissonance (or consonance) increases as the importance or value of the elements increases.

(3) The presence of dissonance gives rise to pressures to reduce or eliminate the dissonance. The strength of the pressures to reduce the dissonance is a function of the magnitude of the dissonance.[4]

He is saying that when two simultaneous cognitions fit, there is consonance. When they do not fit, there is dissonance. When dissonance occurs, efforts are made to make the cognitions fit. The individual "may raise his allowable dissonance level, push the dissonant elements into the background of his conscious, ignore the consequences of such dissonance, shift his beliefs to coincide with the evidence he has received, or reject one of the elements that effected the dissonance."[5]

A theological example of dissonance is the well-known paradox created by two biblical truths—the sovereignty of God and the free will of man. Throughout theological history this cognitive dissonance has been alleviated in various ways, either by ignoring one or the other, by raising the allowable dissonance level and maintaining that tension and paradox are inevitable, or by focusing on one and de-emphasizing the other.

Roger Brown has added a new emphasis to this theory of attitude change which he calls "the principle of differentiation." That is, you differentiate an idea like S into S_1 and S_2. For example:

> A white Southerner who believes Negroes to be mentally inferior, lazy and dirty . . . encounters one who is bright, industrious and neat. Without taking the more painful route of openly (or even covertly) admitting that he was wrong, he can simply differentiate between educated and uneducated Negroes.[6]

What has occurred is that he has alleviated the emerging dissonance level by differentiating.

Cognitive dissonance, though a helpful theory regarding change in persons, errs when it fails to recognize the significant number of people who live on dissonance and attempt very little equilibrium in the face of this fact. It also overstates the case by explaining everything, whereas not everything can be so categorically handled.

2. Boulding's Image

Man cannot be differentiated from the lower animals by his increased capacity for intake of information. Human eyes and ears are perhaps no better than those of other mammals, and the human nose is most certainly worse. Man is a symbol-using creature. It is his capacity for organizing information into large and complex images which is his chief glory.

According to Kenneth E. Boulding, "Behavior depends on the image." [7] Image may be defined as "a value-oriented vision of some part of the world; it is the totality of 'knowledge,' empirical and non-empirical, that one has of himself, others and things which determines his behavior toward them and related objects."[8]

Shared images are essential for communicative purposes. Alienation occurs when the image of persuader and that of persuadee grow dissimilar. In the words of Boulding, "the meaning of a message is the change which it produces in the image." When a message hits an image, one of four things can happen.

> In the first place, the image may remain unaffected. . . . Second . . . it may change the image in some rather regular and well-defined way that might be described as single addition . . . a third type of change of the image . . . might be described as a revolutionary change. . . . A spectacular instance of such a change is conversion. . . . A fourth possible impact of the messages on the image [is that] they may also have the effect of clarifying it, that is, of making something which previously was regarded as less certain, more certain, or something which was previously seen in a vague way, clearer.[9]

Images can be differentiated into images of fact and images of value. An image of fact would be, for instance, that premarital sex is a common phenomenon. An image of value would be that premarital sex is sinful. "The image of value is concerned with the *rating* of the various parts of our image of the world, according to some scale of betterness or worseness. . . . It is what the economists call a welfare function."[10]

Societies are bonded together by a "public image"; that is, "an image the essential characteristics of which are shared by the individuals participating in the group."[11]

S. I. Hayakawa maintains that the fundamental motive of human behavior is the preservation of the symbolic self, not self-preservation as many teach. He says, "If a man symbolizes himself as a certain kind of captain of industry, he must have that tenth, eleventh or twentieth million dollars. . . . If a man symbolizes himself as a certain kind of daring sportsman he must obviously perform feats challenging to his skill and courage."[12] Boulding affirms it is the image which in fact determines what might be called the current behavior of any organism or organization. "The image acts as a field. The behavior consists in gravitating toward the most highly valued part of the field. . . . We behave according to some image of the consequences of our acts." He concludes that "the whole art of persuasion is the art of perceiving the weak spots in the images of others and of prying them apart with well-constructed symbolic messages."[13]

3. Burke's Consubstantiality

Kenneth Burke is a contemporary humanist whose philosophical view of communication, though often obscurely stated, is nonetheless most provocative. He maintains that men are divided from one another and seek unity. People must come together to share values and beliefs which become the basis of society. If there is unity, there is also a need for communication, particularly persuasion. Man is a rational, symbol-using animal. He makes, uses, and misuses symbols. The essence of communication is the use of symbols for the purposes of appeal. Communication takes place, according to Burke, through identification. You establish the identity of some person, thing, or notion through the signs of consubstantiation. Burke says:

> A is not identical with his colleague, B. But insofar as their interests are joined, A is *identified* with B. Or he may *identify himself* with B even when their interests are not joined, if he assumes that they are, or is persuaded to believe so.

> Here are ambiguities of substance. In being identified with B, A is "substantially one" with a person other than himself. Yet at the same time he remains unique, an individual locus of motives. Thus he is both joined and separate, at once a distinct substance and consubstantial with another.[14]

The word "consubstantiality" is taken from the Lutheran lexicon to describe the Lord's Supper. The Roman Catholic term "transubstantiation" means that the bread and the wine become "in fact" the body and blood of Christ. The Lutherans teach, according to their doctrine of consubstantiation, that Jesus Christ is distinct from, but identified with, the bread and the wine. Burke is saying that two individuals never become identical, but that they develop a commonality, a similarity, an identification.

The rhetorician may have to change the audience's opinion in one respect, but his success is dependent on his ability to identify with his audience in other respects. Some of their opinions are needed "to support the fulcrum by which he would move other opinions."[15] Wise communicators consciously or unconsciously have included within their argument signs of consubstantiality which are indicators to the audience that they share much, although their disagreement may also be very real. The points of agreement become the common route that must be acknowledged and followed in order to attain a persuader's purposes.

Walter R. Fisher takes the concepts of Kenneth Boulding and Kenneth Burke, unites them, and concludes:

> One may hypothesize that rhetorical discourse will be persuasive to the extent that the image it creates regarding a subject corresponds with the image already held by the audience, the degree to which the image it implies of the audience corresponds with the self-image held by members of the audience, and the degree to which the image assumed in the message and its presentation of the communicator is attractive to the audience. Rhetorical communication accomplishes its ends through the means of "signs of consubstantiality," which are, most probably, more or less immediately accepted or rejected.[16]

For the preacher this implies a reference to a common tradition, a common authority, or a common life style.

TYPES OF CHANGE

Responses to a persuader's message may range from decidedly marked changes of behavior in the direction advocated to the lack of any change at all to a negative reaction or an extreme boomerang effect. Changes may be expressed as observable value shifting, attitude shuffling, or any type of new behavioral pattern. Hovland and Janis isolate four kinds of observable effects of persuasion:[17]

(1) **Opinion**—a change in attitude or an individual's verbalization of attitudes and values.

(2) **Perception**—"A man may drive through a New York slum and see the people there as dirty, ragged, drunken derelicts. After he listens to a speech by a social worker who has worked among the poor, he may begin to see the same people as sober and dressed in clean, worn clothes."[18]

(3) **Affect**—changes in emotional states (mood, laughter, tears, shivers running up and down the spine, etc.).

(4) **Action changes**—changes in an individual's overt physical behavior.

Voting for a particular candidate, donating money to a particular church, feeding the poor, visiting prisoners are types of action changes.

Discussions of change usually recognize three familiar constructs: attitudes, beliefs, and values. Let us look at them in order.

(1) **Attitudes.** Attitudes are generally considered predispositions to action, to response, or to behavior. It is a positive or negative feeling, affect, or evaluation which we associate with an object or event. Robert T. Oliver says that an attitude may be briefly defined as "a pre-established readiness to act in given situations toward a predetermined goal."[20] Action and attitude cannot be equated. Action is overt and attitude is a predisposition. In addition there is not always a complete correspondence between a man's attitude and his activity. His attitude can be measured on a questionnaire, but his public behavior may be inconsistent with that attitude. It does seem helpful, however, to retain the notion of attitude as a "conceptual bridge between an individual's psychological states and his overt behavior."[21] A man's attitude changes when it ceases to perform the function for which it was designed. Attitudes change more easily than beliefs and values. They are the least stable of the three.

(2) **Beliefs.** A man's beliefs are those things which he conceives of as true; his disbeliefs are those which he conceives of as false. One is committed to a given belief when his curiosity rests, when he no longer is curious enough about a topic to engage actively in research on it. We may say that he is committed to a present belief. An attitude is a predisposition; a belief is a commitment which has been expressed through an attitude. Beliefs are concrete expressions of values. Values are often abstractions; beliefs are values expressed in the realities of day by day living. Some beliefs are primitive (e.g., the sun will rise tomorrow). Others are derived from authority. Much of Christian belief is of this nature (e.g., Jesus Christ rose from the dead on the third day. Salvation is by faith through grace. Immortality is the hope of the Christian. There is a heaven to gain and a hell to shun). Other beliefs are derived, based on second-hand information. And then there are inconsequential beliefs which are based on arbitrary matters of taste.

Beliefs change when the authorities are called into question and are no longer authoritative, when second-hand information is rendered unacceptable, when inconsequential beliefs are not necessary to the maintenance of a reigning life commitment.

(3) **Values.** Values are the most stable and the least subject to change. Milton Rokeach says values are "abstract ideals, positive or negative, not tied to any specific attitude, object or situation, representing a

person's beliefs about ideal modes of conduct and ideal terminal goals."[22] Others say it is a standard on which consciously or unconsciously we base our choices. They express what men believe as right or wrong, important or unimportant, wise or foolish, good or bad, just or unjust, great or mean, beautiful or ugly, true or false, and therefore underlie all choices made by individuals.[23]

Walter R. Fisher distinguishes sixteen separate categories of values.

(a) Puritan and pioneer values. "Pleasure for its own sake is immoral."
(b) Value of the individual. "We ought to value the integrity and worth of every individual."
(c) Achievement and success.
(d) Ethical equality.
(e) Equality of opportunity.
(f) Effort and optimism.
(g) Efficiency, practicality and pragmatism.
(h) Rejection of authority.
(i) Science and secular rationality. "Rational man using scientific knowledge to the full could secure the economic welfare of all."
(j) Sociality.
(k) Material comfort.
(l) Quantification. "The biggest is always the best."
(m) External conformity.
(n) Humor.
(o) Generosity and considerateness.
(p) Patriotism. Either "love it or leave it" or "change it or lose it."[24]

This represents a variation on the usual lists of ideal modes of conduct identified as values: truth, beauty, justice, reason, humility, honor, happiness, and freedom. All men establish a value system which is the hierarchical organization or rank ordering of values in terms of importance. For one person truth, beauty, and freedom may be on top of the list; for another it may be prosperity, order, and cleanliness. Beliefs, attitudes, and values are organized together to form a functionally integrated system within man. Man has a set of values which are expressed existentially in terms of beliefs and then overtly recognized through attitudes.

Change takes place in reverse order. Attitudes, beliefs, and values are changed in that order. It is a well-substantiated finding of social psychology that individuals who have well-established attitudes, beliefs, and values act to maintain them. The more extreme the attitudes, the more difficult they are to change.[25] The persuader is involved in a process of strengthening the values that will move the listener in his predetermined direction, and weakening those that will oppose this movement.

It may be helpful to distinguish some other types of change. *Replacement behavior* is a movement in life from one behavior to another which replaces it. For example, a movement from unbelief to belief, a movement from prayerlessness to prayer, drunkenness to sobriety. Some behavior is *additional:* it replaces nothing in particular but becomes a form of behavior which is new to the person and does not supplant any other. Some change is only *regional.* Those who share a theological position may differ in their geographical expression. For example, many northerners practice mixed bathing, but look down on Christians who smoke. Southerners, on the other hand, may smoke, but refuse to have mixed bathing. Some changes are *temporary.* The teetotaler who visits Europe may drink wine in Rome but return to his own country and maintain total abstinence. Some change is simply *seasonal.* The child who plays baseball in summer, football in the fall, and basketball in the winter cannot be accused of changing his values, or his beliefs, or even his attitudes. It represents nothing of the sort. Value changes represent a revision at the base, a motivational revision where reigning affection is converted. Regional, temporary, and seasonal changes are environmental. They represent pattern changes but may not represent a value revision at all. The variations within these three may simply be ways of applying or expressing fixed or stabilized values.

INFLUENCES EFFECTING CHANGE

Persuasion as goal-oriented communication generally has identifiable steps. The first of these is gaining and maintaining attention; second, the selection of needs or problems; third, suggestion of a solution by which the needs may be met or the problems solved; fourth, a request for action. John Dewey says there are five steps: (1) a felt difficulty—awareness that something is wrong—a sense of need for a change; (2) analysis of the cause of the difficulty and a definition of the need; (3) a survey of possible ways of satisfying the need; (4) evaluation of the ways—leading to one selected as the best—at least under the circumstances; (5) the preferred solution is acted upon.[26] There are a myriad of influences that effect the changes that work their way into the steps used by the persuader. Let us note a few of these.

1. Need

Persuasion must of necessity isolate some need and uncertainty, disequilibrium, problem, dissatisfaction, unhappiness, or inadequacy. Boulding says, "Where life is disorganized, where there is dissatisfaction and discontent with the processes of existing faith, then there is search for change."[27] Common lists of man's needs usually include hope, judgment, entertainment, recognition, listening, and therapy. A. H. Maslow says there are five basic needs and he gives them in rank order: (1) physiological, (2) safety, (3) belongingness and love, (4) esteem, (5) self-actualization.[28] Needs may be brought into the persuasive situation by the persuadee. As such he is a seeker in search of help, saying, "Help me." On the other hand, needs may be created by the persuader and the attitude of the persuadee is "prove it." Then again, existing needs may be intensified, defined, focused, confirmed, refined, or modified by the persuader.

Ministerial sensitivity in the form of audience analysis grapples with the needs of a congregation. The task of preaching is to raise the question in the minds of the listeners to which the gospel is the answer. Dwight E. Stevenson recognizes the spiritual needs of man:

> We are Abraham driven out of Ur; but we have gone only halfway to the promised land. We cannot go back; we lack the will to go forward. It is our destiny to be a little lower than the angels; it is our fate that we often fall a great deal lower than the beasts. There is no human being who is not caught in this tragic tension—tragic because it involves the stark alternatives of man's destiny or his undoing. God in Christ has entered this tragic situation in order to speak to man in the midst of his pilgrimage.[29]

2. Data

Changes in behavior often result from the impact of data presented in the persuasive situation. This data may be logical, lending itself to greater validity and viability while minimizing irrationality and incoherence. It may be emotional or existentially oriented. Such data can communicate happiness, joy, peace, tranquility, as well as guilt, anxiety, uncertainty, and ambivalence. Existential data provides critical evidence of situations where lives have been changed and persons healed of brokenness. Data may also be characterized by authority. The impact of authority can be seen in such situations as teachers with students, parents with child, employer with employee, or preacher with layman. It is also recognized that individuals of higher educational level are more persuaded by logical argument than those of lesser educational attainment.[30] Good evidence, however, must be combined with adequate delivery. Poor delivery, even though combined with good evidence, is ineffective.[31]

3. Motives

People's lives are changed for many reasons. Motives differ dramatically. Some of the motives that impel people are directed toward self, health, and physical well-being, self-preservation, the desire to possess power and wealth, reputation, self-respect, welfare of one's family, community, nation, or religious group. Brembeck and Howell speak of five general classifications of motives: (1) subsistence motives such as profit, health, safety; (2) social approval motives which are within the home, church, state, and nation; (3) conformity motives—a negative form of social approval developed from the fear emotion conditioned in infancy; (4) mastery motives—to excel, to rival, to compete, to dominate, to gain prestige, to seek authority; (5) sex motives; and (6) mixed motives, which are a combination of the other five. [32] Successful persuaders know not only a set of motives, but how and why they are derived. They are also able to discover which motives are operative within a given audience. Walter Fisher speaks of four master motives in public address.

(1) **Affirmation**—concerned with giving birth to an image, when a communicator addresses potential believers in an effort to get them to adopt a new image. Woodrow Wilson's advocacy of the League of Nations is an example.

(2) **Reaffirmation**—concerned with revitalizing an image. It describes a situation where the communicator attempts to revitalize a waning faith already held by his audience. Lincoln's Gettysburg Address or Martin Luther King's address, "I Have a Dream," are good examples here.

(3) **Purification**—concerned with correcting, where a communicator attempts to refine an ideology. John F. Kennedy's Houston Ministerial Address was of this nature.

(4) **Subversion**—concerned with undermining existing motives. These are situations in which a communicator attempts to destroy an ideology. Antony's Funeral Oration is a case in point. [33]

Unfortunately, although human beings tend to arrange their drives or motives in a hierarchy of preference, there is no guarantee which motive will be the master motive in any given situation. The apostles appealed to motives centering in God in Christ: Romans 12:1; 15:30; I Corinthians 1:10; 10:31; II Corinthians 10:1; and I Thessalonians 2:11 and 12.

4. Frame of Reference

All persuasive messages are received and acted upon from a particular frame of reference. For example, on Sunday morning a man may agree with the minister that giving to the poor is an excellent idea. On Monday night the same individual may feel that giving money to lower classes only makes them ask for more. His behavior is inconsistent, but it is explainable when the differences between the two reference groups are pointed out. [34]

Positive reference groups are groups to which an individual aspires or to which he belongs. Negative reference groups are groups to which he does not aspire and which he may wish to avoid. For example, a church committee meeting may divide two individuals over a decision regarding helping the needy. One may speak from a positive frame of reference with respect to the John Birch Society. Another may use this as his negative frame of reference. The polarity which this generates is obvious. Communicators concerned about changing attitudes and beliefs on the part of the listeners do well to recognize the standpoints of individuals in their congregation and to what frame of reference they may appeal. A political frame of reference may hinder a communicator's efforts to effect a decision regarding something distinctly spiritual. The entire decision and response is colored by outside commitment. Unfortunately it is impossible to predict with any accuracy which of the available reference frames will actually be used to evaluate a given message by any individual. However, when the communicator has information about probable reference groups in an audience, his message can call attention to that reference group in his attempt to not only identify with his hearers, but also to share a frame of reference.

Similar to the frame of reference influence, but not exactly identical with it, is what has been called group pressure. Deviations on the part of individuals within a group are often met with punishment and pressure brought to bear on individuals who do not conform. When a group is looked upon as very important, the pressure is extremely great. Likewise, persons will sometimes change under the influence of conformity pressure. If at one or more points a person is not conforming with a group he wishes to be identified with, the very same group pressure can account for changed behavior.

5. Participation

Active participation as contrasted to passive observation leads to learning. John Dewey said that we learn by doing. Actively playing a role involves a person in change. Wilbur Schramm says,

> It is believed that if a subject can be made to participate to the extent of making an effort to receive the information . . . then learning and attitude change are very likely to result. If a subject can be given a channel by which to express the desired attitude . . . write a letter, join a club, march in a parade—then the attitude will probably be more likely to stick.[35]

Very few things are as persuasive as participation. If I hope to change behavior, I need to engage the other person whose behavior I seek to alter in the decision to make that change. Involve a person in the process of change, and he shares in the task of persuading himself. Communicators have recognized the wisdom of evangelist Billy Graham who consciously or unconsciously recognizes the value of learning theory. He does not simply ask people to make a decision for Christ. When he makes his plea to the audience he asks them to come forward and go to the front of the stadium or hall. This participation on the part of the individual facilitates the response desired and tends to produce faster, more effective learning.

Participation requested by the persuader should be in reasonable steps. That is to say that a persuasive communication which calls for a large step can be broken down into smaller units, and better results may be expected. Reinforcement is helpful in establishing response. The persuader can guarantee greater and more lasting commitment to a decision and a change if there is an opportunity for reinforcement in the form of praise, intrinsic reward, or some other form of positive reinforcement. It may be positive or negative, "but positive reinforcement seems to produce better results than negative reinforcement."[36]

6. Ego Involvement

Studies by Muzafer Sherif and Carl I. Hovland indicate that the greater the degree of ego involvement, the less likelihood there is of opinion change through communication. Conversely, with little ego involvement there is greater potential for change.[37] That is to say, the greater the degree of open-mindedness to change the more likelihood there is that a man will be changed. When he is closed in his mind regarding a subject, or a behavior, the likelihood of his changing is greatly lessened. Ego involvement is highest where the rejection factor is highest.

In a study conducted by Kenneth K. Sereno, it was discovered that highly involved individuals change their attitudes on a topic in the direction advocated by the persuader less often than lowly involved subjects.[38]

7. Mass Media

Marshall McLuhan has insisted in all of his writings that we are being changed though ever so subtly by the media around us. We "become what we behold." This change is seldom recognized, according to McLuhan, but is significant. Messages influence us and we are aware of them. Media influence us but we are not aware of the significant character of the change that is occurring.

Berelson and Steiner have questioned McLuhan's theory by emphasizing the lack of evidence supporting the persuasive influence of mass media communication.[39] It just may be that Berelson and Steiner, along with many of the other critics of McLuhan, have used instruments prejudiced in their direction and that there is a great deal of truth in McLuhan's theory.

Why then do changes occur? Generally a felt need precedes change. When an individual senses that some option holds out a satisfaction for his need, his attitude is modified and this then is expressed in one or a combination of the changes that we have noted. It may be a confrontation with new or fresh ideas, with data, evidences, authority, logic, changed lives and the promise of some fulfilling behavior which triggers dissatisfaction with his existing life style. Similarly, when a new dimension in living is sufficiently enticing, it may be annexed and not serve as a substitute behavior.

At what point does the change occur? It occurs when the weight of evidence in favor of B (new behavior) logically and emotionally outweighs option A (present behavior). Or it occurs when the amount of evidence in favor of B can no longer be rejected, resisted, refuted, rationalized away, or denied. Again, change may occur when the need is so intensified that some viable solution is sought, and B appears to be the best among the available known options.

RATE AND DURATION OF CHANGE

Is change a process or an immediate response? If it is not coerced, it may be argued that it is always a process. An exception may be cited when a person responds to a particular evangelist the first time he hears the gospel of Jesus Christ presented, disclaiming vehemently that he had ever heard it before. It may be shown that some prior experiences laid the foundation for the decision or there were some felt needs which made the individual impressionable or a candidate for immediate response. The process of change began at the moment when need was realized or initially felt.

The apostle Paul, according to Acts 9, had a radical, immediate change in his life. It was characterized by an abruptness, an about-face, a sudden shift, a transformation of his whole life. On occasion this does occur and generally it applies in the area of evangelism. Some changes are deferred, which is to say that preaching or teaching or other events serve as influences which in time are expressed. Truth is a time bomb which goes off at the time of need. Some change, and perhaps most change, is gradual. II Corinthians 3:18 says, "And we all, with unveiled face, beholding the glory of the Lord, are being changed into his likeness from one degree of glory to another; for this comes from the Lord who is the Spirit."

Much change is the result of a cumulative effect, the impact of numerous influences. Usually changed behavior results from a number of factors which combine their influence to make the change a reality. Charles F. Kemp says that we should not assume that change happens all at once. It may be the influence of many sermons or ideas that gradually and unconsciously begin to have an effect.

> Karl de Schweinitz, the social worker, in his classical little book on *The Art of Helping People Out of Trouble,* points out that people were a long time in becoming what they are, and we ought not expect sudden transformations. He said that with some it may take "months and years of effort." The preacher should be just as realistic.[40]

Some change is so gradual as to be almost imperceptible. But change it is indeed. It is essential for the sake of lasting behavioral change that modification be based upon a changed value rather than upon coercion or an emotional state. When change is not supported by a value adjustment, the individual will lapse into earlier patterns when coercive elements are removed or the spell of the emotional experience is over. Lasting change must be built upon the structure of changed value. Obviously the categories are not mutually exclusive but often simultaneous, and they regularly influence one another. For example, during the spell of an evangelistic service with its mood music, charismatic preaching, and manipulative techniques, some respond in an emotional state which may be devoid of significant understanding, conviction, genuine desire, or sense of need. But in short order the person reverts to an unconverted life pattern. He had had a change of short duration built upon a questionable foundation. The parable of the sower and the four soils recorded for us in Matthew 13 depicts all soils being potentially fruitful; the difference was in cultivation and preparation.

At times it is possible to defer a decision. Psychologists call this phenomenon "suspending closure." August campaigning by a politician is meaningful but really does not count until November when the elections are held. Yet even in this type of setting the persuader is attempting to secure commitments and is not simply involved in "planting the seed." Sometimes it is impossible and even unethical to suspend closure on a decision. It is 7:30 P.M. on election day and you have not voted, and the polls close at 8:00 P.M. To delay is unthinkable for a responsible citizen. You are driving on a side street when a child darts into your path. The decision allows no luxury of waiting for all of the evidences. You put on the brake and do so quickly. It is the right thing to do, obviously. There is, however, a gray zone. Appeals to prepare to meet your creator are sometimes ethically questionable. Neither the persuader nor the persuadee has absolute certainty when that will occur. It may be five minutes or fifty years. To delay on the basis of time being on your side, which may be youth's logic, is subject to modification abruptly. War, auto accident, or disease, for example. By the same token, the persuader may use the potentiality of death in a manipulative fashion which is coercive advantage-taking of the fear motive.

In summary, we may say that it is not possible to know in advance whether change will be immediate, deferred, or gradual. All types are potential in any given persuasive situation. It is manifestly unfortunate when a persuader feels he has failed because his listeners do not immediately take up the banner and march.

CHANGE THROUGH PREACHING

The ultimate goal of preaching is not the transmission of information, but the transformation of persons; not simply data exchange, but behavioral change. This means that preaching is done for a change in attitudes, beliefs, and values expressed verbally and nonverbally on the part of the persuadee. Preaching calls for radical transformation; not simply changes of life fashion, but a whole new foundation for existence.

James S. Stewart says, "Remember that every soul before you has its own story of need, and that if the Gospel of Christ does not meet such need nothing on earth can. Aim at results. Expect mighty works to happen." [41] The Bible assumes that change can take place. Jesus said to Nicodemus, a ruler of the Jews, "Truly, truly, I say to you, unless one is born anew, he cannot see the kingdom of God" (John 3:3). Paul said to the church at Corinth, "If any one is in Christ, he is a new creation; the old has passed away, behold, the new has come" (II Cor. 5:17). The Letter to the Ephesians says, "For by grace you have been saved through faith; and this is not your own doing, it is the gift of God—not because of works, lest any man should boast. For we are his workmanship, created in Christ Jesus for good works, which God prepared beforehand, that we should walk in them" (Eph. 2:8-10).

Peter spoke of the divine power which allowed men to become "partakers of the divine nature" (II Peter 1:3, 4). Change in the New Testament is very common. Most characteristically the concept of change or conversion is in the context of men turning to God as in Acts 9:35 and 15:19. It is often associated with repentance, Acts 3:19 and 26:20; and believing, Acts 11:21. It talks about moving "from darkness to light," Acts 26:18; from idols to God, I Thessalonians 1:9; from vain things to a living God, Acts 14:15. Paul can say that "when a man turns to the Lord the veil is removed" (II Cor. 3:16).

Biblical change, sometimes referred to as conversion, is "turning to God . . . more than a change of mind, more than undergoing some experience; it is a concrete change to a new way of life, as the word 'turn' suggests—a turning in one's tracks and going in a new direction."[42] While the preacher is calling people to change, he in turn is being caught up in change. Cronkhite says, "The persuader should not set about to persuade without accepting the probability that he himself will be to some extent persuaded."[43]

Preaching by the disciples provided them with an opportunity for their own growth.

> We know really well only something which we have to teach. We never learn or understand anything so well as that which we have to formulate and explain to others. We have deep and lasting impressions only of things we have expressed. In preaching to others, the disciple himself is strengthened.[44]

ETHICS OF CHANGE (or persuasion)

Great controversy has raged over the ethics of persuasion. It is commonly argued that persuasion has been unethical when it appealed to the emotional side of man. Others indict such culprits as name-calling, glittering generality, transfer, testimonial, plain folks' approach, card-stacking, and bandwagon techniques.[45] It is generally agreed that it is unethical to be dishonest. There is no excuse for deliberate deceit, for intentionally misleading an audience, regardless of the end in view. The end does not justify the means. When you speak out of honest convictions, you have a right to be heard. If you speak from falsification or fabrication, you are unethical and do not deserve a hearing. A cheap, temporary success may be recorded but the price is far too high.

It is also unethical to deceive the audience about your intention. When a speaker has a goal, a predetermined end for his listeners, and seeks to deceive them regarding this intention, he has flirted with untruth. His purposes should be aboveboard and honest. On occasion the evangelistic invitation has been most unethical. The minister will ask people to simply raise their hands while every head is bowed and every eye is closed. Then later in the service he will ask the same persons to come and stand before the congregation to show the integrity of their intention. Such action is completely unethical and hence unworthy of Christian usage.

Persuasion which either overtly or covertly attacks the basic freedom of response in the individual or subjugates his self-determination is also unethical.[46] That is to say, it is unethical for the persuader to downgrade the humanity of the persuadee and not allow him the freedom of choice. All persuasion must have the possibility of being rejected. In other words, a speaker should grant to the listener freedom to agree or disagree, to change or not be changed. If he does not grant him that freedom, he is unethical. The ethical test is a matter of measuring one's willingness to accept rebellion with equanimity. Ethical communicators react in such a way as to enhance the self-determination forces within the persuadee. The servant of God is obligated to accept the person even though that person chooses to reject the message.

NOTES

1. Thomas M. Scheidel, *Persuasive Speaking* (Glenview, Ill.: Scott, Foresman and Company, 1967), p. 1.

2. Winston Lamont Brembeck and William Smiley Howell, *Persuasion: A Means of Social Control* (Englewood Cliffs, N.J.: Prentice-Hall, Inc., 1961), p. 24.

3. Eric Hoffer, quoted by Don Fabun, *The Dynamics of Change* (Englewood Cliffs, N.J.: Prentice-Hall, Inc., 1967), I, 28.

4. Leon Festinger, *A Theory of Cognitive Dissonance* (Stanford, Calif.: Stanford University Press, 1957), pp. 18, 78.

5. George A. Borden, Richard B. Gregg, Theodore G. Grove, *Speech Behavior and Human Interaction* (Englewood Cliffs, N.J.: Prentice-Hall, Inc., 1969), pp. 46-47.

6. Gary Cronkhite, *Persuasion: Speech and Behavioral Change* (Indianapolis: The Bobbs-Merrill Company, Inc., 1969), pp. 60-61.

7. Kenneth E. Boulding, *The Image* (Ann Arbor: The University of Michigan Press, 1956), p. 6.

8. Walter R. Fisher, Class Notes, "Recurrent Motives in Communication," Los Angeles: University of Southern California, 1969, p. 2.

9. Boulding, pp. 7, 8, 10.

10. Boulding, p. 11.

11. Boulding, p. 64.

12. S. I. Hayakawa, *Symbol, Status, and Personality* (New York: Harcourt, Brace and World, Inc., 1963), p. 37.

13. Boulding, pp. 115, 134.

14. Kenneth Burke, *A Grammar of Motives and a Rhetoric of Motives* (Cleveland: The World Publishing Company, Meridian Books, 1962), pp. 544, 545.

15. Burke, p. 56.

16. Fisher, pp. 2, 3.

17. C. I. Hovland and I. Janis, eds., *Personality and Persuasibility* (New Haven, Conn.: Yale University Press, 1959), pp. 1-28.

18. Hovland and Janis, pp. 1-28.

19. Scheidel, p. 41.

20. Robert T. Oliver, *The Psychology of Persuasive Speech*, 2nd ed. (New York: Longmans, Green and Company, 1957), p. 44.

21. Erwin P. Bettinghaus, *Persuasive Communication* (New York: Holt, Rinehart and Winston, Inc., 1968), p. 22.

22. Milton Rokeach, *Beliefs, Attitudes, and Values* (San Francisco: Jossey-Bass, Inc., Publishers, 1968), p. 124.

23. Otis M. Walter and Robert L. Scott, *Thinking and Speaking*, 2nd ed. (New York: The Macmillan Company, 1968), pp. 217-218.

24. Walter R. Fisher, Class Notes, University of Southern California, Winter 1969.

25. Cronkhite, p. 139.

26. John Dewey, *How We Think* (Boston: Heath, 1910).

27. Boulding, p. 172.

28. A. H. Maslow, *Motivation and Personality* (New York: Harper and Brothers, 1954), Chapter 5, "A Theory of Human Motivation."

29. Dwight E. Stevenson, *In the Biblical Preacher's Workshop* (Nashville: Abingdon Press, 1967), p. 33.

30. Cronkhite, p. 138.

31. James C. McCroskey, "A Summary of Experimental Research on the Effects of Evidence in Persuasive Communication," *Quarterly Journal of Speech*, LV (April 1969), 175.

32. Brembeck and Howell, pp. 83-91.

33. Fisher, pp. 4, 8, 10, 12, 15, 16.

34. Bettinghaus, p. 37.

35. Wilbur Schramm, *The Process and Effects of Mass Communication* (Urbana: University of Illinois Press, 1961), p. 213.

36. Bettinghaus, pp. 56-57.

37. Muzafer Sherif and Carl I. Hovland, *Social Judgment* (New Haven: Yale University Press, 1961), p. 196.

38. Kenneth K. Sereno, "Ego-Involvement, High Source Credibility, and Response to a Belief-Discrepant Communication," reprinted from *Speech Monographs*, XXXV (November 1968, No. 4).

39. Scheidel, p. 56. Cf. Berrard Berelsen and Gary A. Steiner, *Human Behavior: An Inventory of Scientific Findings* (New York: Harcourt, Brace and World, Inc., 1964), pp. 287, 542, 575.

40. Charles F. Kemp, *Life-Situation Preaching* (St. Louis: The Bethany Press, 1956), pp. 26-27.

41. James S. Stewart, *Preaching* (London: The English Universities Press, Ltd., 1955), p. 42.

42. J. Marsh, "Conversion," *The Interpreter's Dictionary of the Bible,* 1. George A. Buttrick, ed. (New York: Abingdon Press, 1962), 678.

43. Cronkhite, p. 205.

44. Michel Philibert, *Christ's Preaching—and Ours,* trans. David Lewis (Richmond, Va.: John Knox Press, 1964), p. 29.

45. Alfred McClung Lee and Elizabeth Briant Lee, eds., *The Fine Art of Propaganda* (New York: Harcourt, Brace and Co., 1939), pp. 23-24.

46. Paul W. Keller and Charles T. Brown, "An Interpersonal Ethic for Communication," *Preaching,* V (January-February 1970), 33-40.

BEHAVIORAL CHANGE—THE APPLICATION

MARKS OF A SUCCESSFUL APPLICATION

1. Appeals to Shared Values
2. Based upon Careful Audience Analysis
3. Shares in the Language of Today
4. Is Practical

TYPES OF APPLICATION

1. Direct Application
2. Indirect Application

PLACEMENT WITHIN THE SERMON

1. Outset
2. Sprinkled Throughout
3. Conclusion

COMMON MISTAKES

CHAPTER FIFTEEN • THE APPLICATION

CHAPTER FIFTEEN / BEHAVIORAL CHANGE—APPLICATION

A sermon rises or falls in its application. In fact, it is questionable whether a sermon is really a sermon unless it contains some form of application. Some have argued—and I believe correctly—that unless a discourse has an application it is a declamation or monologue, not a sermon. Spurgeon said, "Where the application begins, there the sermon begins."[1] The gospel of Jesus Christ was never intended as mere information which could simply be transmitted from generation to generation. Rather, it must bring the hearer under its claims, search his heart, and mediate a divine encounter. It is reprehensible to provide faithful exegesis and careful exposition and then to slight the application. Unless the sermon motivates some action or decision, it has not fulfilled a basic canon of preaching. As we noted earlier, preaching is "the communication of biblical truth by man to men with the explicit purpose of eliciting behavioral change."

Application is neither exegesis, theology, nor theological exegesis. When a man teaches that the reference to "water" in John 3:5 is a reference to the baptism of John, which was a baptism unto repentance, the preacher is performing an exegetical task which pertains to historical, cultural, and grammatical matters. Or, if he teaches that Matthew 16:18 may be variously interpreted as the Roman Catholics do to refer to a transmissible authority resident in the Pope, or as Calvin did when he insisted that it was upon Peter's confession that the church would be built. Or, when he contends that the reference is to Peter as representative of the Twelve as argued from the metaphor of Ephesians 2:20, he is involved in theology, not application. Theology and exegesis are foundational for, but not identical with application.

Application, furthermore, is not what the apostles did when they took Joel 2:28-32 and applied it to Pentecost (Acts 2:15-16), Psalm 16:10 and applied it to Christ (Acts 2:31). Contemporary preachers are not applying truth when they establish instances of promise and fulfillment. What then is application?

Application is *personal*. It answers the question "What shall we do?" which was asked following Peter's sermon on the Day of Pentecost (Acts 2:37). It is distinctly a relational issue. From the listener's perspective, he is attempting to discover the relation between the gospel and himself. From the preacher's perspective, it is the relationship between the gospel and his audience. It is always personal. It is "you," not "they." In the Sermon on the Mount (Matt. 5:1—7:29) Jesus used the personal pronoun "you" no less than one hundred times, not including the word "your," which is also frequently used. There was no mistaking the personal nature of His message. It was geared to His listeners. "The Sunday sermon will lack purpose and never recover its meaning until it is understood by all as an instrument for the instruction of disciples."[2] The concern of the speaker is with his listeners: What are their needs? What is their condition before God? What does the lordship of Christ mean to them? The listener has a right to ask, "So what?" If there is no answer forthcoming, there has been no sermon. The gospel is addressed to individuals, and the application underscores that fact.

Application is also *present tense.* It is not simply, What shall we do? but, What shall we do now? The gospel is specifically related to the audience at hand. Only rarely should the application be future tense. "Perhaps this, too, as well as the authority in his manner and words, was a difference noticed between Jesus' teaching and that of the scribes. Perhaps the scribes taught as many preach today, in the past tense."[3] It is not simply "thus *said* the Lord," but "thus *saith* the Lord." Without this dimension, sermons sound like hollow echoes out of the past. The truth of the gospel must become incarnate in the surging, seething, revolutionary day in which the message is delivered. Truth, revealed in its temporary setting, whether B.C. or first century A.D., is inserted into the present, into our time, into our day. Jeremiah spoke to sixth century B.C. people living in Palestine, Babylon, and Egypt. Jesus spoke to first century people dwelling in Galilee and Judea. In every age the preacher must "paint the Good News with local color"[4] in order to meet the real needs of his times, not necessarily what his contemporaries consider to be relevant for them. Jesus spoke and was crucified. They felt His message was irrelevant. In a sense they were right. His message was irrelevant to their wants, though not to their needs.

Application is also *dynamic.* Exegesis is a frozen form; that is to say, its truth remains intact year after year. A sermon's exegesis is the same regardless of when it is preached. The same is true of exposition. The theological truth of Scripture, because it is both universal and timeless, can be established and settled. There is no fluidity involved. Application, however, is dependent on the setting, the persons addressed, the time, the culture, and the needs of the given environment. Truth does not change. We always ought to love our neighbor. Application inevitably changes. The questions may be asked, What neighbor? When? In what setting? From what perspective? In what fashion? Even Acts 2:38, where Peter tells the assembled crowd at Pentecost to "repent, and be baptized," is a time-bound application. Men must always repent, but repent of what? Sin takes on a different complexion for each person, for every age, and in every culture. I cannot take an old sermon manuscript and preach it without rethinking, rewriting, and adjusting the application. Exegesis, exposition, and theology, when accurate, remain basically intact. Application, on the other hand, has a dynamic nature which must be honored. It is the truth about God in relation to the persons immediately before me in their setting and in the light of their needs. Applications can never be frozen forms.

The authors of *Steps to the Sermon* suggest a helpful exercise as part of sermon preparation. Using a sheet of paper lined down the center, the preacher places on one side of the sheet the truths he has discovered in the passage and on the other side the relationship of these truths to life.[5]

MARKS OF A SUCCESSFUL APPLICATION

Every communicator should do his utmost to guarantee a high degree of persuasiveness. At the same time he ought to be concerned about fending off unnecessary alienation from his listeners. To change them without alienating them is his goal. Therefore, the question ought to be asked, What should I do to be as successful an agent of change as possible? Paul Tillich reminds us that there are genuine stumbling blocks that people must face as they make a decision regarding the gospel. It is the preacher's task to remove the wrong stumbling blocks, "namely, the wrong way of our communication of the Gospel—our inability to communicate. What we have to do is overcome the wrong stumbling block in order to bring people face to face with the right stumbling block and enable them to make a genuine decision."[6] All too frequently we find people who reject the gospel because it was never properly communicated to them.

A successful application has the following hallmarks:

1. Appeals to Shared Values

Researchers hypothesize that "communication is likely to be very successful when it reinforces attitudes already in existence. It may play a significant role in formulating new attitudes where previously there were none. But it usually fails to change deep-seated attitudes already in existence."[7] If this hypothesis is correct—and many maintain that it is—it means that the task of application is best accomplished when we are cognizant of the values held by the audience and gear our message to these values. Messages are ignored, rejected, or distorted when the attitude of the speaker is at variance with the attitude of the listener. Occasionally a message is unnecessarily rejected. The fault lies with a misunderstanding on the part of the persuader. In sharing a message based already upon shared values, he did not enunciate this commonality. Instead, he noted the variance between the behavior he maintained and the behavior of his listeners. He should have begun by drawing attention to those shared values, beliefs, and attitudes already in existence; once these were established he could then show the wisdom of his proposed behavior. In this way the persuader cooperates with the persuadee. "You can persuade others to do far more than they originally intended to do, but only if you help them guide themselves along *their route* toward *your conclusion.*"[8]

This is not manipulation. It is understanding that shared values, commonly held beliefs, and attitudes that are identical often become the bases upon which new behavior, new practices, and new commitments are made. If we challenge a man to move immediately from where he is to where he ought to be without showing the bases upon which this is done, we lessen the possibility of change.

One example will suffice. A sermon on social-prophetic issues is controversial by its very nature. The controversy is lessened when the preacher can show the audience that his application to social issues is predicated upon a belief in the Bible and a commitment to the message of Jesus Christ. That is, "you who accept the Bible and Christ as I do recognize what this implies. . . ." Unless this step is taken, the audience may likely express hostility because the proposed message is at variance with their present practice.

2. Based upon Careful Audience Analysis

At no point in the preaching event is slipshod audience analysis more costly. Audience analysis has *some* bearing upon subject choice, method of development, exegesis, and exposition; but it has *utmost* bearing upon the application of the message as it relates to the assembled auditors. Audience analysis is imperative before an appropriate application can be made. The nature and needs of a congregation should be known in rather minute detail so as to make the truth as helpful as possible. When this is not practiced, preachers "evangelize the already evangelized," teach the obvious, provide answers for unasked questions, discuss irrelevant issues, or otherwise "scratch people where they do not itch." It is a matter of not only knowing the audience in depth, but discovering how to use that knowledge in a constructive manner. A man must match his perceptiveness with wisdom in implementation.

3. Shares in the Language of Today

The communicator cannot afford to ignore the cultural thought patterns of his audience. James E. Sellers says that we are ministering to a post-Christian society in which even churchgoers are outsiders.[9] Traditional Christian symbols may have to give way to newer symbols "that outsiders can understand."[10]

Present-day writers have done an admirable job of speaking a language that people comprehend. They have spoken of our day as a "wasteland" from which there is "no exit." It is an "age of anxiety." One has spoken of the "neurotic character of our times," and another insists that we are having "an encounter with nothingness." Those symbolic expressions are easily understood. If the gospel is to apply to moderns it must be in language that arises out of the experiences in which they have participated. This calls for an identification of the preacher with his congregation to such a degree that he can participate in their concern without becoming identical with it. The

Christian gospel is thereby applied to current needs in the modern idiom by a man who has kept himself current.

4. Is Practical

Application should be within immediate reach of the congregation. Realism, not idealism, should characterize the application. Occasionally sermonic proposals are overly demanding and impossible for the listener, creating frustration rather than providing a challenge. Some of these sermons demand a complete response when a partial response would be far more feasible. Erwin P. Bettinghaus notes, "Many tasks or responses which the persuasive communicator may wish to elicit can be broken up into smaller units and have better results than if complete responses were expected." [11] The value of audience analysis to sermonic applications cannot be overstated. What is my congregation's present state? What can be expected of them? Where, from their present condition, can they move and how far can they move? Application within the sermon is then related to their condition and the possible changes. What is the next step? What can I do? Sermons should provide helpful, reasonable guidelines for implementation of Christian truth. For example, most congregations welcome practical suggestions regarding prayer, sharing their faith, Christian ethics, the Christian family, and related subjects.

TYPES OF APPLICATION

Sermons may be broken into three types: those that have direct application to the listener, those that make indirect or suggestive application, and those that make no application at all. In the light of what we have said thus far, we may seriously question whether the latter is a sermon in any purist sense. The school of preaching that fits this last category insists that the task of the preacher is simply to "rehearse the mighty acts of God." "Sermons" of this type are strong biblically, exegetically, and theologically; but practically they are woefully deficient. This task, they argue, is left to the Holy Spirit. People are not called to respond. They are to hear a proclamation. One wonders if it is even possible to preach in this fashion because there is always a suggestive nature to doctrinal, theological, and biblical teaching. However, if it is possible (and I have serious reservations) to declare and proclaim without applying, let us label it a theological treatise, a doctrinal discussion, or a religious lecture. It is not a sermon by our criteria. Sermons make either direct or indirect application of the gospel.

1. Direct Application

Whitesell says, "It is better to make definite, searching application than to imply or hint at it." [12] For example, "You are a sinner who needs salvation." "You are a Christian who must learn to forgive." "You are a

Christian and must learn to love your neighbor." When Jesus spoke, He made definite demands upon His listeners. He expected people to drop their nets, get out of bed, invite Him to dinner, or to follow Him; there was no doubt that something momentous had occurred. He expected something definite to be accomplished. Harvey Cox says:

> Our preaching today is powerless because it does not confront people with the new reality which has occurred and because the summons is issued in general rather than in specific terms. It is doubtful, however, whether proclamation which is not highly specific can be thought of as preaching in the biblical sense at all.[13]

This type of preaching takes various forms:

(1) **Elucidation.** This type of sermon has carefully defined directives. It is an explicit exhortation which clarifies the issues and leaves the listener with a minimum of ambiguity or confusion regarding his expected response. Billy Graham's evangelistic ministry is of this nature. His sermons conclude with explicit steps that must be taken if a person is to become a Christian or is to enter into the reality about which the evangelist has spoken. Very little confusion regarding expectation arises. A communion sermon, for instance, might state, "As we partake, let us confess our sins and give gratitude to God for the gift of life provided through the sacrifice of Christ on the cross." Such is explicit and leaves very little confusion.

Much protest rhetoric has been of this nature. In May 1970 I heard a young radical rhetorician on the UCLA campus say, "The United States has acted irresponsibly in Vietnam, and now Cambodia. Students have been killed on the Kent State campus. Let us march on the ROTC building." The response was immediate. When they arrived at the ROTC structure, they threw rocks at the windows, tore down the doors, and smashed property inside the building. The response to the persuader was immediate and definite. He had elucidated the steps in careful, even meticulous, unconfused fashion.

Isaiah in a sermon which recorded his vision and revelation from Jehovah said: "Wash yourselves; make yourselves clean; remove the evil of your doings from before my eyes; cease to do evil, learn to do good; seek justice, correct oppression; defend the fatherless, plead for the widow" (Isa. 1:16-17). In Jeremiah's "great temple sermon" recorded in Jeremiah 7:1–10:25, he makes a direct application to his listeners as it comes from the Lord. "For if you truly amend your ways and your doings, if you truly execute justice one with another, if you do not oppress the alien, the fatherless or the widow, or shed innocent blood in this place, and if you do not go after other gods to your own hurt, then I will let you dwell in this place, in the land that I gave of old to your fathers for ever" (Jer. 7:5-7). Peter was equally explicit in his sermon on the day of Pentecost. The crowd asked, "What shall we do?" And his answer was, "Repent, and be baptized every one of you in the name of Jesus Christ for the forgiveness of your sins; and you shall receive the gift of the Holy Spirit" (Acts 2:38).

(2) **Interrogation.** Questions proposed for the auditors by the preacher become a form of direct application. The preacher may ask, "What is your response? What will you do?" In a sense, interrogation is indirect because it allows the listeners to choose and does not tell them specifically what they must do or decide in a certain way, although this is probably implied. It is direct because it calls them to make a personal decision or response. The questioning method of application is very common. It must therefore be used with discretion, lest it lose its usefulness through overuse.

(3) **Hyperbole.** Overstatement, which attempts to arouse the listener out of lethargy and into some activity or response, is a helpful form of direct application. The speaker does not anticipate a literal response in intensity or scope. In the Sermon on the Mount Jesus said, "If your eye offend you, pluck it out" and "if your hand offend you, cut it off." He was enunciating the radical nature of discipleship. His statements were never intended to be literally applied. Protest rhetoric often does the same. The speaker may say, "Let's burn the city down." Such direct applications are intended to arouse people from inactivity to some activity rather than total obedience to the suggestions.

2. Indirect Application

Direct application specifies what you must do: one, two, and three; it is overt, explicit, and direct. Suggestive or indirect application gives stimulation in a particular direction but trusts the listener to make his own specific decision. It recognizes the uniqueness of every situation and trusts the Holy Spirit to complete what the sermon has begun. Rather than being overt, it is subtle. Frequently it states the case in general terms and allows the congregation to apply it in its specifics. There is good reason for using this approach.

Frank Dance maintains that "the most persuasive thing in the world is participation. If I want to change behavior, I must engage the other person whose behavior I want to change in the decision to change his own behavior. I will not change his behavior by telling him to."[14] In this way the people are involved in the process and help to persuade themselves. Carl Rogers once argued that "self-discovered and self-motivated behaviors are, in the long run, the only ones which produce significant changes."[15] Carl Larson relates an interesting study that was conducted by Mervin Ziegler.

His question was, "What is it that causes some sermons to be ineffective?" One of the results of Ziegler's studies was that the sermons which contained applications to the daily lives of the congregation were the sermons that were unanimously rejected by the congregation. The frequency of rejection and the intensity of rejection exactly paralleled the amount of daily application contained in the sermon. I would suggest that individuals are becoming more and more reluctant to accept that kind of application, religious or otherwise, to their daily lives. That kind of prescription implies that one person is in a position to tell others just what they should do with their daily lives.[16]

Although we are in no position to check the validity of Ziegler's study, and are not yet ready to accept all the ramifications of Larson's conclusions, the point is well made that direct application is not always as commendable as one might think. Gary Cronkhite, a communication behaviorist, says, "The greatest attitude change may be obtained by giving an audience *just enough* justification to elicit the desired behavior, so that they will feel compelled to reduce their own dissonance by further attitude change."[17]

The weight of these evidences is rather insignificant. Good preaching need not make explicit application, but may often serve its purpose—and more effectively so—through implicit, subtle, and suggestive application. The preacher becomes a midwife who assists in the encounter between God and man. Man must do the responding; the preacher is to assist, not do it for him.

Four common types of suggestive applications will be noted:

(1) **Illustration.** A concrete example is drawn out of contemporary life in order to bridge the chasm from the biblical world. Because this form of application is suggestive and not explicit, its force is in direct ratio to the illustration's ability to establish listener identification, or what Burke has called "consubstantiality." That is, the illustration preferably ought to be typical, not unique; believable, not stranger than fiction; current, not dated; possible, not unlikely; life-situational and not theoretic.

An illustration carefully shared need not be explained. If it needs explanation it is faulty. An illustration simply shared becomes its own form of application.

(2) **Multiple choice.** In this instance a speaker enumerates the possible options, then encourages the listener to make his choice. Elijah, to the Israelites gathered at Mount Carmel, said, "How long will you go limping with two different opinions? If the Lord is God, follow him; but if Baal, then follow him" (I Kings 18:21). In Joshua's sermon recorded in chapter 24 of the Book of Joshua, he enumerates three possible options: the Lord, "the gods which your fathers served beyond the River," or "the gods of the Amorites" (vv. 14-15). Isaiah told the people of Israel, "If you are willing and obedient, you shall

eat the good of the land; But if you refuse and rebel, you shall be devoured by the sword; for the mouth of the Lord has spoken" (Isa. 1:19-20).

Modern preachers can do the same by suggesting the available opportunities or options open to the listener, and then allowing the listener to make his decision based upon the evidences and personal need.

(3) **Narration.** Often a biographical sermon, artistically prepared and carefully presented, will carry the listeners through a dramatic experience while driving home lessons, though often unconsciously for them. A narrative sermon could be preached on Abraham and his faith; on David and his lust, greed, and penitence; on Jonah and his parochialism; on Zacchaeus and his willingness to make amends when he met Christ; on Peter and the lack of correlation between his profession and his performance; on Judas and betrayal; on Thomas and doubt; on Demas and the subtle lure of the world. Each of these and many, many other biblical personages provide indirect, subtle forms of application. A narrative sermon is significantly weakened when the speaker finds it necessary to append points of application. Narrative sermons, wisely presented, have these implicit suggestive applications throughout the sermon and it is unnecessary to insult the listener by tacking them on.

(4) **Testimony.** A speaker makes an indirect application of the message by witnessing to his own decision. He tells the people what the gospel he professes means to him. Joshua said, "As for me and my house, we will serve the Lord" (Josh. 24:15). Paul in a message given to Agrippa said, "I would to God . . . all who hear me this day might become such as I am" (Acts 26:29).

Which approach is best—the direct or the indirect? The evidence seems to suggest that increasingly the indirect method has value for today's sophisticated listeners. Hovland, Janis, and Kelley conclude,

> With an audience composed of highly intelligent individuals, there may be less need to have the implications of the premises spelled out and less benefit from conclusion drawn by the communicator. On the other hand, with less intelligent individuals, there is the likelihood that they will be unable to arrive by themselves at the correct conclusion from the premises alone.[18]

A balance needs to be developed between making certain that the gospel and its implications are known and the recognition of the role that the individual and the Holy Spirit play in that application. Subtle, indirect applications have significant value and should therefore be developed along with the more common direct applications.

PLACEMENT WITHIN THE SERMON

Sermonic applications may appear at any point within the sermon. An analysis of printed sermons reveals, however, a discernible pattern. Applications occur at the outset, are sprinkled throughout the message, or appear in the conclusion of the sermon.

1. Outset

The "basic pattern" sermon, because it is deductive in nature, frequently states a proposition in the introduction. In a sense, this is an application of the biblical truth being examined. It is generally focused and personalized later in the sermon, but the application is formally stated in germinal fashion at the outset. Often it tells what you need to do with the body of the forthcoming sermon, and is given to a consideration of the reasons why you should respond in this fashion. The application stated in the proposition is deductively proved through the body and then frequently summarized in the conclusion. Jesus' sermon at Nazareth began with the following words, "Today this scripture has been fulfilled in your hearing" (Luke 4:21). The Lord had read Isaiah 61:1, 2, closed the Scriptures, sat down, and His first words were of application.

Jeremiah's temple sermon has an introduction which makes direct application to the listeners. "Amend your ways and your doings, and I will let you dwell in this place. Do not trust in these deceptive words: 'This is the temple of the Lord, the temple of the Lord, the temple of the Lord.' For if you truly amend your ways. . ." (Jer. 7:3 ff.).

Peter's sermon to the household of Cornelius began with a proposition, "God shows no partiality, but in every nation any one who fears him and does what is right is acceptable to him" (Acts 10:34-35). Peter then proceeds to review the earthly ministry of Christ, including His crucifixion, resurrection, and ordination by God as the Messiah. The sermon concludes with a specific application which follows up the application stated at the outset in the proposition. "Every one who believes in him receives forgiveness of sins through his name" (Acts 10:43). The response was immediate. The Holy Spirit descended on the Gentiles, to the amazement of the Jews; and many of the household of Cornelius were baptized.

2. Sprinkled Throughout

Many sermons attempt some indirect or direct application throughout the message.

A typical pattern is as follows:

Introduction—interest secured, theme introduced, and direction established.

I. Major Point
   A. Then—exegetical comments (definition, clarification, theology, history, and the like)
   B. Now—application (illustration and exhortation)
II. Major Point
   A. Then
   B. Now
III. Major Point
   A. Then
   B. Now
Conclusion—summary (recapitulation—final word of application).

Amos's message, which was a judgment against Israel (Amos 3:1—6:14), had application sprinkled throughout the entire message. Early in his address he noted Israel's failure to return to God: "Come to Bethel, and transgress; to Gilgal, and multiply transgression; bring your sacrifices every morning, your tithes every three days . . . for so you love to do, O people of Israel!" (4:4-5). In the middle of the sermon he calls Israel to repentance: "For thus says the Lord to the house of Israel: "Seek me and live . . . ' " (5:4). He speaks of the fact that they have built houses, but shall not dwell in them; they have planted vineyards, but shall not drink their wine. All because of their sinfulness. He continues: "Hate evil, and love good, and establish justice in the gate; it may be that the Lord, the God of hosts, will be gracious to the remnant of Joseph" (5:15). In the last section of this sermon, another application is made: "Take away from me the noise of your songs; to the melody of your harps I will not listen. But let justice roll down like waters, and righteousness like an everflowing stream" (5:23-24).

The Sermon on the Mount (Matt. 5:1—7:29) is an interesting volley between the past and the present. Applications are sprinkled throughout the entire sermon. Of particular interest is the section 5:21-48. Here Christ speaks of the sixth commandment, "it was said" but "I say unto you." This is repeated with the seventh commandment, with a reference to oaths, retaliation, and love for neighbor. For example, "You have heard that it was said, 'You shall love your neighbor and hate your enemy.' But I say to you, Love your enemies and pray for those who persecute you" (Matt. 5:44).

Artistically developed narrative sermons also sprinkle application throughout the entire message. Subtle elements are interspersed throughout the sermon, but no direct applications are made.

3. Conclusion

Some sermons postpone the application until the conclusion. Obviously, in most sermons the preacher will not entirely postpone the application to the few moments of the conclusion. "He will have been moving steadily toward it throughout, and the carefully chosen last point will have brought him to the goal, the issue."[19]

Peter's sermon at Pentecost (Acts 2:14-42) had no overt direct application until the crowds cried for one, and then Peter obliged them. Paul's sermon in the synagogue at Antioch of Pisidia (Acts 13:14-43) begins by recounting Israel's history—Egyptian bondage, wilderness wanderings, movement into the promised land, the provision of King Saul, David and through him Jesus, John the Baptist the forerunner, the killing of Christ, the resurrection, and postresurrection appearances. From this body of the sermon, Paul gives an application in the conclusion. "Let it be known to you therefore, brethren, that through this man forgiveness of sins is proclaimed to you, and by him every one that believes is freed from everything from which you could not be freed by the law of Moses" (Acts 13:38-39).

Paul's sermon to the learned at the Areopagus (Acts 17:22-34) in Athens has subtle application in the body, but it is not until the conclusion that the direct application is made. "The times of ignorance God overlooked, but now he commands all men everywhere to repent, because he has fixed a day on which he will judge the world in righteousness by a man whom he has appointed, and of this he has given assurance to all men by raising him from the dead" (Acts 17:30-31).

The motivated sequence pattern, popularized by Monroe, concludes quite naturally with a "therefore." It terminates logically with specific applications to the listeners.

Paul in his Letter to the Romans shared an inductive type message. In the first eleven chapters he gave them theological data (sin, salvation, the life in the Spirit, sanctification, etc.). Chapter 12 states the ethical application: "I appeal to you therefore, brethren, by the mercies of God, to present your bodies as a living sacrifice, holy and acceptable to God, which is your spiritual worship. Do not be conformed to this world but be transformed by the renewal of your mind, that you may prove what is the will of God, what is good and acceptable and perfect" (vv. 1, 2).

No rigid statement of policy can be established regarding placement of the application in the sermon. It is sufficient to note that it may be at any point, but should be handled with care in the light of the type of development chosen by the sermonizer. A deductive sermon may begin with it. An inductive sermon generally concludes with it. A narrative sermon often has it throughout. Of course variations and hybrids are common and acceptable.

COMMON MISTAKES

A few faults seem to plague preachers at the point of application. For some it is the problem of predictability. This occurs when the sermon's application is unimaginatively conceived, when congregations are never surprised because everything moves along after an established pattern. One layman said of his pastor, "After I have heard the first part of his sermon I can preach the last part. I know what he is going to say." This is unfortunate. Rather than living with a useful pattern, he is languishing in a deadly rut.

Another fault is insulting the audience. This occurs when the preacher takes pains to spell out the obvious. It is an insult to a congregation to tell them what they could have discovered by themselves. It is a judgment upon the ability and wisdom of the congregation. In essence he is saying, "Listen, stupid people, here is what I mean. Here is what you must do." For most people, an application does not need to be labored. The people who hear us are not made of stone. They are not helpless children who need every thought developed and explained.

> If what I am talking about has life and reality in it, my hearer will apply it to his own situation for himself. He knows himself better than I know him, and he can often apply it to himself better than I can. The conclusion he draws for himself will likely have more relevance, and will certainly meet less resistance, than any I could give him.[20]

Another commonplace fault of preachers is that they let their application degenerate into moralistic additions to otherwise helpful sermons. They append little "preachy" additions to sermons which are at once offensive and childish.

In the final analysis, change is the work of God. At the same time, He has called preachers to faithful stewardship in their proclamation of the gospel. The tension is apparent in Paul's Letter to the Philippians. "Work out your own salvation with fear and trembling; for God is at work in you, both to will and to work for his good pleasure" (Phil. 2:12-13). Such is the interesting paradox with which every preacher has to work. He is to be faithful in presenting the gospel, clarifying the options, and providing an opportunity for response. Meanwhile he trusts God the Holy Spirit to do His own work.

As Daniel D. Walker says, "The layman should leave the church on Sunday morning not so much impressed with what happened *during* the hour he spent there as with what is going to happen *because* of the hour he spent there."[21]

NOTES

1. Faris D. Whitesell, *Power in Expository Preaching* (Fleming H. Revell Company, 1963), p. 91.

2. Michel Philibert, *Christ's Preaching—and Ours*, trans. David Lewis (Richmond, Va.: John Knox Press, 1964), p. 40.

3. Henry Grady Davis, *Design for Preaching* (Philadelphia: Fortress Press, 1958), p. 208.

4. James T. Cleland, *Preaching to Be Understood* (New York: Abingdon Press, 1965), p. 77.

5. H. C. Brown, Jr., H. Gordon Clinard, Jesse J. Northcutt, *Steps to the Sermon* (Nashville: Broadman Press, 1963), p. 59.

6. Paul Tillich, "Communicating the Christian Message: A Question to Christian Ministers and Teachers," *Theology of Culture*, Robert C. Kimball, ed. (New York: Oxford University Press, 1959), p. 213.

7. George A. Borden, Richard B. Gregg, Theodore G. Grove, *Speech Behavior and Human Interaction* (Englewood Cliffs, N.J.: Prentice-Hall, Inc., 1969), p. 241.

8. Robert T. Oliver, *The Psychology of Persuasive Speech*, 2nd ed. (New York: Longmans, Green and Co., 1957), p. 111.

9. James E. Sellers, *The Outsider and the Word of God* (Nashville: Abingdon Press, 1961), p. 21.

10. Sellers, p. 23.

11. Erwin P. Bettinghaus, *Persuasive Communication* (New York: Holt, Rinehart and Winston, Inc., 1968), p. 63.

12. Whitesell, p. 92.

13. Harvey Cox, *The Secular City* (New York: The Macmillan Company, 1966), pp. 122-123.

14. Frank Dance, "Communication Theory and Contemporary Preaching," *Preaching*, III (September-October 1968), 31.

15. Donovan J. Ochs, "Videotape in Teaching Advanced Public Speaking," *The Speech Teacher*, XVII (March 1968), 111.

16. Carl Larson, "Factors in Small Group Interaction," *Preaching*, III (November-December 1968), 18-19.

17. Gary Cronkhite, *Persuasion: Speech and Behavioral Change* (Indianapolis: The Bobbs-Merrill Company, Inc., 1969), p. 58.

18. Carl I. Hovland, Irving L. Janis, and Harold H. Kelley, *Communication and Persuasion* (New Haven: Yale University Press, 1964), p. 103.

19. Davis, p. 193.

20. Davis, pp. 206-207.

21. Daniel D. Walker, *Enemy in the Pew?* (New York: Harper and Row Publishers, 1967), p. 94.

BEHAVIORAL CHANGE—DIALOGUE PREACHING

BIBLICAL PRECEDENCE

DEFINITION OF DIALOGUE PREACHING

VALUES OF DIALOGUE PREACHING

FORMS OF DIALOGUE PREACHING

1. Chancel Dialogue
2. Congregational Dialogue

SUGGESTIONS

1. Dialogue Preaching Is Not for Everyone
2. Most Should Try Dialogue Preaching
3. Dialogue Preaching Is Not a Panacea
4. Dialogue Preaching Is Time Consuming
5. Dialogue Preaching Is Enhanced by Certain Architectural Forms
6. Teach People about Preaching

CHAPTER SIXTEEN • DIALOGUE PREACHING

CHAPTER SIXTEEN / BEHAVIOR CHANGE—DIALOGUE PREACHING

Modern man has canonized dialogue. This development was inevitable. Educators, influenced by the philosophy of "learn by doing," have replaced lectures with seminars and individual learning experiences with group learning experiences. No area of education has been left untouched by this trend. A dialogical climate has affected education at all levels—grade school, high school, and college.

The electronic era in which we live has helped to create a dialogue conscious society. Marshall McLuhan insists that a hot medium (like speech, a newspaper, or radio) has a very different effect on the recipient than does a cool medium (such as the seminar, the telephone which brings a personal message, or a soap opera on the afternoon television program). Hot media are high in definition, low in participation. Cool media are low in definition, high in participation. An entire society has moved almost unconsciously from the Gutenberg era with its privileges of seclusion and detachment into the electronic era with its demands for involvement characterized by the TV child and his "participation mystique." That society has discovered the truth of Marshall McLuhan's dictum that "the medium is the massage."

The church and its preaching, to the surprise of no one, have been influenced. Pastors who bemoan the fact that nothing seems to happen as the result of preaching will try anything to break the dull routine. Dialogue preaching has emerged as one of the viable answers. This, according to certain cynics, is laudable due to the inadequacy of some preachers who neither like to preach nor have congregations that like to hear them. On the other hand, it is a positive movement which has grappled seriously with the character of a dialogue era. Such a trend within the church is supported by communication theorists who have long maintained that communication is a two-way process. The sender and receiver (preacher and auditor) are involved in a dynamic relationship. Preaching is a two-way street. It is not an active speaker and a passive listener. This monological illusion is being challenged in our day. And, rightly so. The parishioner is not content to be a passive receptacle of religious information. He wants, and deserves, a slice of the action.

Wayne N. Thompson says, "No method of changing attitudes can be guaranteed, but the uniformity of the findings suggests that the statement 'discussion is likely to be effective in producing changes' is a modest, well-supported generalization."[1] Attitudes are more likely to be changed when there is participation and involvement, rather than spectatorism and passivity.

H. J. Leavitt and R. A. H. Mueller conclude that feedback increases accuracy and results in greater source and receiver confidence in what they are doing.[2] Group dynamics document the value of personal interaction in the group process and psychologists refer to the value of identification, catharsis, and involvement. It is the cumulative effect of such evidences which gives credence to the dialogue preaching movement.

BIBLICAL PRECEDENCE

Communication as dialogical involvement is not new. Dialogue was an early part of Hebrew ritual. The psalms were frequently spoken, chanted, or sung in temple or synagogue worship. Liturgies developed in which there was an interchange between speakers or singers. Examples are to be found in Psalm 24 and Psalm 136. The prophet Isaiah offered a dramatic proposition to his audience, "Come now, let us reason together, says the Lord" (Isa. 1:18). This was an appeal to dialogue with opportunity to share, respond, interact, and come to a basis of self-understanding, with the possibility of divine forgiveness.

Albert M. Windham in an unpublished masters' thesis titled "Preaching Is Not a One-Man Show" says that

> of some 125 teaching incidents recorded in the gospels, approximately 54% were initiated by the hearers, the teaching that followed was not a lecture or sermon, but a conversation with question, answer, objection, debate, agreement and rejection.[3]

The Gospels are full of dialogue and not much concerned with long and brilliant sermons. The apostles were constantly involved in animated conversation as they preached in the marketplace or synagogue. It seemed quite natural for someone to call out to Peter as he finished his sermon on Pentecost, "Brethren, what shall we do?" (Acts 2:37). The democratic nature of the New Testament church implied this type of participation. An act of sharing the Christian message seemed normal at Corinth. "When you come together, each one has a hymn, a lesson, a revelation, a tongue, or an interpretation. Let all things be done for edification" (I Cor. 14:26). This is not a formula for a worship dominated by a preacher with a soloist mentality, but a suggestion for an orderly interaction of the laity concerning the application of faith to life. There was a freedom to share as people were moved by the Spirit. Ephesians 4:15 and 16 enunciates this attitude and practice: "Rather, speaking the truth in love, we are to grow up in every way into him who is the head, into Christ, from whom the whole body, joined and knit together by every joint with which it is supplied, when each part is working properly, makes bodily growth and upbuilds itself in love."

In time, the informal gave way to the formal and dialogue yielded to monologue. Wayne E. Oates traces the retrogression:

> The original proclamation of the Christian message was a two-way conversation in which Christians bore witness to what God had done

in raising Christ from the dead. He had called them out of darkness into the light of the knowledge of God in the face of the living Christ. In return, those to whom they witnessed were free to converse with them, to inquire of them, and to discuss the meaning of the Scriptures in the light of these things. But, when the oratorical schools of the Western world laid hold of the Christian message, they made Christian preaching something vastly different. Oratory tended to take the place of conversation. The greatness of the orator took the place of the astounding event of Jesus Christ. And the dialogue between speaker and listener faded into a monologue. Only in pentecostal churches, street preaching, and mental hospitals are Christian preachers interrupted with responses and questions from the audience. One wonders what would happen if in a Sunday morning sermon some one were to arise and say: "Brethren, what shall we do?"[4]

DEFINITION OF DIALOGUE PREACHING

Webster says that dialogue is "two or more persons . . . conversing or reasoning." It is a "colloquy between two or more." It implies a form of mutual discourse. Reuel L. Howe says:

> Dialogue is that address and response between persons in which there is a flow of meaning between them in spite of all the obstacles that normally would block the relationship. It is that interaction between persons in which one of them seeks to give himself as he is to the other, and seeks also to know the other as the other is.[5]

It is, as Paul Tillich notes, "a matter of participation. Where there is no participation there is no communication."[6]

Dialogue preaching, because it assumes the necessity of participation, has, through various means, set out to accomplish this dynamic interaction between persons. Thompson and Bennett define dialogue preaching as "an act within the context of public worship in which two or more persons engage in a verbal exchange as the sermon or message."[7]

For our purposes, let us look at dialogue preaching in broader terms. Thompson and Bennett have limited themselves to that which occurs in the experience of public worship, but dialogue may serve as an adjunct to worship as well as something distinctly integral to worship. Dialogue preaching is not simply a presentation. It includes a preparation for, as well as a discussion or interaction following, a formal type presentation. It may also be an informal congregational discussion within the context of public worship.

Windham's definition is broader and perhaps more helpful. He says that dialogue preaching is "a cooperative effort on the part of pastor and people in proclaiming the Word of God to themselves and the world."[8] Dialogue preaching is an adventure which encourages interaction between pastor and people, between the Word of God and the needs of men. Frank Dance prefers to call this "participation preaching."[9] Preaching is not something that one person does, it is something that the community of faith does in concert, with each one having a role in this communication between man and God.

Dialogue preaching is not simply an act where people and preacher interact with each other, it is an attitude. Luther, in his preparation of sermons, tried to keep a young German lad (Hans) and a young German girl (Elsa) before his mind's eye. He was concerned to discover what they would say. Would they understand? What questions would they ask?

Harry Emerson Fosdick, writing back in 1928, said that a sermon should be a

> cooperative enterprise between the preacher and his congregation. When a man has got hold of a real difficulty in the life and thinking of his people and is trying to meet it he finds himself not so much dogmatically thinking for them as cooperatively thinking with them. His sermon is an endeavor to put himself in their places and help them to think their way through.[10]

He was quite correct in thinking that "the future . . . belongs to a type of sermon which can best be described as an adventure in cooperative thinking between the preacher and his congregation."[11] A good teacher does not think for his students, he thinks with them. The same applies in the pulpit. The dialogical attitude is sometimes expressed from the pulpit by the preacher when he says, "But some of you will say," or "Let us consider a few questions that inevitably arise," or "Some of you may wonder about this problem," or "Some of you have recently gone through experiences and are asking what we can do." A dialogical attitude is predicated upon the experiences of a dialogical person who moves sensitively among his people and is thereby enabled to experience with them the kinds of life-like problems that punctuate human existence.

A dialogical person is an open person who views truth as relational to others, while the monological person views others with detachment, seeing them as a body of *its*. The dialogical person will try to see his role as a fellow seeker rather than dispenser of easy, clear-cut, unambiguous answers. [12] Dialogue is more than a method, it is a principle. It is an approach to people. A dialogical partnership does not always depend on multiple speakers, but it is imperative that there be an understanding, an openness, an empathy, a willingness to encounter people even though the presentation is in monologue form. "Communication is possible only when pulpit and pew are aware that each depends on the other—consciously, cooperatively, continually."[13]

It is more difficult to foster a dialogical attitude than to construct a dialogical sermon. Dialogue is more dependent on relationship than on manuscript.

VALUES OF DIALOGUE PREACHING

While many see the value of dialogue, some remain skeptical and critical of its existence in the church. Objections to dialogue preaching are numerous. For some it is a departure from a sacred tradition. They point out the example of the Old Testament prophets who addressed multitudes, of Peter who preached to thousands at Pentecost, of Jesus who taught a huge throng on the mount or addressed thousands on one or more occasions. Others frankly confess that they lack the courage to try something novel. They have always done it one way and it is not easy to change well-entrenched behavior patterns. Some are concerned about the negative criticism that will come from their congregation. Some recognize that it takes extensive preparation, and their time schedules are already so full that it seems impossible to work it in. Some feel that it requires skills which they have never had and which they are not likely to acquire. A few object that dialogue preaching is a "cop out" on the part of a few homiletical failures. Good preaching, they maintain, is still possible in the traditional manner. For a few others, it is a concern about roles. They assume that preaching is the private domain of the clergyman. They have been called to this task and the laity have been called to other forms of ministry.

Those who have tried dialogue preaching attest to its values:

(1) It produces a **high interest level** on the part of the congregation. This is to be expected, for freshness and variety initially attract and hold attention. It involves people in ideas rather than allowing them to sit back passively as spectators. Identification with the speaker and points of view expressed often occurs.

(2) **Clarification.** Frequently issues are ambiguous. A dialogical situation tends to sharpen issues and create greater understanding. Interaction between individuals permits that which was obscure to emerge clear and lucid.

(3) It **forces people to face issues** that they might otherwise have tuned out.

> The person who hears his pastor hold forth on fair housing legislation, for example, may well switch to another channel mentally if he is unsympathetic to the idea. But when the argument is proposed by a fellow member in the next pew he will listen, at least, if only because of the novelty of the situation.[14]

This is very important because most persons tune out on ideas that are contrary to their frame of reference or belief structure. It is what we have already discussed as "cognitive dissonance."

(4). It **deepens faith.** If members are allowed the responsibility of sharing in the preaching of the church, it becomes an indispensable means of instruction and deepening of their faith.[15] They learn to live in

Christ rather than becoming sterile, unfruitful members of the body. They have something to pass on because they have received something. Every teacher has discovered the truth of this. You learn best when you are teaching others. The greatest value of dialogue preaching is the change that occurs in the life of participants. If the gospel was given to change people, and dialogue assists in the process, then no greater rationale for dialogue preaching needs to be discovered.

FORMS OF DIALOGUE PREACHING

Three volumes in particular are recommended for anyone concerned about dialogue preaching: Reuel L. Howe, *Partners in Preaching;* Clyde Reid, *The Empty Pulpit;* and William D. Thompson and Gordon C. Bennett, *Dialogue Preaching: The Shared Sermon.*[16] Thompson and Bennett's volume is particularly helpful because it includes an anthology of dialogue sermons. The eight sermons included in the anthology suggest the variety available under the rubric of dialogue preaching.

Dialogue preaching includes two forms: chancel dialogue and congregational dialogue.

1. Chancel Dialogue

Chancel dialogue is an involvement of two or more persons who converse with each other in the context of public worship but who do not involve the members of the congregation. Participants in chancel dialogue should be clearly heard, although they are not necessarily seen by the listeners. On occasion the voice will be heard, but the person will not be seen. He may be in another room of the church building, or standing among the congregation, seated in the choir loft, speaking from the balcony, speaking from the foyer, or as one pastor did, completely hidden and speaking through a microphone. The possibilities are unlimited. It is even possible that chancel dialogue will be conducted by one person. Loring D. Chase of the Westmoreland Congregational Church in Washington, D.C., preached such a sermon. He played both roles by changing his voice to represent first a humorous questioner and second a capricious questioner.[17]

The purpose of chancel dialogue is to get the congregation to respond in some fashion. They do this as they psychologically identify with a presentation or conflict represented by the spokesman.

Four discernible patterns have emerged:

(1) **The dialogue of support.** This has been conducted between clergy, between clergy and laity, between clergy and youth, or between representatives of various faiths. The purpose is essentially to share information about which the participants have a shared understanding. Some have called this team teaching or farmed-out respon-

sibility. No particular difficulties or contrasts are noted. The message is simply distributed between two individuals rather than being delivered by a single preacher. In this way the variety introduced by more than one spokesman invites a hearing. It is likely to be more interesting than one person doing it all. It is not, to my mind, the best form of dialogue preaching. Better yet is a dialogue that involves some form of unanswered question or conflict.

(2) **The dialogue of inquiry.** One is a questioner and the other becomes the resource person. This, as Thompson and Bennett note, can

> easily degenerate into artificiality or condescension, and it can become "stagy" or theatrical. In the ideal form of inquiry, each partner is a responsible participant who happens to have authentic questions or some thoughtful answers on the subject at hand.[18]

(3) **The dialogue of conflict.** The most enthusiastically received form of dialogue preaching is that in which there is a conflict, disagreement, or vigorous opinion differences. When there are opposing forces, a conflict is generated and people identify with one of the expressions. Conflict may be between "good guy" and "bad guy" or it may be between two viable options such as the issue of war when one plays the role of hawk and the other that of dove. Conflict creates tension which involves the listener. Conflict dialogue should not be simply two persons speaking for themselves, but rather they should represent points of view expressed by others in the congregation. This dramatic form need not include two persons who have hostility for each other, but who through friendly interaction have a vigorous discussion of an issue. Congregations near a university setting or consisting of well-educated parishioners will accept this form more readily than other congregational types. This unorthodox presentation of truth may necessitate a careful introduction to orient the congregation.

A Presbyterian church in St. Paul, Minnesota, had such a sermon. The preacher began in very traditional language discussing a rather traditional theme. A young man in the congregation stood up and challenged him. The ushers, fortunately, had been advised of the situation; but some of the ladies sitting around the young man were heard to whisper, "Sit down, sit down." The interaction on that Sunday morning created no small stir, and people are still talking about it. The subject was Easter and the resurrection faith. The young man raised the question about the relevance of such a faith in the midst of a technological and skeptical age.

Biblical characters may be used dialogically. It could be a conversation between David and Saul, or Jesus and Lazarus, between Luke and Silas. Occasionally a trialogue sermon has been attempted, where three points of view are suggested. For example, one person could represent "man," another "conscience," and a third "tempter." The sermon would be unfolded with "man" weighing the two available options in life represented by "conscience" and "tempter." A number of such sermons are included in an anthology titled *Man in the Middle*.[19]

(4) **Composite patterns of dialogue preaching.** Thompson and Bennett include a "stream of consciousness" sermon delivered on Christmas by Robert Raines and Theodore Loder, pastors of the First Methodist Church of Germantown, Philadelphia, Pennsylvania. Or, interspersing the verbal with stereophonic records of music.[20] The reader is encouraged to review chapter 3, "Dialogue in the Chancel," in Thompson and Bennett's book for a careful study of this form.[21]

2. Congregational Dialogue

Congregational dialogue is a form of talkback or feedback that occurs either within worship, prior to it, or following it. Congregational dialogue is intended for both those within and outside the church who wish to get on with their faith but who find the traditional form unacceptable and lacking in challenge. It is very beneficial to the worshiper. He begins to appreciate the fact that Christianity is more than occupying a pew and becoming a passive recipient of predigested religious information dished out from the pulpit without any opportunity for reaction, interaction, or response. With this structure, he finds himself caught up in the process. He shares, he responds, he has the privilege of articulating his faith, and in so doing becomes involved in his faith. Congregational dialogue occurs either prior to the sermon, during the sermon, or after the sermon.

(1) **Prior to the sermon.** Congregational dialogue may be no more than informal conversations which are carried on during the week between the pastor and his people. No preacher should fear to share his sermon text with as many people as possible. This is done not simply to train the people to listen, but more importantly to help him discover their attitudes toward the gospel that will be shared in formal fashion on Sunday. This is to say, he should not live with his text and his idea in privacy during the week, but in "brotherhood with his people in the church."[22]

Some pastors have discovered the wisdom of providing worship folder inserts for their congregation which outline weekly devotional readings correlated with the sermon text of the following Sunday. Readings are provided for each day of the week, and a question given for adults and another for children regarding the Scripture passage that is read on any given day. In one sense the sermon is being preached all over the parish.

Sermon seminars are becoming somewhat popular. These are

generally open to anyone who would like to come early in the week to discuss sermon ideas with the pastor. The First Congregational Church of Berkeley, California, had such a weekly experience with its pastor, Browne Barr. The weekly sessions were led by the pastor who was to preach on the following Sunday. The laity were to study the Scripture passage, to prepare by reading commentaries and bring with them various translations of the Bible plus their own questions, ideas, and personal needs. Approximately thirty-five minutes were given to round table groups of eight to ten persons who responded to the Scripture passage, and then there was a time of feedback to the total group. A fifteen-minute period for individual prayer concluded the session. The pastor then returned to his study armed with the insights and expressions of concern that had arisen from this sermon seminar.[23]

According to Mary M. Eakin a number of benefits accrued. The Bible was viewed as life related. People sensed a close-knit fellowship with one another as they searched for an understanding of their relationship to God. The pastor was grateful for the observations which brought personal insight to his sermons. In addition, the people looked forward with eagerness to the sermon on Sunday.[24]

In the midst of all of the complaints raised against the church in terms of its "administrivia," I make my next suggestion with some hesitation. A sermon board, in addition to the existing boards within the church structure, should be carefully considered. A sermon board would meet with the pastor early in the week, preferably no later than Tuesday night, to discuss his sermon for the following week. Membership on the board should be no more than seven or eight people, including perhaps a housewife, student, professional person, teacher, blue-collar worker, senior citizen, and so forth. Representation needs to be as broad as the congregation itself. This group would come with the assigned sermon topic and Scripture, having read it and thought it through in order to bring questions to the board session that they have regarding its implementation on Sunday. They would interact with the pastor to tell him how that subject had ramifications in their world of experience. The teacher would raise some issues, the student others. The elderly would raise questions that would not be raised by the young, and vice versa. Each would bring to the sermon his own frame of reference, experience, and insight, thereby humanizing the sermon while giving the pastor a reality factor frequently missing when sermons are prepared from commentaries instead of from people.

By changing the membership on this board every three months, each family in a congregation of four or five hundred could be represented during the course of four or five years.

(2) **During the sermon.** The congregation may be involved during the

message itself. Two possibilities are worth considering. The first is "stop me if you have a question." At the outset of the sermon the pastor mentions to the congregation that he will be willing to answer any questions that arise during the sermon if they will simply raise their hand. The pastor recognizes the question, answers it, and continues his message. This is obviously an occasional variation. It should not develop into a regular practice. Every congregation has the potential for a few who may dominate such an opportunity. If this liability arises, the method should be dropped. But on occasion this does provide a means for audience participation which assists in the process of understanding the gospel.

The second possibility is called "help me preach." The pastor uses a chalkboard or overhead projector in plain view of the congregation. The Scripture passage apropos to the sermon is read; then the minister turns to his congregation and asks, "What is the subject of this passage?" Suggestions are elicited from the congregation and listed on the board. A consensus is sought. Once the subject is determined, questions are raised regarding what the passage says about that subject. Conclusions are recorded on the board. The message is outlined as the people discuss it. Then the question is asked, "What illustrations would you use to illumine these concepts?" People share personal insights, stories they have heard, or experiences with which they are acquainted to fill in the structure with concrete examples. Finally the pastor says, "What truth or truths should we take from this subject or text for our own lives?" Applications are suggested, a consensus is sought, and then the applications jotted down for all to read. This requires a pastor who is secure enough to allow people this form of freedom. It requires careful preparation on the part of the pastor so he can guide them when they misinterpret the Scripture or when they misunderstand its intention. In the process he is teaching them to do what they ought to be doing on their own—studying the Bible and making application to their own lives. At the same time he is involving them in the process of the church's preaching. This, too, is suggested only as an occasional variation, rather than a weekly pattern.

(3) **After the sermon.** Many pastors open up discussion with the congregation after preaching their sermon. A portable microphone generally is provided so that the congregation may raise questions, make comments, question the conclusion, or make further illustrations of the truths set forth. Reinhold Niebuhr did this years ago during his Detroit pastorate. He would give a short sermon on a more or less controversial moral issue or on a perplexing religious question. He would close the service, then have a half-hour to forty-five-minute period of discussion. The group was not large, but as he reflected, "It is a group of unusually thoughtful people, and the way they explore

the fundamental themes and problems of life is worth more than many sermons."[25]

Some churches prefer to have a shorter sermon and thus allow part of the usual service time to be given to discussion. This is recommended. I have tried this many times, particularly on Sunday nights, and discovered that people sometimes want to discuss for an hour or more on a subject, particularly if it is an issue regarding social questions, youth, or controversial doctrines of the church. It is not necessary in this form of discussion for the pastor to give a conclusion of a sermonic nature. The discussion is the sermon. It is wise, however, to summarize the conclusions that have been reached. Thompson and Bennett note the dangers that arise from this type of situation. "(1) Initiating the discussion, especially in a large congregation, is very difficult; (2) some persons tend to dominate any discussion and will dominate it even in the sanctuary; (3) the minister may pose as an answer-box and cut off honest dialogue with the people."[26]

In spite of the dangers inherent within discussion, every pastor should consider this option with a congregation of manageable size. Buzz groups are another form of after-sermon conversational dialogue. An Evangelical Free Church in Covina, California, met in small, deacon-led groups (with an added incentive of a cup of coffee) to discuss the sermon and its relevance to their lives. Groups of this nature need a Diogenes who will puncture pretense, who will not allow the members to discuss second or third handed instead of first handed. Leaders of buzz groups should be handpicked, screened, and primed regarding both their task and the particular subject to be discussed. Some buzz groups will take the message that was only partially completed and then complete it in the small group. The Prince of Peace Lutheran Church in Addison, Illinois, tried this at an 8:00 A.M. service.

> The Pastor or Vicar presents a brief introduction/exegesis on the text. This usually involves some textual/historical criticism and the views of several commentators as to interpretation. No lesson or moral is drawn from the text. Following the brief (no longer than two or three minutes) introduction, the parishioners comment on that passage, relating it to their lives and sharing experiences that might apply. Occasionally they ask questions with regard to textual meaning. The result is a live and active dialogue, without structure from the leaders, in which the congregation literally "writes" its own sermon.[27]

It is also possible to include a Sunday school class which meets following the morning worship service, the subject matter being a discussion of the sermon, its ramifications and application to the class members. Most of these postsermon congregational opportunities require a preacher who is unafraid of questions or unthreatened by a free style give-and-take format. It takes a man who is secure in his own faith and willing to become vulnerable with the people of God regarding the gospel and its demands.

SUGGESTIONS

1. Dialogue Preaching Is Not for Everyone

That is to say that the *practice* of dialogue preaching as an act in public worship is not for everyone, but the *spirit* of dialogue is necessary for everyone. Some men have very little reason to practice dialogue preaching as a method simply because the congregational interest is high, people are experiencing change in their lives, and other means are accomplishing the ends of dialogue within the total church program. One such church has a pastor who told me, "This dialogue preaching is not for me . . . it is fine for others." It would be foolhardy to demand that everyone become a dialogue preacher in method. The only essential for our day is that everyone who professes to preach the gospel be a person whose attitude is dialogical in nature.

2. Most Should Try Dialogue Preaching

A church that is not constantly involved in the process of renewal is consciously or unconsciously experiencing decay. When Jesus spoke of "new wine in new wineskins" He recognized the necessity of the gospel being expressed in the best way to meet the current need. It may be that the traditionalist who has felt comfortable with no other way than the typically monological sermon is threatened by the dialogue. If the preacher was to occasionally implement our suggestions, he might discover a new appreciation of the gospel on the part of his listeners as well as a new challenge to his own ministry. It is a worthy risk.

3. Dialogue Preaching Is Not a Panacea

Dialogue preaching is not the final answer to all the questions that the church faces in our day. It may, however, be one possible answer. God has provided it as a gift to the church, but it is not the only way. Good monological sermons are still necessary. Thompson and Bennett recognize this when they say, "It has stood the test of time, in spite of what its detractors say, and is still one of the church's basic tools for communicating its faith."[28]

Some of the advantages of dialogue sermons would vanish if people could hear good traditional preaching. Gerald Cleator, O.P., acknowledges this when he speaks of a reaction to "low grade preaching" which has been replaced by the dialogue homily.[29] Browne Barr talks about the decay within American Protestantism signaled by the outbreak of talkback sessions. He feels these sessions would be splendid if sermons were intended simply to educate or to direct advice or to increase understanding.

> But in Protestant worship the sermon is offered to move men, not to educate them; to touch them at the springs of their being, not just to proffer them advice or counsel. . . . It is an instrument by which the great hand of the Eternal grasps us, people and preacher alike; a hand which leads or drives us out to the periphery of life . . . a hand which shakes us out of complacency and knocks the carefully nurtured dust off our ease; a hand which opens up with that Word which is sharper than any two-edged sword.[30]

Dialogue sermons have their place. They are a supplement to, not a replacement for, the traditional form of preaching which God has used in the life of the church from its inception.

4. Dialogue Preaching Is Time Consuming

Traditional sermons have been time consuming, but dialogue sermons are even more so. The development of a manuscript or text, preparation with others, the polishing, the timing, the logistics—all these combine to make dialogue preaching excessively time consuming. No one should enter into this experience without careful consideration of this demand.

5. Dialogue Preaching Is Enhanced by Certain Architectural Forms

The pulpit has, for some, become a barrier in communication. A more physically proximate position assists in the interaction between preacher and congregation. Some have turned to a Spurgeon's rail, which is a simple lectern upon which notes and a Bible may be placed. The entire body of the speaker is seen. Nothing stands in the way. It is also preferable to have seating in either a circle or a semicircle. In this way the audience can see and influence each other. A degree of vulnerability is an absolute necessity in in-depth communication.

The message is then shared by one whose dependence on a manuscript or notes is minimal. However, skillful reading of a manuscript is possible. Memorization is time consuming and sometimes dangerous. An outline may be the best method of dialogical preaching. Whatever method is used it should allow the speakers to sound spontaneous and be authentic, human, and conversational.

6. Teach People about Preaching

Very few laymen have ever heard a discussion of the preaching task. They have heard sermons for years, but have never once had an opportunity to discuss either the preacher's responsibility or theirs. A pastor should take out time from his regular preaching program occasionally to talk about the task of preaching from the perspective of the congregation. Untrained people should not be expected to get as much from preaching as those who have been instructed. Since sermons are customary, why not instruction regarding this privilege and its attendant opportunity and responsibility. William Thompson's volume, *A Listener's Guide to Preaching,* can be a readable, helpful, and contemporary guide for study. Place it in people's hands and encourage them to read it thoughtfully. Congregations who become conscious of the task become more interested in the preaching event.

Dialogue preaching may have been meant for a time such as this. God is not limited to methods. His message remains intact, but its communication is either assisted or hindered by the preachers of the church. Dialogue preaching may transform some of those dull, theological treatises into life-like experiences. It may provide some new insights into the Christian faith. It may create a new hearing. It may clarify fuzzy concepts. It may be the means ordained of God to change people from spectators into participants in the gospel of Jesus Christ. If something of life-changing value occurs, it is worth all the time and effort expended in this experimental form. It is worth a try.

NOTES

1. Wayne N. Thompson, *Quantitative Research in Public Address and Communication* (New York: Random House, Inc., 1967), p. 99.

2. H. J. Leavitt and R. A. H. Mueller, "Some Effects of Feedback on Communication," *Human Relations,* 4 (1951), 401-410.

3. Albert M. Windham, "Preaching Is Not a One-Man Show," unpublished M.A. thesis, Wheaton College Graduate School, 1969, p. 42.

4. Wayne E. Oates, *Protestant Pastoral Counseling* (Philadelphia: Westminster Press, 1962), p. 167.

5. Reuel L. Howe, *The Miracle of Dialogue* (New York: Seabury Press, 1963), p. 37.

6. Paul Tillich, "Communicating the Christian Message: A Question to Christian Ministers and Teachers," *Theology of Culture,* ed. Robert C. Kimball (New York: Oxford University Press, 1959), p. 204.

7. William D. Thompson and Gordon C. Bennett, *Dialogue Preaching* (Valley Forge: The Judson Press, 1969), p. 9.

8. Windham, p. 97.

9. Frank Dance, "Communication Theory and Contemporary Preaching," *Preaching,* III (September-October 1968), 29.

10. Harry Emerson Fosdick, "What Is the Matter with Preaching?", *Harper's Magazine,* 157 (July 1928), 137.

11. Fosdick, p. 137.

12. John Thompson, "When Preaching Is Dialogue," *Preaching*, II (July-August 1967), 4-13.

13. James T. Cleland, *Preaching to Be Understood* (New York: Abingdon Press, 1965), p. 126.

14. Thompson and Bennett, pp. 68-69.

15. Michel Bouttier as quoted by Michel Philibert, *Christ's Preaching—and Ours*, trans. David Lewis (Richmond, Va.: John Knox Press, 1964), p. 55.

16. Reuel L. Howe, *Partners in Preaching* (New York: The Seabury Press, 1967); Clyde Reid, *The Empty Pulpit* (New York: Harper & Row, Publishers, 1967); William D. Thompson and Gordon C. Bennett, *Dialogue Preaching: The Shared Sermon* (Valley Forge: The Judson Press, 1969).

17. Thompson and Bennett, p. 38.

18. Thompson and Bennett, p. 50.

19. James A. Pike and Howard A. Johnson, *Man in the Middle* (Greenwich, Conn.: The Seabury Press, Inc., 1956).

20. Thompson and Bennett, pp. 63, 64.

21. Thompson and Bennett, pp. 37-64.

22. Dietrich Ritschl, *A Theology of Proclamation* (Richmond: John Knox Press, 1960), p. 154.

23. Mary M. Eakin, "Sermon Seminar in a Parish Church," *The Christian Century* (January 19, 1966), pp. 75-77.

24. Eakin, p. 77.

25. Reinhold Niebuhr, *Leaves from the Notebook of a Tamed Cynic* (Chicago: Colby, 1929), p. 145.

26. Thompson and Bennett, pp. 67, 68.

27. Thompson and Bennett, pp. 28-29.

28. Thompson and Bennett, p. 10.

29. Gerald Cleator, O.P., "Experiments in Dialogue Homily," *Preaching*, III (November-December 1968), 28.

30. Browne Barr, "Pop Sermons," *The Christian Century*, LXXXVI (September 17, 1969), 1190.

CHAPTER SEVENTEEN • ROLE OF THE HOLY SPIRIT

Every textbook on preaching states or implies that preaching without the Holy Spirit is dead. He inspires preparation, grants unction in delivery, and produces all significant results that follow the preaching event. In the words of John Knox, "True preaching from start to finish is the work of the Spirit."[1] No one writing on the subject of preaching feels obliged to take issue with this thesis. It is uniformly accepted as basic.

Hendrikus Berkhof says the Holy Spirit

> creates a world of his own, a world of conversion, experience, sanctification; of tongues, prophecy, and miracles; of mission; of upbuilding and guiding the church, etc. He appoints ministers; he organizes; he illumines, inspires, and sustains; he intercedes for the saints and helps them in their weaknesses; he searches everything, even the depths of God; he guides into all truth; he grants a variety of gifts; he convinces the world; he declares the things that are to come.[2]

The implication of such a statement is that without the Holy Spirit there is no church. One writer has distinguished no less than one hundred New Testament facts pertaining to the Holy Spirit and His ministry.[3] But how important is the Holy Spirit to preaching? According to William Barclay, "The preacher may be a scholar, a pastor, an administrator, an ecclesiastical statesman, a scintillating orator, a social reformer. He is nothing unless he is a man of the Spirit."[4] It is generally assumed that when the pulpit drops to the level of the platform, it is due to an ignoring of the Holy Spirit as the supreme power behind preaching. Christianity has consistently maintained that the philosophy of humanism, with man as self-sufficient, is foreign to a proper understanding of the preaching role. Communication of the gospel is a message shared in the inspiration of the Holy Spirit.

Two separate studies made of preachers support the thesis that preaching is dependent on the Holy Spirit. Raymond W. McLaughlin's study of selected evangelical ministers in the United States and Canada concluded that Spirit filled preaching was both possible and necessary. His respondents felt that present-day preachers can have the power of the Spirit as did the prophets and apostles of old. Most knew when they were preaching in the power of the Spirit, although some expressed uncertainty. Most of them distinguished preaching in the power of the Holy Spirit from preaching that resulted through thorough preparation, personal magnetism, good psychology, and rhetorical persuasion. Others felt, however, that the Holy Spirit uses these very means.[5]

A more recent study of one small conservative denomination revealed comparable attitudes. The 214 ministers in this study uniformly asserted the primacy of the Holy Spirit in preaching. Representative responses included: "He is the very *life* of preaching"; "without the Holy Spirit all is vain"; "without His working, I would quit"; "He is uppermost." The ministry of the Holy Spirit was recognized particularly in the preparation of sermons (forty-five percent of the respondents), delivery of sermons (forty-nine percent), and the results that come from preaching (fifty-one percent). Incidentally, a very small percentage of the ministers felt they lived up to their ideal standards regarding the Holy Spirit's place in preaching.[6]

Any study of the Holy Spirit is filled with difficulty, for the subject is not of the laboratory variety. One cannot study this subject in the so-called scientific manner. Empirical research is neither likely nor possible. The Holy Spirit has never been, nor is apt to be, an object for scientific analysis. It is simply impossible to establish such things as a "control group" or even a workable hypothesis. That the Holy Spirit persuades and illuminates is acknowledged. How the Holy Spirit affects the human spirit is quite beyond us, for we know nothing concretely about such an act. We acknowledge the fact, but can do nothing with test tubes, hypotheses, or scientific tools to make it acceptable to scientific minds. There is unfortunately a dearth of literature specifically concerned with this subject. Theological treatments of pneumatology are common; treatises, essays, or books on the relation of the Holy Spirit to preaching are not.

Two well-known volumes on preaching by John A. Broadus (*On the Preparation and Delivery of Sermons*) and H. Grady Davis (*Design for Preaching*) disregard the topic. We are limited in our search for information to an article here, a page or two there. We have nothing that is comprehensive or exhaustive. Even the literature we do have often fails to satisfy a serious seeker after truth. Most reporting is extremely subjective, based primarily on experience, opinion, or perception.

The two studies previously cited were doctoral dissertations characterized by compilation, comment, and conclusions. They presented attitudes of preachers which were evaluated and from which conclusions were drawn. Objectively they said nothing of importance. Some of the dissertation data were weakened by sentimentality, passiveness, or distortion of biblical material. Sentimentality emerged when the preacher felt that the Spirit meant everything to him; passiveness when the preacher said he did nothing and the Spirit did all; and biblical distortion was evident where many writers on the subject practiced faulty proof-texting to support their thesis.

A concerned laywoman asked, "How can we know that it is not a man-made sermon rather than the guidance of the Holy Spirit?" In the final analysis we can be certain of only two things. First, when preaching is done in the Spirit, it will build the church, not divide it. Second, it will magnify Christ—not men, methods, or even the Holy Spirit Himself.

THE HOLY SPIRIT AND THE PREACHER

The Holy Spirit begins with a man. He makes the preacher. Denomina-tions don't, seminaries don't, but *He* does. Charles E. Jefferson says, "It is commonplace to say that a preacher must have the Holy Spirit, but it is a commonplace which every preacher will do well to ponder."[7]

Luke's picture of the primitive church explicates the role of the Holy Spirit in guiding and controlling in the worldwide mission. Philip, the evangelist, joined an Ethiopian eunuch and shared Christ with him through the inspiration of the Spirit (Acts 8:29). On the accomplishment of this task, Philip moved elsewhere through the agency of the Holy Spirit (Acts 8:39). Peter was induced to meet Cornelius and minister to his household in Caesarea through the direct guidance of the Holy Spirit (Acts 10:19; 11:22). The Spirit directed the church at Antioch to send out Barnabas and Saul as missionaries to Asia Minor (Acts 13:2). These two missionaries then set out with a consciousness of the Spirit's guidance (Acts 13:4). The Council at Jerusalem, confident that its decision had been due to the direct guidance of the Spirit, sent instructions to the Gentile brethren (Acts 15:28). The strategy of Paul and Silas on their second missionary journey which directed them to Troas rather than Bithynia where they received the call to take the gospel to Macedonia was explicitly in the Spirit (Acts 16:6-7). On a third missionary journey, Paul's decision to leave Asia and revisit Greece was similarly made under the compulsion of the Holy Spirit (Acts 19:21).

On Paul's last journey to Jerusalem, the Spirit warned him of the dangers and difficulties that awaited him (Acts 20:22-23). Church historians remind us that Augustine, Savonarola, Luther, Wesley, Whitefield, Finney, Moody, Brooks, and Graham are further evidence that the Holy Spirit empowers and uses men. What specifically then does God the Holy Spirit do in the life of the preacher?

1. He Changes the Preacher

Theologically speaking, the doctrine of regeneration or salvation is where the Spirit of God begins in the life of a man. Titus 3:5 says, "He saved us, not because of deeds done by us in righteousness, but in virtue of his own mercy, by the washing of regeneration and renewal in the Holy Spirit." The process of change—namely, sanctification—continues throughout a man's life. This is a state of being "in the Spirit" (Rom. 8:9). This does not denote a condition of prophetic ecstasy. "It includes the whole content of the Christian life, the deep personal union with Christ made possible by grace. It is a state in which the Spirit of God dwells in the believers."[8]

The preacher as a Christian possesses the Holy Spirit as a guarantee and first installment of the total redemption which is to be his inheritance. It is the ground of his Christian hope. He is set apart as God's property, uniquely owned by God, the seal of the Spirit being his assurance of final redemption (II Cor. 1:22; Eph. 1:13; 4:30). The preacher is changed as God the Spirit molds, shapes, and conforms him to the "image of Christ." The fruit of the Spirit is manifested in such things as love, joy, peace, patience, kindness, goodness, faithfulness, gentleness, and self-control (Gal. 5:22-23). Even the secular rhetoricians have noted that the good speaker ought to be a good man. Quintilian said:

> The first essential for such an one [the perfect orator] is that he should be a good man, and consequently we demand of him not merely the possession of exceptional gifts of speech, but of all the excellences of character as well.[9]

The preacher is to be known by the fruit of the Spirit, not the works of the flesh (Gal. 5:19-23). Such virtues, of course, are to be sincere and not clerical role-playing. People quickly detect insincerity in a preacher. A man needs to be more than professionally virtuous; his whole life should be one of sincerity and developing holiness as the Spirit changes his entire personality.

Raymond W. McLaughlin notes that

> modern communicators support the notion that the sum total of a man's words and deeds constitutes a message. When there is an inner contradiction between words and deeds, the deeds tend to communicate much more effectively than the words. Part of the answer to the problem of communication, then, is to build deep-seated piety and integrity into one's whole life. Each pastor must live without conflicts within and before God.[10]

2. He Calls Him to Serve

Just as Jesus said to Peter and Andrew, "Follow me and I will make you become fishers of men" (Mark 1:17), so He has called men in every generation to serve as His ambassadors. For some the call is not nearly so explicit. For all, the call needs to be a reality. Without a call a man has no *oughtness* about his service. The Spirit has been sent to call men to serve. The Book of Acts reminds us that the Holy Spirit does this very deed.

3. He Illuminates Scripture

The Holy Spirit as teacher guides the servants of Christ to teach them all things (John 14:26), to lead them into the truth (John 6:13), and in the process, of course, He magnifies Christ (John 16:14).

4. He Empowers His Witness

Jesus, at the time of His ascension, made the promise, "You shall receive power when the Holy Spirit has come upon you; and you shall be my witnesses in Jerusalem and in all Judea and Samaria and to the end of the earth" (Acts 1:8).

5. He Changes People Through Him

Beginning at Pentecost and continuing through the Book of Acts and the Epistles, we have repeated witness to the fact that the Spirit changed people through the medium of preaching. The role of the Holy Spirit has gone full cycle in the life of a preacher when he is changed, called, Scripture is illuminated, his witness empowered, and people are changed through his ministry. This was true of Peter. Peter was changed by the power of God and then heard the call to "follow me" (Matt. 4:18-20). Scripture was illuminated and he declared on Pentecost that this event had been prophesied in Joel 2:28-32. Without the inspiration and illumination of the Spirit of God this identification would never have been possible. The three thousand who believed and were baptized according to Acts 2:41 were impressive testimony to the fact that God does empower preaching.

This full cycle of the Holy Spirit's place in the life of the preacher is also illustrated in Paul. According to Acts 9:1-20, his life was changed through a unique encounter with Christ. He was then called to serve (Acts 9:15). His preaching was empowered, not in personal eloquence, but "in demonstration of the Spirit and power" (I Cor. 2:4). It is at once apparent that people were changed through the ministry of Paul when one considers the existence of the Ephesian church, the Galatian church, the Corinthian church, and clusters of believers all over Asia Minor. We have no reason to assume that God's work has changed on this count from the first century to the twentieth. He still changes potential preachers, calls them to serve, illuminates Scripture, empowers their witness, and finally changes people through these Spirit-led human instruments.

THE HOLY SPIRIT AND THE SERMON

What, you ask, distinguishes preaching from other forms of public address? Three truths seem apparent. There is a subject matter distinction. Preaching, by its definition, is a "communication of biblical truth." Paul instructed Timothy to "preach the word" (II Tim. 4:2). Commitment is made by the preacher to the Bible as his authoritative guide. The subjects he treats and the interpretation he gives are both dominated by a commitment to the Bible's own witness. The Bible judges preaching, not vice versa. The subject matter is biblically derived and Christocentric. An insight into apostolic preaching is given in John 20:31; Acts 1:8; 8:35; and 26:22-23. It found its focus in Jesus Christ. Christian preaching is always of this nature: it witnesses to Christ and Christ alone. People are then called to commit themselves to the person of Jesus Christ.

A second distinguishing mark of preaching is that there is an incarnational expectation. Paul wrote to Timothy regarding the expectations of a minister of Christ Jesus. He told him to train himself in godliness (I Tim. 4:7), to be an example in speech, in conduct, in love, in faith, and in purity (4:12), and in all other matters to take care of himself (4:16). Using an advertising analogy, "Does the soft drink commercial announcer actually drink the product he advertises?" Helmut Thielicke asks, "Does the preacher himself drink what he hands out in the pulpit?"[11] This incarnational expectation is increasingly true of political, legal, and protest speakers though not yet of some spokesmen in advertising, entertainment, and elsewhere. It is expected that the preacher should not only speak the truth but should also live it. Correlation between profession and practice is an implied norm. The preacher, if authenticity and integrity are honored, must not toy with the luxury of the advertising man who can say one thing and do another. When correlation is absent, communication breaks down.

The third mark which distinguishes preaching from other forms of public address is the role of the Holy Spirit. This is Paul's testimony: "I did not come proclaiming to you the testimony of God in lofty words or wisdom. . . . I was with you in weakness and in much fear and trembling; and my speech and my message were not in plausible words of wisdom, but in demonstration of the Spirit and power, that your faith might not rest in the wisdom of men but in the power of God" (I Cor. 2:1, 3-5). The church in Jerusalem prayed and "they were all filled with the Holy Spirit and spoke the word of God with boldness. . . . And with great power the apostles gave their testimony to the resurrection of the Lord Jesus, and great grace was upon them all" (Acts 4:31, 33). The Holy Spirit may not be an absolute stranger to other forms of public address, but nowhere else is He promised as the constant, faithful support, guide, and inspiration. He is a unique ally of the biblical preacher. The apostolic message was summed up in Peter's simple words, "The things which have now been announced to you by those who preached the good news to you through the Holy Spirit sent from heaven" (I Peter 1:12). This means literally that the true preacher does not simply use the Spirit, he is used by the Spirit. He is mastered by divine power.

In what areas, then, does the Holy Spirit relate Himself to the sermon? The most comprehensive statement on this subject comes from Faris D. Whitesell, who says that

> he can guide us in choosing the right Scripture passages for each occasion; guide us in the selection of books to buy and use in studying the Bible; give us illumination and insight in studying the passage; aid our memory to recall parallel passages and fitting illustrations; give us joy in concentrating on the text and the strength to push through the writing or verbalizing of the sermon; give us boldness and confidence at the time of delivery; inspire us with new thoughts during delivery and cause us to omit less appropriate ones. He can unify the audience, create attentiveness, open hearts, and apply the Word in both expect-

ed and unexpected ways. The Holy Spirit can convict, convert, comfort, inspire, reprove, correct, and instruct in righteousness. He can fix the Word in the minds and memories of hearers so that it becomes fruitful like the seed on good soil. How foolish to try to prepare sermons and preach them apart from the power of the Spirit![12]

A similar statement is found in *A Manual for Preaching,* by Lloyd M. Perry.[13] It is difficult to imagine a more comprehensive statement. Little is left to chance. However, for our purposes, let us look at the role of the Holy Spirit in three areas: preparation, delivery, and results.

1. Preparation of the Sermon

Every biblical preacher can testify to the ministry of the Holy Spirit in sermon building. This is not to be construed as an elimination of the responsibility of labor, but preachers have discovered that there is a cooperation of the Spirit in the man's own labor with the text of Scripture. Knox says, "The preacher devotes a solid week perhaps to listening to what the Spirit is seeking to convey. The sermon is his response...."[14] The Spirit is active in topic selection. The preacher will seek to be open to Spirit-directed themes and choices. The Holy Spirit bears witness to Christ. Themes that are not Christ centered cannot be certain of commanding His cooperation. A. J. Gordon says, "Ought it not therefore to be the supreme question with the preacher, what themes can assuredly command the witness of the Holy Spirit, rather than what topics will enlist the attention of the people?"[15] While Gordon's concern relates to the basic theme of the sermon, it may also have ramifications for nonbiblical or non-Christ-centered material in a sermon. Can we automatically assume interest on the part of a congregation simply because we are sharing biblical truth? Is the role of nonbiblical data justifiable only so far as it supports, draws attention to, or clarifies the biblical categories? We are compelled to answer these questions in the affirmative. It may, on occasion, however, be necessary to create interest, to jar lagging interest, or to enlist nonbiblical support. We need not feel guilty about using "secular" illustrations, nonbiblical material, or other content which is not explicitly Christocentric or biblical to such a degree as it *is* intended to support, buttress, and create interest in that which does have the guarantee of the Holy Spirit's cooperation.

The Spirit works with the written Word to reveal Christ the incarnate word. Illumination is no audible voice nor miracle. It is instead

> ... the touch of the Holy Spirit upon native and resident powers of the soul which had been rendered ineffectual through sin. ... It is the removal of a veil; it is light dissipating darkness. It is illumination granting the powers of spiritual perception. The total inward man now *sees* revelation as revelation; he *intuits* truth as truth; he *hears* Scripture as the truth of God.[16]

This ministry is essential if the preacher is to correctly understand, interpret, and apply the biblical message. At times this involves more than simply the preacher. All the people of God have been promised the illumination of the Spirit. Sometimes this self-disclosure of God is corporately understood. Most often, however, the preacher is thrown open to this illumination in a private encounter. The Spirit is not intended as a substitute for hard, unremitting work. Starkey tells of a young minister who testified before a group of his colleagues that he never prepared his sermons. He simply trusted the Spirit to put the right words in his mouth. An older man countered by saying that the Holy Spirit had only spoken to him once in the pulpit. After a poor sermon he had heard, "Heinrich, you're lazy."[17] The Holy Spirit will not do what we ought to do. James Stewart adds that we can count on the aid of the Holy Spirit to give us utterance only when we reflect upon the fact that "the promise is conditional upon the loyalty of common days. The Spirit of the Lord will be upon us in the proportion as our work has been earnest and faithful and ungrudging."[18]

There is no conflict between preparation and the work of the Spirit. The preacher is faithful and the Spirit is also faithful. There is cooperation. There is no either-or. The man who uses his mind provides the Holy Spirit with more material with which to work. The Holy Spirit illuminates Scripture to the man who gives himself to hard, unremitting, exegetical, scholarly tasks. When a man's mind grows lazy, the Spirit of God will not overcompensate for this. It represents a blending of his own commitment and the Spirit's faithfulness. Only a fool would allow dependence on the work of the Holy Spirit to be an excuse for personal laziness. Gerald Kennedy contends that one of the marks of the Spirit in a preacher's ministry is that he hungers for excellence.[19] When open to the Spirit, a man will discover topics, content, illustrations, passages of Scripture that may be helpful in the declaration of the gospel. The task is to study diligently, providing the Holy Spirit with material to use, and to study receptively in order that there may be a minimum of distortion between the Holy Spirit's purpose and our understanding of that purpose. We always stand in need of correction and direction. To prepare without the Holy Spirit is to prepare without God's promised ally for that task.

2. Delivery

Power in the pulpit has traditionally been identified with God's Spirit. Apostolic preaching was dynamic and persuasive. The dynamic influence did not come from human eloquence and artful rhetoric; it came to the people "not only in word, but also in power and in the Holy Spirit and with full conviction" (I Thess. 1:5). God has intended that it would be so in our day, so that we still hear a man's voice but it is the voice of the ambassador of Christ and hence is the voice of Christ Himself. The Holy Spirit works through the human words of the preacher, making them His own words.

"The Spirit's activity is His own secret, and it is sufficient for us if we preach the Gospel and hear it preached, and trust in the gracious promise of our God that he will speak to us."[20]

The discipline of the preacher plus the crisis of the preaching event provide the Holy Spirit with the material He uses in the dynamic moment of sermonic delivery. The preacher at such a time is to be real, not a simulation of someone else. He must communicate sincerely and be genuine in the pulpit. Yet many are confused at this point. Gordon Johnson speaks of those who put on

> an organ voice and a grand manner to give a spurious air of profundity to unimportant thoughts. It is almost ludicrous to hear a man make little bits of nothing sound like mighty concepts. On the other hand, many have such shallow convictions that they say important things as though they were nothing. . . . We are dealing with the greatest issues of human experience and sometimes speak of them as though they were minor household decisions.[21]

While the preacher should not attempt to be other than himself, he ought, however, to be his best self. Samuel W. Shoemaker says that we should pray sometimes to "get loose" under the Holy Spirit, so that "He says fresh, vivid, exciting, moving and convincing things through us, and so that there is fire in it all that leaps from Him to us and from us to them." [22] In those times a minister is his best self with all of his faculties in operation under the control of the Holy Spirit. It is at such times that people can be moved, made aware, and so changed that life is never the same. No sermon technique can do this; but when the Spirit of God is offered the best that we have, He can work according to His own sovereign purpose.

Structure and content in a sermon are inadequate in themselves. Polished sermons delivered in lackluster, wooden fashion without the impulse, direction, and power of the Spirit, are useless pieces of dead art. The goal of sermon delivery is to mediate the presence of God. There is an encounter which the preacher seeks to establish between himself and the listener. At best this is an encounter between man and God, and the preacher steps out of the limelight so as to allow the presence of God to be recognized. Spirit directed preachers can do this. Those who are self-centered and self-controlled remain in the spotlight.

When a man works under the direction of the Spirit, he has a freedom to speak as the Spirit directs. He may change his content in the dynamic event if the Spirit so dictates. He is not limited to his manuscript or his preparation, although generally the Spirit uses what has been faithfully prepared in the study. However, the Spirit may illuminate the spokesman as he delivers the message, and in those moments the preacher should feel a freedom to move as the Spirit directs so that the purposes of God may be accomplished and not simply a manuscript delivered.

The word *unction* is often used to describe that mystic plus in preaching.

This concept is difficult to define and has sometimes been erroneously confused with volume or personal gifts. This much we know: men either have unction or they do not have it.

> It is a thing apart from good sermon outlines, helpful spiritual insights, wise understanding, or eloquent speech. It can use all these media—and dispense with them—it is rare, indefinable, and unspeakably precious. One of the things which distinguishes preaching from all other forms of public address is that preaching can have unction. That it has it so rarely is the shame of us preachers and proves the poverty of our prayers.[23]

Unction seems to be a gift that the Spirit gives. Without Him there is none.

3. Results

Christianity has always affirmed that human nature can be radically and permanently changed. Drunkards can become sober. The impure can become pure. The unlovely can become lovely. He who is plagued by temper can learn the secret of self-control. Thieves, adulterers, murderers, and likable pagans (which includes most of us) can be changed through the gospel as it is applied in the life of individuals by the Holy Spirit.

William D. Thompson is correct: "The preacher does not control response, the Holy Spirit does."[24] And what may we expect the Holy Spirit to do? He brings conviction. According to I Thessalonians 1:5, when the Word is preached in power and in the Holy Spirit it brings "full conviction." Dale Moody says, "The power (dynamis) is derived from the Holy Spirit. There is as much difference between preaching 'in the Holy Spirit' and preaching by human strength alone as there is between living 'in the Spirit' and living 'in the flesh.' "[25] Jesus promised the Holy Spirit, asserting that He would "convince the world of sin and of righteousness and of judgment" (John 16:8).

When a person is aware of his sinfulness, his alienation from God, and has a personal sense of guilt, it is likely that the Holy Spirit has been at work in his life. The Holy Spirit also regenerates, according to John 3:5-8; I Corinthians 12:13; and Titus 3:5. Conversion is an act, the results of which are seen by men, which occurs in a man but is a result of God the Spirit's response to the faith that a man places in Jesus Christ as his Saviour. The act of regeneration is accomplished by God the Holy Spirit, producing change that man himself is incapable of.

In the fourth chapter of Acts we find an illustration of the Holy Spirit coming to restore and refresh a body of believers. These had become discouraged following the persecution and jailing of leaders of the apostolic band after the mighty outpouring of the Spirit on the day of Pentecost. When the Spirit came upon them they found a fresh sense of purpose, their spirits were revived. Leon Morris defines revivals:

when the Holy Spirit does a new thing, when He shatters men's complacency, and brings life where before all were dead. Men and women are deeply stirred. Sinners are converted. Nominal Christians are shaken out of their formalism and brought into genuine experience of the Spirit's power. . . . That is the work of the Spirit. He and He alone can revive the Church.[26]

Paul in his Letter to the Galatians contrasts two life styles: that which is characterized by the fruits of the flesh and that which is known as the fruit of the Spirit. Interestingly enough, Christian character is thought of as a cluster of virtues and not individual virtues in isolation. The fruit of the Spirit—love, joy, peace, and the like—is the creation of God and is not something that a man produces on his own by way of bootstrap theology, or by simple addition of certain character traits. Yieldedness on the part of man allows the Spirit of God to transform his personality and produce what man on his own can never create. The Holy Spirit guides (Acts 16:6-7), strengthens (Eph. 3:16), sometimes hinders (II Thess. 2), and otherwise works sovereignly to accomplish the purposes of God among men, using preaching as an instrument through which He accomplishes these tasks.

Spirit directed preaching avoids two extremes: *coerciveness,* which implies a lack of trust in the Spirit's wisdom or ability, and *bald proclamation,* which betrays a misunderstanding of the legitimate means enlisted by the Spirit in the accomplishment of His purposes. Manipulation occurs when excessive emotional appeals are employed to move men. Such preaching places trust in the preacher, not in the Holy Spirit.

On the other hand, declaration without offer, or recital without a call to decision is unbiblical sacramentalism. The Holy Spirit changes people, but He does use various means to accomplish change. We must trust the Holy Spirit to make the truth real to the hearers and to produce the changes that are according to His will.

SUMMARY

In the final analysis we have the emergence of an inevitable paradox. Two truths emerge which must be diligently honored. One is that the preacher must be faithful and the other is that the Holy Spirit is sovereign. The role of persuasion and the role of the Holy Spirit combine to create a difficulty which must be acknowledged. We cannot capitulate to either without due regard for the other. The two remain and must remain in tension. No resolution is forthcoming.

The Christian faith has always testified to two truths—the necessity of human faithfulness and the sovereignty of the Holy Spirit. In Matthew 25 Jesus tells the parable of three men who were given gifts: one was given approximately $5,000 (5 talents), another $2,000 (2 talents), the third $1,000 (1 talent). After an extended period of time the master returned to check regarding their use of their gifts. The first had taken his $5,000 and gained another $5,000; the second had taken his $2,000 and gained another $2,000; the one with $1,000 had buried it and returned it intact to the master. The master answered him, "You wicked and slothful servant! You knew that I reap where I have not sowed, and gather where I have not winnowed? Then you ought to have invested my money with the bankers, and at my coming I should have received what was my own with interest" (Matt. 25:26-27).

The implication of the parable is that it does not matter how much you have been given. What is essential is how you have responded in terms of faithful stewardship. Responsibility is bestowed in proportion to a person's native endowments; and these may be misused, abused, or properly used. God demands personal excellence from all of His servants. It is expected that a faithful servant will give his best to the preaching task. This naturally follows, for God has chosen to use human instruments to accomplish divine purposes. As Andrew Bonar says, "No soul will be in Heaven without a human thumb-mark upon it."[27]

The second truth is that the Holy Spirit is sovereign. Jesus Christ in describing the role of the Holy Spirit in conversion said to Nicodemus, "The wind blows where it wills, and you hear the sound of it, but you do not know whence it comes or whither it goes; so it is with every one who is born of the Spirit" (John 3:8).

Stewart says:

> Just as it is impossible to control the wind or dictate to its direction, so no man, no Church, can domesticate the Spirit of God or delimit His sphere of operation . . . that is God's way. "The wind bloweth"—not where we timidly suggest or dogmatically demand that it should, not where the most up-to-date computer decrees—"where it listeth."[28]

As a modern translation puts it, "The wind blows wherever it wishes."[29] If the Holy Spirit is sovereign, then it follows that His work is dynamic, creative, and demands a naiveté on the part of God's servants. We cannot freeze a method because there is no guarantee that this will be God's purpose or God's instrument. Occasionally the Spirit will fracture our schemes and disrupt our plans. He defies preprogramming and this demands risk, faith, and flexibility on the part of His servants.

One pastor said to his congregation that

> the future is always uncertain except in the eyes of the rigid tradition-alist. But God is no traditionalist, and I cannot believe the Holy Spirit will forever be bound by our fixed human forms and traditions. Progress always risks traveling some untested roads . . . we must not try to put the Holy Spirit into unchanging, rigid, man-made forms. The life of the Spirit is larger than all our forms . . . how has the Holy Spirit been boxed in by our traditional forms? Worship is actually the

flow of spiritual life that exists among a people of God. Life is diverse, and life flows in changing patterns and expressions. Life is characterized by freshness, myriad forms and expressions. So ought the spiritual life of a people.[30]

Because the Holy Spirit is, as Wayne E. Oates says, "the Spirit of innovation and creativity,"[31] it follows that there can never be a static approach to preaching in the life of the church. It is dynamic, developing, and flowering. "A faith directed and protected by the Holy Spirit is necessarily a faith re-thought, re-expressed, re-minted in each generation."[32]

All of our preconceptions, presuppositions, biases, and beloved hypotheses must be kept in abeyance so that the Spirit can do what He chooses to do and we do not get in His way.

What then ought we to do? Should we seek for another Pentecost, as some have done? The answer is no.

> Sometimes people sigh for, or pray for "another Pentecost." They might as well pray for "another crucifixion." Each represents a divine action which brooks no repetition. At Pentecost God gave the Spirit to the Church in full measure. The gift has never been withdrawn.[33]

We ought, however, to keep ourselves as pure instruments because we are the temple of the Holy Spirit (I Cor. 6:19). We should strive to be obedient to what we know of God's will and seek the power and provision of God to make possible what He has commanded. At the same time we should be sensitive to His leading and discover ways of entering into a cooperation with the promised Holy Spirit.

We have a sure guarantee if we are faithful. Preaching, based on the Word of God and testimony of Christ, has the promise of the Spirit's cooperation. For God has promised to honor the Bible and to honor Christ. To those ends the Spirit was sent and of these truths we may be certain.

NOTES

1. John Knox, *The Integrity of Preaching* (Nashville: Abingdon Press, 1957), p. 89.

2. Hendrikus Berkhof, *The Doctrine of the Holy Spirit* (Richmond: John Knox Press, 1964), p. 23.

3. Arno C. Gaebelein, *The Holy Spirit in the New Testament* (New York: Publication Office "Our Hope," n.d.), pp. 109-113.

4. William Barclay, *The Promise of the Spirit* (Philadelphia: The Westminster Press, 1960), p. 106.

5. Raymond W. McLaughlin, *Communication for the Church* (Grand Rapids: Zondervan Publishing House, 1968), p. 199.

6. J. Daniel Baumann, "Preaching Within the Evangelical Free Church of America," unpublished doctoral thesis, Boston University School of Theology (1967), pp. 160-165.

7. Charles E. Jefferson, *The Minister as Prophet* (New York: Thomas Y. Crowell Co., Publisher, 1905), p. 62.

8. G. W. H. Lampe, *The Interpreter's Dictionary of the Bible,* 2 (Nashville: Abingdon Press, 1962), 636.

9. *The Institutio Oratoria of Quintilian,* trans. H. E. Butler (Cambridge, Mass.: Harvard University Press, 1953), I pr. 9.

10. Raymond W. McLaughlin, "Piety and Preaching" (Denver: Conservative Baptist Theological Seminary, 1970), p. 12.

11. Helmut Thielicke, *The Trouble with the Church,* ed. and trans. John W. Doberstein (New York: Harper & Row Publishers, 1925), pp. 2-3.

12. Faris D. Whitesell, *Power in Expository Preaching* (Westwood, N.J.: Fleming H. Revell Co., 1963), pp. 144-145.

13. Lloyd M. Perry, *A Manual for Preaching* (Grand Rapids: Baker Book House, 1965), p. 1.

14. Gordon G. Johnson, "The Holy Spirit in Preaching," *Bethel Seminary Quarterly,* X (February 1962), 31.

15. A. J. Gordon, *The Ministry of the Spirit* (Philadelphia: American Baptist Pub. Society, 1896), pp. 144, 145.

16. Bernard Ramm, *The Witness of the Spirit* (Grand Rapids: Wm. B. Eerdmans Publishing Company, 1959), pp. 84, 85.

17. Lycurgus M. Starkey, Jr., *The Holy Spirit at Work in the Church* (New York: Abingdon Press, 1965), p. 83.

18. James S. Stewart, *Preaching* (London: The English Universities Press, Ltd., 1955), p. 102.

19. Gerald Kennedy, *For Preachers and Other Sinners* (New York: Harper and Row, Publishers, 1964), p. 108.

20. T. H. L. Parker, *The Oracles of God* (London: Lutterworth Press, 1947), p. 140.

21. Johnson, p. 32.

22. Samuel W. Shoemaker, *Beginning Your Ministry* (New York: Harper and Row, Publishers, 1963), p. 120.

23. W. E. Sangster, *Power in Preaching* (London: The Epworth Press, 1958), pp. 109,110.

24. William D. Thompson, *A Listener's Guide to Preaching* (Nashville: Abingdon Press, 1966), p. 96.

25. Dale Moody, *Spirit of the Living God* (Philadelphia: The Westminster Press, 1968), p. 83.

26. Leon Morris, *Spirit of the Living God* (Chicago: Inter-Varsity Press, 1960), pp. 68, 69.

27. James Stewart, *Evangelism Without Apology* (Grand Rapids: Kregel Publications, 1960), p. 72.

28. James S. Stewart, *The Wind of the Spirit* (New York: Abingdon Press, 1968), pp. 12, 13.

29. John 3:8a, Good News for Modern Man (New York: American Bible Society, 1966).

30. Dwight Small, *Excerpts from a Sermon,* No. II, 1, 2, 3.

31. Wayne E. Oates, *The Holy Spirit in Five Worlds* (New York: Association Press, 1968), p. 69.

32. William Barclay, *The Promise of the Spirit* (Philadelphia: The Westminster Press, 1960), p. 97.

33. Morris, p. 55.

History, according to Marshall McLuhan, can be broken into three periods: (1) the primitive era, when people lived absorbingly with one another, face to face; (2) the Gutenberg era (approximately 1500-1900 A.D.), when society moved toward a print dominated existence; (3) the present electronic era, which is characterized by mass communication.

Who knows what the next period of human history will be? The velocity of change is almost unbelievable. Some prognosticate that by the end of the twentieth century, in the next thirty or forty years, we will have seen compressed into this short period literally millenniums of change in which a new civilization will arise as it explodes into being. And man is well advised to develop some orientation which will enable him to cope with the radical nature of change which is inevitable in tomorrow.[1]

What is ahead for the church? It is not difficult to find opinions, for there are prophets everywhere. It is common to hear that the church as presently structured is unrenewable. It will die and must inevitably be replaced by a "tomorrow structure." Steven Rose, Gordon Cosby, Clyde Reid, George Weber, and others have said this for years; many are now beginning to take them seriously. In a lecture by a high school teacher in California it was stated, "We are in for one of three things: revival, revolution, or the rapture." It seems to me that revival would be a pleasant prospect, revolution has already occurred, and the end of this age may be imminent. God could draw the curtain on human history at any moment.

An elder statesman within the conservative wing of the Christian church, who is both knowledgeable and sensitive to national climate, prophesied at a retreat: "The evangelical church will go underground in the next ten years." One can only surmise that such a movement may be healthy, to recover a portion of the vitality of the primitive church. Then it was unpopular to be a Christian; as a result the church developed integrity and emerged as a significant power within a hostile society.

I see a number of things in the future of the church. It seems inevitable that the church will experience a period of purging. Church rolls will be pared down, membership statistics will not be nearly as impressive as they were in the 1950s and 1960s. Christians will have to stand up and be counted. The lines are being drawn between those who take seriously the claims of Christ and those for whom this kind of commitment is primarily social.

The letter to the Ephesian church in the Book of Revelation speaks of those who have lost their first love. Some of these will depart from the church rolls. The Book of Revelation also speaks of lukewarm Christians who will depart. Men will either call Christ "Lord," or they will leave the church. I do not anticipate that mediocrity or nominal Christianity will suffice in a revolutionary era. While in the past it has been fashionable to have Christians in Western culture known by their language and taboos, it will now be necessary for Christians to make a wholesale commitment to the Lordship of Christ. This form of revolutionary faith liberates the believer to really be what grace intended him to be—in love with God and people, vulnerable for Jesus' sake.

A great deal of experimentation is also on the horizon. We have begun to find value in dialogue preaching and in involving of the laity in preparation, evaluation, and implementation of sermons. Drama and even silence are finding increased acceptance in the church. There is the possibility of worship in small mission oriented task force units, which are occasionally supplemented by mass meetings for special purposes. The extensive use of mass communications and audio-visual aids of every conceivable sort and type will become commonplace.

There is a desire on the part of some to enter into authentic communal existence like that known in the early church when they "loved one another." Although the drive may be similar to that of hippie movements, the application will inevitably be different. The quest will be for a life-style in which people can know vulnerability as a reality. In such a life-style, role-playing is taboo and love between God's people is spontaneous. In it people can learn to weep with those who weep, but more importantly discover how to rejoice with those who rejoice, which is far more difficult. In such settings a moratorium will be declared on labels which only feed pride and serve to divide people prematurely.

It seems curious to me that the "love-ins" should have been sponsored by people who, in the main, do not know Christ, whose sacraments are taken from the drug culture, whose language is often profane, and whose morals are frequently questionable. The early church had love-ins, unbesmirched by certain present-day excesses. Is it not likely that the Christian church which takes the gospel seriously will discover ways of being real with each other and recover the *koinonia* that the body of Christ ought to have experienced all along?

Sunday evening services will go through significant revision. Some churches have already discontinued them. Others will use Sunday nights as teaching opportunities, developing lay seminaries. For some it will be out-reach time through neighborhood Bible studies conducted throughout the community. A mid-week service will be spent by the pastor training his laymen to be teachers and hosts of Bible study groups. We will probably see less preaching, but hopefully better preaching. We have been guilty of communication overkill—speaking too frequently and applying too little. Good preaching with ample opportunity for discussion and implementation is far better than much preaching and little feedback in word and act.

We are also in for a trimming of denominationalism to essentials. There is something healthy about denominational distinctives. I do not applaud a one-world church. This is unhealthy. It does not allow for the varieties of personality needs. By the same token, the denominationalism which we presently see has gone beyond the place of peak efficiency and has succumbed to a form of institutionalism and uncritical self-perpetuation. In the next decade denominational literature, outreach, and programs must be, and inevitably will be, pared down so that they serve the purposes of God rather than inverted and ingrown needs. The church as denominationally identified is not healthy when it exists simply to feed itself. The church is a means. Denominations should exist to help accomplish the purposes of the gospel, not to feed their own self-image or selfish ends.

As we look into tomorrow, it is necessary that we build today the sort of future shock absorbers that will allow us to cope creatively with the radical change which is just around the corner. In the light of this, I plead for two things: *A confidence in God* and *an openness to the future.* God's instruction to Joshua as he embarked on a venture of faith may be the very words we need to hear again as we anticipate the unfolding mystery of tomorrow. "Be strong and of good courage; be not frightened, neither be dismayed; for the Lord your God is with you wherever you go" (Josh. 1:9). The unknown is frequently accompanied by uneasiness, some hesitancy, and even fear. A neurotic anxiety which knots the stomach, sours the spirit, and spreads gloom like a cloud cover is unnecessary for one who affirms the truth: "He goes before . . . " (John 10:4). God's man is one whose focus is upon the object of faith, not the act or subject of faith.

God's man discovers that his faith is not in his own gifts, status, role, denomination, education, reputation, or experience. Rather, it is placed irrevocably in Christ. He is a man who is discovering that it is foolish to defend or carry his own faith; he allows his faith to carry him. Our age is little impressed with rational defenses of Christianity, though it is significantly impressed by a faith that changes people. God's man, because of his faith in Jesus Christ and his reliance upon God, is carried by a life-giving, liberating, joy-granting experience. He is carried by his faith; he does not carry it as a burden nor find any pressure to defend it. His life and the gospel do that. God's man needs a spirit characterized by a frequently sung but rarely believed chorus, "I don't know what the future holds, but I know who holds the future. It's a secret known only to God." A new epoch of usefulness lies ahead for the man who will focus upon his God, love His people, and hence discover what it means to be a genuine servant of the Word.

The second future shock absorber, in addition to a confidence in God, is *an openness to the future.* Søren Kierkegaard says:

> He who fights the future has a dangerous enemy. The future is not; and it borrows its strength from the man himself and when it has tricked him out of this, then it appears outside him as the enemy he must meet.[2]

It is folly to stand in the way of change, progress, or revolution. You cannot deny it, you cannot impede it, you can only enter into the challenge of revolution by becoming a revolutionary servant of Christ. Change is ahead. Some will face anxiety and even breakdown due to the excessive stimulation of environmental change. A decision overload will drive some people to frustration. Fortunately, this is not inevitable. When one's confidence is in God and in the Spirit whom He has sent, one can be open to change. The Holy Spirit is sovereign, unpredictable, and unfettered by comfortable behavior patterns. The person through whom He works is not troubled by this possibility. I feel personal sorrow for two groups: (1) the unmovable traditionalists who cling tenaciously to the past and resist any attempt at change. To such the comfort of recognized patterns, familiar structures, and "business as usual" will be used to feint off the anxiety of future (and even present) change. The church will inevitably die if it depends on such folks, regardless of their sincerity and commitment. They cling to a dangerous precipice with breaking fingernails. We forget the lessons of church history when we worship the past. When there is revival, there is shake-up. Life can never again be the same. (2) I feel sorrow also for the novelty seekers who live from one high to another. Their life is a series of adventures in which they seek change for its own sake. They have a low threshold of boredom. They are impatient with tradition and restlessly eager for the new. When we ask a man to be open to the future, we are not suggesting that life is a series of novel experiences and changes which daily punctuate his existence, but that he be open where changes are necessary, where the Spirit dictates that changes take place.

God's man is not a faddist. He is, however, open to the possibility that the Spirit of God may shuffle the schedule, change the service time, change methods, change anything and everything conceivable with the exception of certain universals. God's man for tomorrow is one who is learning the difference between that which is established and absolute and that which is changeable and therefore relative.

What will remain intact? The human predicament, regardless of the future, is alienation from God. This will not change. The anxiety of being human—namely, the anxiety attending time, space, causality, and substance—is part of the syndrome. Revolution may put new expression and dimension into sin, but it will not remove it. Man's problem always has been and will continue to be sin, with its inevitable alienation from God. The divine solution will not change regardless of the culture. Christ died to bridge the impossible chasm between creator and creature. A new way of salvation is not forthcoming. In this respect it is still the "old time religion." God's grace, Christ's provision, and man's redemption through repentance and faith will always be true.

I simply suggest that a man keep open at the right places. Some things will not change, need not change, and should not change. Much certainly can and will change, and we must have the ability to discern the difference between that which is and must be enduring and that which is and can be different. Permanence is found in the Saviour, not in structures. We worship God and not the scaffolding of the church. J. C. Hoekendijk puts it rather bluntly:

> What then shall we do? It seems to me that we have to cultivate a healthy skepticism toward all traditional forms and procedures; we must prevent ourselves being hypnotized by familiarity. Therefore we must put the fundamental questions: not begin halfway with the question, "How shall we continue to do in the future what we used to do in Egypt?"[3]

Change for its own sake may only feed a personal need. Change must be for the sake of God, the gospel, and the people for whom the gospel is intended. Change ought to be dictated by the Spirit who is the innovator and who alone is capable of dictating healthy change.

We must keep the windows of the church wide open so that the wind of the Spirit may blow and we may be moved by it. To shut the windows is death; to keep them open is life. When the Spirit moves among us, we must be willing to respond as He dictates.

I do not know what the future holds for the servants of Christ in His church. I do know that the Christian whose confidence is in God and not in tradition, the one whose faith in the Spirit is undaunting and who therefore has an openness to the future, need not be unnecessarily threatened. Let me conclude with the words of Herbert Butterfield:

> There are times when we can never meet the future with sufficient elasticity of mind, especially if we are locked in the contemporary systems of thought. We can do worse than remember a principle which both gives us a firm Rock and leaves us the maximum elasticity for our minds: the principle: Hold to Christ, and for the rest be totally uncommitted.[4]

NOTES

1. Alvin Toffler, *Future Shock* (New York: Random House, 1970).

2. Søren Kierkegaard as quoted by Don Fabun, *The Dynamics of Change* (Englewood Cliffs, N.J.: Prentice-Hall, Inc., 1967), p. 30.

3. J. C. Hoekendijk, *The Church Inside Out,* trans. Isaac C. Rottenberg (Philadelphia: The Westminister Press, 1966), p. 178.

4. Herbert Butterfield, *Christianity and History* (London: Bell Publishing Company, 1949), p. 146.